STRAVINSKY THE MUSIC-MAKER
Writings, Prints and Drawings

STRAVINSKY THE MUSIC-MAKER
Writings, Prints and Drawings

HANS KELLER
and
MILEIN COSMAN

With a Preface by
HUGH WOOD

Edited by
MARTIN ANDERSON

TOCCATA
PRESS

Parts of this book were first published in *Stravinsky at Rehearsal* (Dennis Dobson, London, 1976) and in *Stravinsky Seen and Heard* (Toccata Press, London, 1982).

British Library Cataloguing in Publication Data
A catalogue record for this book is available from the British Library.

ISBN-13: 978 0 907689 69 0

Set in 11 on 12½ point Minion Pro
by Kerrypress Ltd, Luton, Beds

Printed and bound in Great Britain
by
CPI Antony Rowe, Chippenham, Wiltshire

Contents

Preface
HANS KELLER AND MILEIN COSMAN: A HAPPY STORY

Hugh Wood

For many readers under 50 Hans Keller is no more than a name – and for some younger ones, perhaps not even that. Yet for 35 years he played a leading part in the musical life of Britain, and his influence since then has been widespread and profound. Fortunately his widow Milein is still very much with us: five minutes in her company is enough to prove her livelier than many of her younger friends. This may be the first time that a joint portrait of this remarkable couple – who pursued, and were triumphant in, independent careers, but who also achieved on occasion the closest collaboration – has been attempted. It is a happy story.

Both Hans and Milein were children of that tragic diaspora provoked by the Nazis, which before the 1939 war scattered artists, scientists and intellectuals from central Europe all over the world. The whole story has been brilliantly told by Daniel Snowman in his book *The Hitler Emigrés.*[1] He gives there a context for these two lives; and by taking his narrative forward to the 1960s and '70s he demonstrates how much British scientific and cultural life owes to this remarkable generation of exiles.

Hans Keller came from Vienna, from a prosperous and music-loving family in Döbling.[2] His father, Fritz Keller (1878–1938), a well-known architect, used to play piano duets with his son and accompany his violin-playing, and the family had many musical and artistic friends, including the composer Franz Schmidt, to whose work Hans was to give a lifelong devotion.[3] On 12 March 1938, the day after Hans' nineteenth birthday, Hitler marched his troops into Austria, to be greeted with hysterical fervour by many Viennese. The horror of the next few months has been told by Hans himself. In a radio talk long afterwards which moved all who heard it, he spoke quietly,

[1] Chatto & Windus, London, 2002.

[2] Keller discusses his family and childhood in 'My Family, You and I', *The New Review*, Vol. 3, Nos. 34–35, January–February 1977, pp. 13–23.

[3] Keller's 'Personal Recollections' of Schmidt introduced Harold Truscott's *The Music of Franz Schmidt*, Vol.1: The Orchestral Music, Toccata Press, London, 1984. A German Wikipedia page gives more details of Fritz Keller's career: http://de.wikipedia.org/wiki/Fritz_Keller_(Architekt).

eloquently and always factually of his detention by the Gestapo and his eventual narrow escape to England – where (mercifully) he already had relations. The account may be read in Keller's book *1975* (*1984 minus 9*)[4] in the chapter called simply 'Vienna, 1938'.

His sister had married an Englishman, Roy Franey; Hans joined them in Herne Hill, where they lived with Hans' mother in a house his father had designed (Fritz Keller, already mortally ill, had died before Hans left Austria). With Hitler's invasion of the Low Countries came internment: Hans spent nine months on the Isle of Man, amid a galaxy of intellectual and creative talent which included three members of the soon-to-be-formed Amadeus Quartet. After his release he used his violin-playing to gain an LRAM, and then became a freelance orchestral and chamber musician who also did some teaching. But his intellectual interests at that time centred on psychology, psychiatry and sociology. He did fieldwork, particularly in group psychology, and his earliest published writing was on these subjects.[5] The turning point came in 1945, and in a rather surprising way. As a good Viennese steeped in Viennese classical tradition, he was particularly enthusiastic about *Così fan tutte*. But an expected performance of *Così* at Sadler's Wells turned out to be that of a new opera by a young composer completely unknown to him: *Peter Grimes*. From then on, Keller wrote more and more about music (though psychoanalysis was never to be very far away). But it was Britten rather than Mozart who set it all off: the *coup de foudre* had been instant and lasting.

The first Edinburgh Festival took place in 1947. Keller was due to attend as critic. Milein Cosman, already embarked on her career of mainly musical but wide-ranging portraiture, was to go too – sent by the same publication, *New Life*, which described itself as 'A Jewish Pictorial Monthly'. Since she lacked a ticket for Bruno Walter's performance of *Das Lied von der Erde*, the magazine put them in touch, and that is how they met.[6] From now onwards their lives were to be intertwined.

For three years (1949–52) Keller – together with Donald Mitchell – edited a lively, combative little magazine called *Music Survey*, which eventually sank in a flood of invoices. Nothing like this fiery publication exists today. The degree of passionate commitment, the eagerness to examine and criticise a

[4] Dennis Dobson, London, 1977; re-issued by Toccata Press, London, in 1986 as *Music, Closed Societies and Football*. The text of Keller's talk had previously appeared in *The Listener*, Vol. 91, No. 2348, 28 March 1974, pp. 397–99; the original broadcast (now held in the British Library Sound Archive as T6548W) took place on 3 February 1974.

[5] It has been republished as *Music and Psychology: From Vienna to London, 1939–52*, ed. Christopher Wintle (with Alison Garnham), Plumbago Books, London, 2003.

[6] In his final interview, Keller spoke – with difficulty: he was already very ill – about their meeting: 'I had seen [the name] "Milein Cosman", and I thought to myself this would probably be an old Jew with a long beard: the drawings looked to me like work by a mature artist' (*cf.* Mark Doran (ed.), 'Hans Keller in Interview with Anton Weinberg', *Tempo*, No. 195, January 1996, pp. 6–12).

Hans Keller with score, by Milein Cosman, 1984

performance – and *a fortiori* a composition – these drives have long since vanished from the earth. Then came *Benjamin Britten* from the same partnership[7] – the target of much hostile criticism at the time. In 1956 came the 200th anniversary of Mozart's birth and, in a symposium edited by H. C. Robbins Landon and Donald Mitchell, Keller's article on Mozart's chamber music applied both psychoanalysis and serialism to its subject in an entirely original way.[8]

In 1959 Keller's life altered from freelance to employee. William Glock, himself newly appointed as Controller, Music, at the BBC, asked Keller to join

[7] Donald Mitchell and Hans Keller (eds.), *Benjamin Britten: A Commentary on his Works from a Group of Specialists*, Rockliff, London, 1952/Philosophical Library, New York, 1953.

[8] 'The Chamber Music', in H. C. Robbins Landon and Donald Mitchell (eds.), *The Mozart Companion*, Rockliff, London, 1956, pp. 90–137.

his staff. Keller's degree of success in transforming the BBC Music Department can be assessed by reading Alison Garnham's pioneering volume *Hans Keller and the BBC.*[9] These were the years of the creation of Functional Analysis: an attempt to by-pass the use of words in analysis in favour of a direct demonstration of how a piece of music works, and is articulated, in terms of music alone. It would have pleased Mendelssohn (another of Hans' passionately defended causes), whose wisdom on words *v.* music is well known. After the changes of BBC policy brought about by a report called *Broadcasting in the Seventies* Keller continued to fight on against the long slide towards mediocrity from which the BBC has never recovered. And broadcasting administration had, after all, only been one aspect of his multifarious activities; the others – the production of articles and reviews, the teaching of composition, the coaching of young players – continued to be pursued right up to his death from motor neurone disease on 6 November 1985.

Even before his years at the BBC Hans had become something of a public figure and was then occasionally seen on television. His combative and argumentative personality – always at the unconditional service of ideas – disconcerted some who did not know him personally. English people, on the whole, distrust anybody who is passionately concerned with anything except football (Hans scored there, too: the only reason which would draw him back to his native Vienna would be to follow his local team). The beady gaze of *Private Eye* was soon to be turned upon him and he became Hans Killer, Professor of Soccer Hooliganism at the University of Schoenberg. But get closer, and a different picture emerged. Once one had passed a certain initiation test – showing the will and ability to stand up to him in argument, and thus learn to dodge the flying chunks of paradox which came whistling past one's ears – then his friendship, which was warm and unconditional, taking no account of relative age, rank or status, was assured and it lasted. He was never, in a sense, off-duty, but it was the joyful duty of thinking that he took with him, wherever he went, even (or especially) on holiday. Besides an immense number of published articles (and several books left unpublished at his death) and a sizable list of public lectures he leaves behind the results of being a prolific letter-writer (they are all being collected by Alison Garnham) and a practitioner of that rarer art – the memorable, meaningful postcard, following in the steps of Bernard Shaw and Evelyn Waugh. The subject matter could be weighty or trivial, the point at issue large or small, the tone friendly or stern. But to read anything, printed or unprinted, is to bring back the sound of that unforgettable voice and the warmth and energy of that personality.

[9] A. M. Garnham, *Hans Keller and the BBC: The Musical Conscience of British Broadcasting, 1959–79*, Ashgate, Aldershot, 2003.

Milein Cosman painting Stravinsky, 1970

Milein Cosman was born in Germany in 1921. Her actual birthplace was Gotha, but her parents lived in Düsseldorf and she was brought up there. Drawing was always a passion: she tells the story of being told off by a teacher for drawing in class when she was meant to be reading *Mein Kampf* along with the other pupils. Other anecdotes demonstrate what a cat-and-mouse game it was to be a Jew in Nazi Germany. Wise Jewish families soon saw that it was better to have their children educated abroad. Milein went off to a school in Switzerland, run by an idealistic German friend of Rabindranath Tagore; later she went to the League of Nations school in Geneva. She came to England in 1939, to enter the Slade School of Fine Art just as it was leaving its Gower Street home for a war-time stay at the Ashmolean Museum in Oxford.

Oxford in wartime was the home of a number of memorable characters, many of whom were friends and acquaintances of Milein. There was Michael Hamburger, the translator and poet; Michael Meyer, the translator; Joseph Horovitz, the composer (who also studied drawing at the Slade at that time); and – soon to be killed in North Africa – the poet Sidney Keyes (1922–43). He fell in love with her, but his feelings were not returned; nevertheless, some of his best poems are inscribed to her.

After graduation from the Slade, the usual sort of money-earning jobs followed: giving lectures to W.E.A. evening classes and (splendidly) working on a milk float by day. Her freelance life continued in London where she sought every chance of getting her drawings into newspapers and magazines. It was on such an assignment that she came to Edinburgh in 1947. Before that she had had her first meeting with Hans – outside Goodge Street tube station. Many years later, she was to say 'He looked like a very thin Indian who had forgotten his turban. I remember thinking "I'd really like to draw that man!"' There were to be many opportunities to do so in the years that lay ahead. One of the chief attractions of the Hans Keller symposium held at Vienna in April 2001 was a whole room of Milein's drawings and paintings of Hans which – without the aid of words – gave a comprehensive biography of the man.

The collaborations with her husband were only one aspect of a remarkably wide-ranging career, in which the portraying of musicians played a leading but by no means exclusive role. Julian Hogg, an old friend of Milein's over many years, has put together a list on which over five hundred names appear. He points out that 'any list that includes Adenauer, Strauss, W. H. Auden, and Jimmy Greaves, and which ranges between Giacometti and Benjamin Britten's parrot must be slightly unusual'. Her drawings are to be found in the USA, in Canada, Japan, Italy, her home town of Düsseldorf, and as part of a Stravinsky exhibition in Basel; the most notable collection of her drawings has been on permanent display at the Palais des Beaux-Arts in Brussels since 2007. In this country the Victoria and Albert Museum, the British Museum and the National Portrait Gallery head the list. Her tally of participation in group exhibitions has a welcome local flavour – the Hampstead-based Camden Printmakers was an excellent show. An exhibition in the restaurant of the Wigmore Hall of 2005 later became a permanent display there. Its 46 items provided a comprehensive survey of the musical world of the latter half of the last century, headed by four etchings and one oil painting of Stravinsky, but including a wide range of internationally known artists all of whom have played an active part in the musical life of this country.

The year 2008 saw a major retrospective of Milein's work. From January to March it was shown at the Austrian Cultural Forum, Knightsbridge; then from April to June, with some adjustments, at Burgh House (Hampstead Museum). This exhibition of between 80 to 100 paintings, prints, drawings and sculptures spanned 60 years of her output, including some early work from her 'Slade' days. It was greeted with wide critical acclaim.

In 2006 Milein established the Cosman Keller Art and Music Trust, a charitable body which aims to encourage and advance education in the fields of art and music, as well as to preserve, publish and exhibit her and Keller's work. The Trust has already supported some valuable work. It forms the climax of many collaborations with her husband which were a feature of their

Hans Keller by Milein Cosman, 1948

life together. First of all came the *Musical Sketchbook* of 1957.[10] Here the range of musicians portrayed is already wide and each portrait is accompanied by a page-worth of pocket biography or comment. Hans is only one of a number of contributors; notable amongst the others is Paul Hamburger. Some of the other texts have dated; not so the drawings, save in terms of Milein's later work, in which mastery is more carelessly and rapidly displayed; in contrast,

[10] Bruno Cassirer, Oxford.

these are precise and sometimes a bit careful. They come from the earliest years when the Kellers could be seen hard at work at rehearsal or during the concert itself. He would be listening hard and on occasion taking notes; Milein would be in some corner or other sketching the players. At a bad or boring concert Hans might well scribble a note and pass it over to his next-door neighbour. I remember a particular studio concert from the BBC's more idealistic and exploratory days, when two young men were doing strange things to a large gong with microphones attached (guess who). Misbehaviour became more than a pleasure: it was a duty. One of those scribbled notes came across of which he was a master. I used to preserve such missives. Milein on the other hand used to spend the time in a more constructive manner – I still have the sketch which on that occasion she did of me.

The previous incarnation of the book to which this is the preface was *Stravinsky Seen and Heard.*[11] Its first half, 'Stravinsky Heard', is a long essay – or series of essays – which in its earliest form dates from 1956, and was concerned with Stravinsky's Dylan Thomas setting 'Do Not Go Gentle', from his *In Memoriam Dylan Thomas*, which had been published the year before, in 1954. But it deals with many other Stravinskian, and indeed generally musical, matters as well. At the invitation of Sir William Glock Stravinsky came to London in 1958, 1959 and 1961 to conduct the BBC Symphony Orchestra. Milein's contribution, 'Stravinsky Seen', consists largely of drawings she did at rehearsals for *Oedipus Rex* on a single day – 6 November 1959. There were also later drawings dating from November 1965, which was Stravinsky's last visit to London, and two etchings of him, done much later, in 1981. As was always her habit, the drawings were done at speed and on the spot, and thus have enormous dash and spontaneity. This was a *jeu d'esprit* which also had the permanent value of immortalising the moments when a great musician was in action.

In 1975 Keller was invited to serve on the jury of the International String Quartet Competition which was held in Prague. His account of this experience provides one of the chapters in *1975 (1984 minus 9)*. Its dust-cover and frontispiece both gave telling portraits; and in the centre of the book, directly after the Prague article, are the dozen pages of Milein's 'Prague Sketchbook 1975' – the generally sombre tone of which perhaps (consciously? unconsciously?) reflecting the prevailing dark tone of Hans' narrative about the communist establishment there at the time.

In *The Jerusalem Diary* (eventually published posthumously by Plumbago Books in 2001, but dealing with two visits in 1977 and 1979) the process of

[11] Toccata Press, London, 1982. *Stravinsky Seen and Heard* was itself an expansion of Keller's and Cosman's *Stravinsky at Rehearsal*, Dennis Dobson, London, 1962. *Cf.* p. 21, below.

integration has gone much further.[12] This is an account of the Kellers' stay in the Mishkenot Sha'ananim – a residence dedicated and available to artists and thinkers in Jerusalem. The pursuits of both were built into the invitation: Hans was to write a book on the Mendelssohn Violin Concerto (still to appear!) and Milein took the opportunity to draw what she wished. The diary itself was an unforeseen by-product of the invitation. It was entirely typical of Hans, with his very regular and strenuous working habits, that he should have had enough energy left over to write this vivid and lively day-to-day account. His delineation of characters whom they met is as sharp as one of Milein's sketches. This time there are 36 pages of drawings, which are both more detailed and more various than the Prague ones. They catch the personalities of old men and soldiers, violinists, singers, people at work and play. They are both instantaneously conceived and permanently memorable.

[12] *The Jerusalem Diary: Music, Society and Politics, 1977 and 1979,* ed. Christopher Wintle and Fiona Williams, The Hans Keller Trust/Plumbago Books, London, 2001.

application of the tools of psychoanalysis to music and musicians, his individualist, liberal humanism[1] – are threaded through his writing, unifying it on a grand scale.[2]

As Hugh Wood relates in his Preface, Keller's first writings were in psychology and sociology, not music.[3] One of the towering intellectual figures in the Vienna in which he grew up was Sigmund Freud, who fled to England in June 1938, only five months before Keller himself escaped. Keller grew up in a family whose circle of friends was well aware of Freudianism,[4] and so it is hardly surprising that Keller's psychoanalytic position was solidly Freudian. In fact, the theory of music he soon developed reveals a Freudian allegiance in its terminology – reflecting Freud's distinction between the 'manifest' content of the dream and the 'latent' dream thought that is only revealed through analysis:

> Meaning, according to my theory of music, can invariably be defined in terms of demonstrable tensions, and indeed relations, between what you hear and what you had expected to hear – between manifest foreground and latent, well-implied background.[5]

Keller's psychoanalytic approach to Stravinsky was not that of the enlightened amateur. He once wrote that 'my psychological interests have [...] always been overriding',[6] and at an early stage he even hoped to train as an psychoanalyst, but as a young man in England found the long and intensive 'training analysis' that was required well beyond his purse. Characteristically, he resolved to analyse himself, later explaining: 'The form it took was that I sat down every day for an hour, with a pencil, and wrote free-associations: whatever came into my mind. [...] Five years of it – changed my life'.[7] With advice from an influential analyst, Willi Hoffer, and having been granted access to the library of the Institute of Psychoanalysis, Keller acquired what

[1] A friend and colleague at the BBC, the composer Robert Simpson once admiringly spoke in conversation of Keller's 'strong sense of justice'. Keller was also an active member of the campaign that in 1964 succeeded in having capital punishment abolished in the United Kingdom.

[2] This book is confined, too, to his writings: Keller, of course, was also a frequent broadcaster, with Stravinsky among his subjects. A first collection of his radio talks, *Chamber Music: Selected Broadcasts (1959–79)*, is in preparation from Alison Garnham.

[3] Indeed, his first significant published article was a discussion of male bias in psycho-analysis: 'Male Psychology', *British Journal of Medical Psychology*, Vol. 20, Pt. 4, (1946), pp. 384–88.

[4] As early as 1913 the doctor and astrologer Oskar Adler had directed Webern to a course of analysis with Alfred Adler (no relation). Oskar Adler (1875–1955) was a boyhood friend of Schoenberg, his first teacher and quartet-leader; later he was also Keller's teacher and a member of the string quartet in which the teenage Keller played with Franz Schmidt. After the *Anschluss*, Schoenberg tried to help Adler escape to California; in the event he came to Britain, settling first in the Lake District and then in London. *Cf.* Hans Keller, 'Not a Genius', *The Spectator*, Vol. 242, No. 7853, 13 January 1979, p. 22

[5] In 'Stravinsky the Downbeater', *The Listener* Vol. 78, No. 2012, 19 October 1967, pp. 509; *cf.* p. 102, below.

[6] *1975 (1984 minus 9)*, *op. cit.*, p. 87; he goes on to explain that since he is a musician, music is not an 'interest'.

[7] In Doran (ed.), *loc. cit.*, p. 10.

Hoffer[8] described as 'unequalled knowledge of psychoanalytic literature'.[9] Indeed, Hoffer thought so highly of Keller's analytic abilities that he even placed a young schizophrenic patient with him; Keller's notes on this brief period of (unsuccessful) treatment have been published.[10]

Keller's early writings had explored issues of group psychology and psychoanalysis, which he proceeded to expand into aspects of music, invoking the 'Polycrates complex' identified by the English psychoanalyst J. C. Flügel[11] in an essay which attacked the critics of Britten's music head-on: 'Resistances to Britten's Music: Their Psychology'.[12] Such an approach was new in the staid and gentlemanly world of writing about music in Britain, and Keller's approach was seen almost as an *ad hominem* attack. It set the tone for the kind of criticism for which Keller, analysing the musician to explain his or her performance, became feared. Keller saw it simply as a question of intellectual honesty, writing in one of the earliest of the essays collected in this book of his desire[13]

> to state the truth without regard for its reception, to winter one's truths as it were until the spring sun dispels the fog with which they will inevitably be surrounded. If the observer in question happens to be a psychologist as well as a musician, thus able, may be, to offer a few scraps of truth about the unconscious which, by its very nature, is damp and productive of fog, it will be a lengthy winter indeed. However, after ages of elaborate theories of cognition, it is time that we embarked upon its indiscreet practice.

Since the observer in question was indeed a psychologist – or, at least, an unconventional psychoanalyst – as well as a musician, one who found 'Stravinsky's absorption of Schoenberg's technique [...] arguably the profoundest surprise in the history of music',[14] it was almost inevitable that

[8] The Austrian-born Hoffer (1897–1967) worked with Anna Freud in Vienna and continued to work with the Freud family after the *Anschluss* forced them, like him, to flee to Britain. Obtaining a British medical qualification in 1943, Hoffer taught as Consultant Psychotherapist at the Maudsley Hospital from 1954 to 1962. He was elected Editor-in-Chief of *The International Journal of Psychoanalysis* in 1949, resigning the post in 1957 to spend three years as President of the British Psychoanalytical Society; in 1957, too, he was elected an Honorary Vice-President for life of the International Psychoanalytical Association.

[9] *1975 (1984 minus 9)*, *op. cit.*, p. 87.

[10] 'Notes on a Case of Dementia Praecox (Bleuler's Schizophrenia) and Attempts at a Musico-psychological Treatment', in *Music and Psychology*, *op. cit.*, pp. 233–34

[11] Flügel (1884–1955) outlined the 'Polycrates complex' – incorporating the compulsion to see good fortune 'paid for', rooted in the 'need for punishment' of the guilt-ridden (the Freudian *Strafbedürfnis*) – in *Man, Morals and Society*, Duckworth, London/International Universities Press, New York, 1945.

[12] *Music Survey*, Vol. 2, No. 4, Spring 1950, pp. 227–36; republished in *Hans Keller: Essays on Music*, ed. Christopher Wintle (with Bayan Northcott and Irene Samuel), Cambridge University Press, Cambridge, 1994, pp. 10–17.

[13] 'Schoenberg and Stravinsky: Schoenbergians and Stravinskyians', *The Music Review*, Vol. 15, No. 4, November 1954, pp. 307–10; *cf.* p. 35, below.

[14] 'Stravinsky Heard: I. Stravinsky's Change of Mind', *Stravinsky Seen and Heard*, *op. cit.* p. 9; *cf.* p. 125, below.

Keller would seek its source, and that is what these essays do, investigating other aspects of Stravinsky's creative character along the way.

In the enlightened polystylist years of the early 21st century, such excitement over a 'mere' change of artistic direction might seem something of an exaggeration. And why regard Stravinsky's change of mind as a shift of polar radicality? Hugh Wood's opening observation that 'For many readers under 50 Hans Keller is no more than a name'[15] applies also to the time in which he lived: it is difficult in these liberal climes to recall the degree to which music was indeed polarised after the Second World War. Hitler's conscription of 'German' music to the cause of Nazi propaganda meant that for many composers and commentators, and for decades after the War, music was inevitably politicised. Embracing serialism allowed them to distance themselves from the cultural attitudes of the Third Reich, both before and after the War. Ernst Krenek later confessed that, although he often wavered in his support of the twelve-tone technique in the late 1930s, 'it was doubly impossible to abandon it at a time when the adversaries, Nazi or otherwise, would have howled in triumph at every sign of wavering'.[16] That antagonism was extended after the War to any circumstance where a connection with the Reich might be perceived – even audiences: Hans Werner Henze observed that some music professionals held in contempt 'the public who had assented to the Nazi terror and who had participated in this blood-and-soil pseudo-culture'.[17] Modern, abstract art, it was argued by writers like the American art-critic Clement Greenberg, was 'innocent', inviolable because it resisted the projection onto it of political values.[18] Echoing Schoenberg's own millennial claims for dodecaphony, the proponents of modernism thus argued that serialism was the only path that music could follow if it expected to be taken seriously; if those same audiences which had cheered Hitler didn't understand it, so much the better. The further fact that on the other side of the Iron Curtain, in an echo of Nazi policy, the Soviet Union was also subjugating the craft of composition to political ends gave the modernist cause an added urgency – and made it a political tool itself: the American forces occupying post-War Germany sponsored the summer courses in new music at Darmstadt (thus, of course, giving the lie to Greenberg's argument that modernism was somehow 'innocent'); and the West German orchestras and radio

[15] *Cf.* p. 9, above.

[16] *Cf.* his 'Self Analysis', *New Mexico Quarterly*, No. 23 (1953), p. 32.

[17] Quoted by Hubert Kolland in 'Die Schwierigkeit, ein bundesdeutscher Komponist zu sein' ('The Difficulty of being a West German Composer'), in Hanns-Werner Heister and Dietrich Stern (eds.), *Musik 50er Jahre*, Argument Verlag, Berlin, 1980, p. 52.

[18] Greenberg argued (in 'Art Chronicle: Our Period Style', *Partisan Review*, Vol. 16, No. 11, November 1949, p. 1138) that modern art showed a 'radical inadaptability to the uses of any interest, ideological or institutional'.

stations promoted the *avant garde* almost in deliberate contrast to the prisoner status of music in the East.[19] By extension, tonality itself was now suspect, a compromise in the eyes of the modernists with the corrupted standards of the recent totalitarian past and the devil over the dyke; hence the contempt in which commentators like Adorno[20] held the Neoclassical Stravinsky. It was in this highly charged atmosphere[21] that Stravinsky began to compose serially – no wonder the musical world sat up and took notice.

Inevitably, there is a degree of overlap in the material republished here but there is remarkably little repetition, and when Keller did recycle his material, he generally examines his subject from a different angle or presents it to a different audience. The sternly technical analysis of rhythm in the *Symphony of Psalms* that appeared in a musicological journal in 1957 and re-appeared in a Leeds Festival programme-note the following year is a case in point: first deployed as part of a discussion that defined Stravinsky's rhythmic invention by way of a comparison with Gershwin's, it went on to figure in Keller's only analytical examination of the full-length work – an examination, one might add, that has not been available to the general reader since 1958. One article, 'Towards the Psychology of Stravinsky's Genius', even had three leases of life: it was published in *The Listener* (Vol. 56, No. 1444, 29 November 1956, p. 897), was republished in part in *Stravinsky at Rehearsal* and then resurfaced again in 'Stravinsky Heard', Keller's part of *Stravinsky Seen and Heard*; there, incorporating '*In Memoriam Dylan Thomas*: Strawinsky's Schoenbergian Technique' (*Tempo*, No. 35, 1955, pp. 13–20), it formed chapter I.[22] On each occasion that a passage re-emerged, he used it as the launchpad for an expansion of his argument; I have preferred to let him repeat himself than do damage to the train of new thought it engendered.

[19] Toby Thacker's *Music after Hitler, 1945–55* (Ashgate, Aldershot, 2007) examines the interplay of music and politics in post-War Germany and methodically demystifies the idea of the apoliticality of music in a struggle for political hegemony.

[20] *Cf.* Keller's comments on pp. 35–40, below. The French avantgardist composer and conductor René Leibowitz (1913–72), a student of Webern, wrote witheringly that Neoclassical composers 'may be disposed of with a shrug, for clearly the musicians who have chosen Stravinsky as their teacher can themselves only be ineffectual, or else so unperceptive that it comes to the same thing' ('Béla Bartók, or the Possibility of Compromise in Contemporary Music', *Transition Forty-Eight*, No. 3 (1948), p. 121). On Leibowitz, *cf.* note 2 on p. 35, below.

[21] Danielle Fosler-Lussier's *Music Divided: Bartók's Legacy in Cold War Culture* (University of California Press, Berkeley and Los Angeles, 2007) offers an excellent examination of the polarisation of attitudes to tonal and atonal music either side of the Iron Curtain, particularly as refracted through the reception of Bartók's music. An interesting personal distinction between Bartók and Stravinsky can be found in their reactions to the exhibition of 'Entartete Musik' ('Denegerate Music') mounted by the Nazis in Düsseldorf in 1938: Stravinsky complained that he had been included, and Bartók complained that he had been left out.

[22] *Cf.* pp. 45–48, below. This piece has also been republished in the collection *Music and Psychology, op. cit.*, pp. 221–23; the part that resurfaced in 'Stravinsky Heard' can be found on pp. 133–41, below. The other two items in *Stravinsky the Music-Maker* which have already been republished are 'Rhythm: Gershwin and Stravinsky' and 'Stravinsky *v.* Stravinsky' (in the shorter version originally published in *The Listener* – *cf.* p. 109, below) in *Hans Keller: Essays on Music, op. cit.*, pp. 201–11 and pp. 103–5 respectively.

A 'Note' in the 'Strawinsky Number' of *Tempo* (New Series, No. 8, Summer 1948, p. 6) states: 'For reasons of uniformity, we have used throughout this issue the spelling of Strawinsky's name which he himself uses'; this is also the form that appears on the Boosey & Hawkes scores of the time.[23] At one stage, Keller likewise seems to have preferred the name with a 'w': in *Music Survey*, for example, he writes 'Strawinsky' in a contribution of his own[24] (but does not editorially impose it on others). And in the typescript of the programme note for the *Symphony of Psalms* he wrote for the Leeds Festival in 1958,[25] it can be seen that Keller wrote 'Strawinsky' throughout – only for the text to be printed with the 'v'. Although I have corrected the 'Schönberg' imposed on Keller by *The Music Review* and *The Listener*,[26] I have therefore preferred to leave the spelling of Stravinsky's name as it appears in the original publication.

The source of each article is given at its outset. Hans Keller's footnotes are indicated with a concluding –HK; the others are editorial, as are titles in square brackets.

[23] *Tempo* was founded as the house publication of Boosey & Hawkes, whose original close association with Universal Edition, Vienna, had led to a preference for German transliterations from Russian in its scores. *Tempo* was still insisting on 'Strawinksy' when it published Keller's 'Strawinsky's Performance of *Agon*' in 1958.

[24] *Cf.* p. 34, below.

[25] It is held in the Hans Keller Archive of the Cambridge University Library.

[26] *Cf.* note 1 on p. 35, below.

Acknowledgements

Christopher Wintle, Hans Keller's Literary Executor and a trustee of the Cosman Keller Art and Music Trust, provided the list of articles which allowed this project to begin; Mark Doran then supplied several more, provided all the texts and many of the references, and typeset the music illustrations, apart from the analysis of 'Do Not Go Gentle', which was set by Mark Henegar. Julian Hogg, Chairman of the Trustees of the Cosman Keller Art and Music Trust, and Jane Cassini, Archivist of the Trust, helped plan the lay-out of Part Two, supervised, of course, by the indefatigable Milein Cosman herself. Benjamin Earle identified a stubborn source for me, Maureen Carr found some supportive text from an American interview with Stravinsky, David Hodges of the Radio Times Readers Services supplied four references, Michael Haas and Peter Tregear of the International Centre for Suppressed Music came up with a couple more; Joanna Green of Ipswich Town Football Club established the correct spelling of Ted Phillips' surname; Andrew Porter, Steven Walsh and Galen Brown provided further useful details. Messrs Doran, Hogg and Wintle all made helpful comments, improving both the body of the text and the editorial annotations; many of the sources Mark Doran hunted down for me in Cambridge University Library. Margaret Jones of the Music Department there also deserves gratitude for her helpfulness.

In resetting Keller's serial analysis of 'Do Not Go Gentle', the opportunity has been taken to restore details from the 1955 original that were omitted from the 1982 republication; some mislabelled and wrongly drawn brackets have also been corrected.

This volume is part of The Hans Keller Archive series (General Editor: Christopher Wintle), and the source materials are reproduced by kind permission of The Cosman Keller Art and Music Trust, to which Toccata Press is grateful for a grant towards the production costs. Thanks go also to the Syndics of Cambridge University Library, who kindly granted permission to include previously unpublished material from the Hans Keller Archive.

Martin Anderson
London
November 2010

Part One
HANS KELLER
Writings

I
Symphony in Three Movements

Record review in *The Music Review*, Vol. 9, No. 2, May 1948, p. 145. An asterisk indicated that this recording was 'strongly recommended'.

Symphony in three movements.
New York Philharmonic-Symphony Orchestra, c. Stravinsky.
Columbia LX1042–44. 18s.

Similarly as 'the dissonance, the "foreigner", becomes gradually acclimatized among the consonances, its "hosts", and thus loses its former dissonant character',[1] the development becomes gradually acclimatized among exposition and recapitulation, or statement and re-statement, thus losing its former developmental character, and raising the norm of development. The first movement (a distant sonata form derivative) and the last movement (a rondo's greatgrandchild) of the present symphony (1945) lavishly contribute to this historical process. The simpler second movement stands for both slow movement and *scherzo*. The three movements use interrelated material. White[2] deems the work 'classical', which means, according to my dictionary, 'subordinating content to form'. White is right if my dictionary is right. To my mind, it is wrong; I consider classicism to be marked by balance rather than by subordination. At the same time not even the score's worst enemy (Sackville-West, I gather[3]) can deny that it is a masterpiece. The performance is brilliant; the recording exaggerates in places.

[1] Carner, M., *A Study of Twentieth-Century Harmony*, [Joseph Williams,] London, 1944, Vol. II. –HK

[2] White, E. W., *Stravinsky* [*: A Critical Survey, 1882–1946*, John Lehmann], London, 1947 [republished by Dover Publications, New York, 1997]. –HK
Keller discusses White's next Stravinsky book (*Stravinsky: The Composer and His Works*, Faber and Faber, London, 1966) on pp. 98-100, below, and reviews its second edition (Faber and Faber, London, 1979) on pp. 122–25.

[3] The music critic and novelist Edward Sackville-West (1901–65) had denounced the *Symphony in Three Movements* in the following terms:

> Stravinsky's new symphony was all too precisely what one would expect from a composer who has committed himself to the following categorical statement: 'I hold music to be essentially powerless to express anything whatsoever, be it a feeling, an attitude, a state of mind or a natural phenomenon'. What wonder that a spiritual condition of such evident bankruptcy should produce music of a determined vacuity! Mastery of the orchestra only aggravates the offensiveness of these brittle, charmless, logarithmic movements.

Cf. 'Radio Notes', *New Statesman and Nation*, Vol. XXXIII, No. 828, 4 January 1947, pp. 9–10. For a full and correct presentation of Stravinsky's statement, *cf.* note 4 on p. 83 below.

II
[*Quatre Études* and Octet]

From 'Reviews of Music', *The Music Review*, Vol. 9, No. 4, November 1948, pp. 309–11 – a survey which included discussion of Britten's *Albert Herring*, Op. 39 (1947) and Six Songs from Purcell's *Orpheus Britannicus* in Britten's realisations, as well as Alan Bush's *Meditation on a German Song of 1848* for solo violin and piano or string orchestra, Op. 22.

Igor Stravinsky. *Quatre Études pour orchestre*, pocket score. (Boosey & Hawkes.) 5s.

Octuor pour instruments à vent, pocket score. (Boosey & Hawkes.) 5s.6d.

The first three of the four studies (1929) are the composer's arrangement for orchestra of the *Three Pieces* for String Quartet (1914), while the fourth is an orchestral version of the *Study* for pianola (1917). White[1] points out that

> the four-note tune of the *Dance* [the first study] blossoms into the main theme of the last movement of the Symphony in C (1940); the phrase played by the first violin[2] in the 13th bar of *Eccentric* [the second study] appears slightly transformed as the subject of the opening fugue in the second movement of the Symphony of Psalms (1930); and the main idea of the *Canticle* [the third study], which is a brief chorale, is more fully worked out in the coda to the Symphonies of Wind Instruments (1920).

The difference between the above-mentioned *Excentrique* phrase (C up to E, up to B, down to E flat) and the first subject of the *Symphony of Psalms*' tremendous double fugue (C up to E flat, up to B, down to D) is determined by the respective context of either phrase. In *Excentrique*, the phrase grows out of the previous one-bar phrase first heard in bar 5. In the *Symphony of Psalms* the first fugue subject takes its place in the Symphony's unifying scheme 'of two inter-linked ascending thirds' (minor thirds in the first and

[1] White, E. W., *Stravinsky: A Critical Survey*, London, 1947, p. 58. –HK

[2] White refers to the string quartet version. In the present version the phrase is played by the clarinets. –HK

second movements);[3] the composer, 'remembering the little phrase in *Eccentric*, inverts the second third to form the subject of the instrumental fugue'.[4]

Stravinsky may use unusual rhythmic devices, but he has not so far, we understand, written a $\frac{5}{4}$ bar that contains only 4 crotchets. The present pocket score, however (*Cantique*, bar 5), would make us believe that he has. In fact in both these scores quite a number of white notes are printed pitch dark, owing no doubt to the small size of the notes.

White should not perhaps have concentrated almost exclusively on the variation movement of the octet (1923; 'for wind instruments' goes without saying, doesn't it?), though the movement does of course 'deserve special attention, as it is the first time Stravinsky has used this particular form'.[5] But there are other things deserving special attention, for instance the intriguing rhythmic unity that underlies the various metric ingenuities of the first movement's Lento. One would advise the reader not to be frightened off by, say, the fact that from number 1 to number 2 the time signature changes with each bar. If he will replace the time signatures of the first six bars after number 1 ($\frac{2}{8}$, $\frac{3}{16}$, $\frac{2}{8}$, $\frac{3}{16}$, $\frac{2}{8}$, $\frac{3}{16}$) by, simply, $\frac{3}{16}$ throughout, except for a $\frac{1}{8}$ bar to be inserted before the fourth bar after number 1,[6] he will notice that such *laisser-aller* works splendidly. If, moreover, he will continue to count $\frac{3}{16}$ as from the fourth ($\frac{3}{16}$) bar after number 1, and beyond the sixth bar after number 1, he will find the $\frac{3}{16}$ flute motif of the fourth bar after number 1 again as a $\frac{3}{16}$ motif in the seventh bar after number 1, and continuing, in spite of everything, to count $\frac{3}{16}$, he will, it is true, for a bar or two deem us insane, but will nevertheless land smoothly at number 2, resolving the $\frac{3}{8}$ bar into two $\frac{3}{16}$ bars and running on into the following two $\frac{3}{16}$ bars as if nothing (apart from $\frac{3}{16}$) had ever happened. It seems that while he considered us demented, the $\frac{3}{16}$s were flowing underground.

To White's analysis of the second movement[7] I would add that the waltz (third variation) seems to be in part inspired by the waltz from the second movement of Borodin's second string Quartet in D major.

[3] *Op. cit.*, 135. –HK

[4] *Op. cit.*, 135. –HK

[5] *Op. cit.*, 106. –HK

[6] Or, alternatively, in the fourth bar after number 1, on the second and third semiquaver. –HK

[7] *Op. cit.*, 106. –HK

III
[*Orpheus* and Mass]

This survey of first performances ('Including first (public) performances in England') – published in *The Music Review*, Vol. 10, No. 2, May 1949, pp. 130–31 – spent more than half its length on the first UK performances of *Orpheus*, given by the BBC Symphony Orchestra under Ernest Ansermet at the Royal Albert Hall on 16 February 1949, and the Mass, given twice by Elsie Suddaby, Ann Wood, René Soames and Bruce Boyce, with the BBC Chorus and Symphony Orchestra again conducted by Ansermet and broadcast on the Third Programme on 19 February.

Unreported by *Daily Express*, *Daily Herald*, *Daily Mail*, and *News Chronicle*, *Orpheus* elicited reactions from *The Times*[1] and *The Daily Telegraph*[2] from which one could hardly gather that they referred to the same work. There can be little doubt that the *Times* critic was right in noting emotional depth behind the suite's technical mastery, for depth is not easily noticeable where it is absent. Mr. Herbert Murrill[3] said in his analytical programme note that in the *Air de Danse* (*Orpheus*) 'a theme of classical shape is given to the oboes', and Charles Stuart speaks here[4] of 'Stravinsky's neo-antique vein: the idiom of Lully is … transfigured by the keener harmonic values of our own day'. I submit that in this song of consolation Stravinsky reverts, doubtless with full

[1] 'Stravinsky's *Orpheus*', unsigned review, *The Times*, 17 February, 1949, p. 7.

[2] 'New Work by Stravinsky', brief notice by 'R.C.' (Richard Capell), *The Daily Telegraph and Morning Post*, 17 February 1949, p. 3.

[3] Herbert Murrill (1909–52), an organ scholar at Oxford University from 1928 to 1931, was an English composer and administrator and professor of composition at the Royal Academy of Music from 1933. He worked at the BBC from 1936 to 1942 and, after war service in the Intelligence Corps, again from 1946 until his premature death, becoming Assistant Head of Music in 1948 and Head of Music in 1950. Murrill's compositions, which include an early jazz opera, two cello concertos and vocal, chamber and piano music, reflect his fondness for Stravinskian neo-classicism.

[4] Charles Stuart (whose dates have eluded me) was not a contributor to *The Music Review*, so it seems that Keller's 'here' either refers to the programme for the concert in question or means 'on this subject'. In *Music Survey* (*New Series*), Vol. II, No. 3, Winter 1950, Mitchell and Keller published Stuart's combatively pro-Stravinsky article 'Stravinsky: The Dialectics of Dislike', referring in one of their infamous editorial footnotes to 'Mr. Stuart's fiery observations', and agreeing that Stravinsky was 'dangerously (because none too obviously) misunderstood and underestimated' (p. 148). By the time of the subsequent issue, Vol. II, No. 4, Spring 1950, Stuart had appointed to the Editorial Board: his name appears on its masthead for the first time then and thereafter on that of every issue until the last (June 1952, Vol. IV, No. 5), in which no masthead was reproduced.

intent, to the middle section of the Dance of the Blessed Spirits from Gluck's own *Orpheus*. Mr. Murrill also observed that at the end of the work 'the horns develop a new theme'. On the contrary, the theme derives, invertedly, from the beginning. About one thing everyone except the present critic seems agreed, namely, the splendid performances of both *Orpheus* and the Mass. It therefore behoves me to criticize them in some detail. I cannot understand, for instance, how everyone could have swallowed the affected accents on the double-semiquaver, quaver figures at their first appearance in the *Pas-de-Deux*. The intrinsic metric, melodic, and harmonic accents are here quite enough; anything more destroys the logical flow of the music. Similar absurdities were to be encountered in the Mass, a particularly enraging example being the '*Et iterum venturus est* CUM *gloria* …'. I suppose Ansermet thought that since we are inclined to regard the '*cum*' as unaccented, both extra-musically and musically (see, say, Byrd, Bach, Beethoven), and as, moreover, the word here falls on the second half of the first beat, the fact that Stravinsky nevertheless stresses it, must be pushed down our throats. However, the natural accent which the '*cum*' receives harmonically and through the sudden, rising similar motion, will do perfectly well. In general the performance of the Mass, though better than the first one in Milan,[5] was worse than that of *Orpheus*. Children's voices were not employed, which would have been justified if the adult voices had done much better musically than children; but they didn't. The vocal intonation was what in Hollywood prose would be described as a chronic aural pain in the neck. For example, the sopranos were terribly flat in the first '*Christe eleison*', and the female solo voices' consecutive fifths in the *Gloria* were not sufficiently narrow, Miss Wood being here on the flat side, though she was lavishly sharp at the end of this movement. In the *Agnus Dei*, the (expected) aberrations were particularly severe in sopranos and contraltos in the first vocal section, and in the tenors in the second. Vocal balance: the contraltos' middle c's on '*ChriSTE, CHRIste*' were too weak, and so was, most disturbingly, the basses' determinant 1st inversion of the A♭ triad before the end of the *Kyrie*. In fact the basses gave a tuberculous rendering of most of their part. Their c-d semiquavers in the *Credo* were almost inaudible, nor was the succeeding '*Qui*

[5] In the previous issue of *The Music Review* (Vol. 10, No. 1, February 1949, p. 42) Keller reported on the Milan performance:

> Stravinsky's problematic Mass needs a lot of recommendation, but first of all it needs a performance. For you can hardly give this title to the singing of the Choir of the Milan Scala which was scandalously out of tune and distorted in texture. (The latter fault may have been partly due to the broadcast.) In the *Agnus Dei*, whose three invocations are unaccompanied and alternate with the orchestra, the choral rendering became in fact chaotic. To give just one example, the contraltos were unable to find the root in a diminished triad's first inversion, although this note (E) should have been reached in comfortable conjunct motion. The few among us, however, who followed the mess in an advance copy of the score could at least see what we were supposed to be hearing. I was thus able to form the provisional opinion that this long-awaited Mass is a sado-masochistic masterpiece.

propter nos homines ...' anything like distinct. The same goes for '*Et in spiritum sanctum...*' and for '*Et expecto resurrectionem mortuorum*'. Mr. Soames' '*Sabaoth*' did not come out nearly enough; at this point the Milan tenor had an excellent idea of the texture. As for the orchestral and total balance, the worst came to the worst in '*Benedictus qui venit*'. Here the bassoons' all-important double-dotted quaver passage was far too soft in relation to oboes and clarinet, and particularly to contraltos and tenors, despite the fact that Stravinsky has marked the bassoon parts *mf* as against the *p* of the other parts! The B.B.C. may, of course, have to take part of the blame for the frequent lack of balance.

With ardent zest for co-ordination, our worthy colleague, Mr. Alan Frank,[6] said in his interval talk that *Orpheus* and the Mass had one thing in common: they were both chamber-musical. One sympathizes with such a search for chamber music in all sorts of slender and clean scorings, what with there being so little real chamber music about.[7]

[6] Alan Frank (1910–94) joined the music department of Oxford University Press after leaving college and remained there – except for war service in RAF Intelligence – for the rest of his working life, from 1954 as head of department; he retired in 1975. Walton. Rawsthorne and Vaughan Williams were among the composers he handled there. Married to the composer Phyllis Tate from 1935, he was chairman of the Performing Right Society from 1976 to 1978.

[7] Keller squeezed into the last fifteen lines of the final paragraph reviews of a concert featuring Jean Absil's String Trio No. 2 and R. W. Wood's String Trio (given by the London String Trio), Britten's *A Charm of Lullabies* (Nancy Evans and Norman Franklin) and Poulenc's *Babar the Elephant* (Bruce Belfrage and the composer) at the London Contemporary Music Centre, the British branch of the International Society for Contemporary Music, on 8 February; Franz Reizenstein's *Divertimento* (Aeolian String Quartet) from the Exploratory Concert Society at the Conway Hall on 11 March; and a broadcast from the Royal Albert Hall on 2 March of Bax's *Concertante* for cor anglais, clarinet, horn and orchestra, played by Helen Gaskell, Ralph Clark, Aubrey Thonger and the BBC Symphony Orchestra conducted by Sir Malcolm Sargent.

IV
[*Symphony of Psalms*]

Record review in *The Music Review*, Vol. 10, No. 4, November 1949, p. 326; the recording was 'strongly recommended'.

Stravinsky: Symphony of Psalms (1930)
London Philharmonic Orchestra and Choir, c. Ansermet.
Decca AK 1753–55. 14s. 3d.

Emphatically recommended to possessors of the score and of the, I gather, unsatisfactory Columbia set with the composer's own rendering. Whether listeners unsupported by the score and uncastigated by the previous recording will consider their money well-spent I dare not decide. One must, however, thank the engineers for what they have achieved in this partly indissoluble task, though not for the extraordinarily bad surface at the end of side 4. Nor am I sure that the balance, particularly the choir's, could not have been better; its effect could certainly have been improved by fairer choral intonation. But to have a recording of this gigantic Symphony – 'composée à la gloire de Dieu' and 'dédiée au "Boston Symphony Orchestra"'[1] – which is as acceptable as this one, is quite something.

[1] The dedication on the printed score continues: '*à l'occasion du cinquantenaire de son existence*'.

V
[Mass]

Published in the 'Radio' section, *Music Survey*, Vol. IV, No. 1, October 1951, p. 368.

Strawinsky Mass (1948): relayed by Radio Paris and Dijon from the Sainte-Chapelle, 28th May, 1951; c. Marcel Couraud.

By far the most musical and spiritual and vital of the five performances – including the Italian world première[1] and the first three English performances[2] – I have heard. In fact, the intonation was good, even in the middle parts, and the basses were audible. Not so, however, the bassoons' double-dotted quavers in the *Benedictus* which, despite Strawinsky's carefully differentiated dynamics, have not to my knowledge yet been heard. Children's voices were at last employed and made a better job of their parts than the adults on previous occasions, which goes to show that Strawinsky may after all have known what he wanted.[3] But the optional *soli* of the *Gloria* (as distinct from the obligatory ones in the *Sanctus*) were, perhaps wisely, sung by several. One trombone was somewhat rough, but only because it was so very well-meaning. For the rest, the zest, intensity and certainty of the phrasing made the *tempi* seem quicker than required by the metronome markings; yet they weren't: the performance lasted exactly 17 minutes. For the first time, one was invited to understand the work.

One's previous impression[s] of a sado-masochistic masterpiece[4] were vehemently and, as it seemed, finally confirmed, the aspect of mastery gaining a fuller meaning. Since this essentially pandiatonic – i.e. undeveloping – music achieves its static state by overpowering itself, it will always overwhelm those who understand it and seem powerless to those who don't.

Bar 6 of the *Gloria*'s contralto part is misprinted in the Boosey & Hawkes Pocket Score: for g′–a′ read e′–f♯′.

[1] October 27, 1948; see *First Performances, Music Review*, February, 1949. –HK *Cf.* note 5 on p. 31, above.

[2] February 19 and 20, 1949; see *First Performances, Music Review*, May, 1949. –HK *Cf.* pp. 30–32, above.

[3] Mr Denis Stevens informs me that in the Third Programme's own performance of the work on 9th April, 1951, children's voices were used. –HK

[4] February 19 and 20, 1949; see *First Performances, Music Review*, May, 1949. –HK

VI
Schoenberg and Stravinsky: Schoenbergians and Stravinskyians

The Music Review, Vol. 15, No. 4, November 1954, pp. 307–10

I

It is not generally known that Schoenberg was not a Schoenbergian.[1] Unlike many a self-styled twelve-tone expert, he did not teach the twelve-tone technique, and unlike René Leibowitz,[2] he did not consider Schoenberg, Berg and Webern 'the only musical geniuses of our time'. In the interests of musicology, it would be important to know whether Leibowitz fainted when he heard that Schoenberg thought Gershwin a great composer. I gather that Schoenberg was not far from fainting himself when Theodor Wiesengrund-Adorno (*Die Philosophie der neuen Musik*), after due reservations, qualifications, obsessional complications, and beggings of the question at the rate of about two per printed page, modelled Stravinsky into a death-mask of the past and appointed Schoenberg to model the future.[3] Schoenberg was in fact

[1] Keller always used the anglicised version of Schoenberg's name that the composer adopted after he settled in the USA; 'house style' in *The Music Review* (edited by Geoffrey Sharp between 1940 and 1974) was to revert to the original Schönberg. I have restored Keller's (and Schoenberg's) preferred spelling.

[2] *Schoenberg and his School,* trans. Dika Newlin, [Philosophical Library,] New York, 1949, p. xvi. –HK
Leibowitz was a Polish-born French composer and theorist who played a central role in introducing the music of the Second Viennese School to France; indeed, *Schoenberg et son école* (J. B. Janin, Paris, 1947) was one of the first treatises to examine Schoenberg's method in detail in any language. Like Keller, Leibowitz did not appreciate the music of Sibelius, but whereas Keller was content to say that he didn't understand it, Leibowitz went on the attack, publishing – in the composer's 90th year – a pamphlet entitled *Sibelius, le plus mauvais compositeur du monde* (Éditions Dynamo, Liège, 1955).

[3] The Frankfurt-born sociologist, musicologist and philosopher Theodor Wiesengrund (1903–69) studied composition with Bernhard Sekles alongside philosophy (and musicology, sociology and psychology) at the University of Frankfurt from 1921, and in 1925 studied composition with Berg and piano with Edouard Steuermann in Vienna, producing a small body of works in a freely atonal style (orchestral pieces, chamber and choral music, song settings) until he ceased composing in the early 1940s. From 1928 until 1932 he edited the journal *Musikblätter des Anbruch* (simply *Anbruch* after 1929), also writing widely in other publications. In 1934 he fled the Nazi regime (he was of Jewish origin), settling first in England and moving to the United States in 1937. He had appended Adorno (part of his mother's maiden name) to his surname in the 1920s and on his naturalisation as an American citizen truncated Wiesengrund to its initial. Returning to Germany in 1949, he became the leader of the 'Frankfurt School' of Marxist sociological analysis. The tendency of post-War German composers to adopt modernism as a means of distancing themselves from Nazi aesthetics (*cf.* pp. 20–21, above) reinforced the sense of historical inevitability fostered by Adorno's Marxist outlook, and he became an intolerant proponent of musical modernism. His *Philosophie der neuen Musik* (Mohr, Tübingen, 1949) posited Schoenberg and Stravinsky as polar antitheses, the titles of the two essays of

alive to Stravinsky's genius and deplored the infrequent performances of his later works; needless to add, this was pre-*Rake* and may well have been said in view of the *Mass*.

Stravinsky, in his turn, is not a Stravinskyian either, and has always shown the greatest interest in performances of Schoenberg's works, whereas the Stravinskyians have preferred to derive their knowledge of Schoenberg's thoughts and technical procedures from their own jokes about them, thus appropriating a critical method which the music critics have always claimed as their very own. Frank Howes,[4] for example, still lives on the conclusions he has drawn from the joke he once made about 'dodecacophony', and is at present engaged in recurrent declarations to the effect that Schoenberg was not a composer at all, a heroic opinion since, of late, it appears to find itself in the minority of one; not even Schoenberg ever reached this degree of esotericism. Again, Eric Blom[5] would appear to derive a variety of fruitful results from his humorous observation that Schoenberg took himself too seriously, an opinion which one can appreciate in view of the playfully modest negligence with which our respected colleague is wont to treat his own criticisms, at any rate so long as they are not opposed by anybody else. Curiously, Mr. Blom has not yet discovered the worthiest object for his humour – Hindemith, who does take himself too seriously, inasmuch as he tends to develop his theories at the expense of the work of other leading contemporary figures – an approach of which neither Schoenberg nor Stravinsky can be accused. In fact, Hindemith is even more of an Hindemithian than Leibowitz is a Schoenbergian.

II

In this somewhat tedious state of complex party strife in which two of the three great 'party leaders' take no part, it is sometimes easier for the

which the book consists making his position abundantly clear: 'Schoenberg and Progress' and 'Stravinsky and Reaction'. Keller's review of *Philosophie der neuen Musik* appeared in *Tempo*, No. 16, Summer 1950, p. 32 (republished in Hans Keller, *Music and Psychology: From Vienna to London, 1939–52, op. cit.*, pp. 223–24).

[4] Frank Howes (1891–1974) was chief music critic of *The Times* from 1943 to 1960. He was a lecturer at the Royal College of Music from 1938 to 1970 and was made a CBE in 1954. His books include monographs on Vaughan Williams (1954), Walton (1965), the English musical renaissance (1966) and British folk-music (1969) – a choice of subjects indicative of his conservative, nationalist inclinations. A copy of Howes' *Music and its Meanings* (Athlone Press, London, 1958) was owned and critically annotated by Keller (it is now in the Hans Keller Archive of Cambridge University Library).

[5] Eric Blom (1888–1959) was the London music critic of *The Manchester Guardian* from 1923 to 1931, music critic of *The Birmingham Post* from 1931 and chief editor of the fifth edition of *Grove's Dictionary of Music and Musicians* from 1946; in 1949 he was appointed music critic of *The Observer*. His writings include books on Tchaikovsky (1927), Strauss (1930), Mozart (1935) and Beethoven (1938) and *Everyman's Dictionary of Music* (1946); in his entry on Stravinsky in *The Grove Dictionary of Music and Musicians* (3rd edn., ed. H. C. Colles, Macmillan, London, 1928), he had mounted a subjective and unscholarly attack on the composer. Towards the end of Blom's life, Keller revealed that the two of them had had 'many friendly arguments by correspondence': *cf.* 'National Frontiers in Music', *Tempo*, No. 33, September 1954, pp. 23–30.

understanding musician to see the truth than to tell it. Immediately he adopts – as, I think, he must adopt – a point of view in the neighbourhood of (though at a respectless distance from) Wiesengrund-Adorno's, he will be relegated to the realm of the 'Schoenbergians' by Stravinskyians and critics alike. The label itself will not bother him much, first because it has probably been appended on him on previous occasions anyway, and secondly, in view of the fact that he would not, after all, object to being called, say, a Beethovenian. What will disturb him is the circumstance that being labelled 'Schoenbergian', the truths he is trying to communicate will anon be identified with, and submerged under, the views of the Schoenbergians, and in no time he will be cited to have produced the very untruths, half-truths, and three-quarter-truths arrived at by way of invalid inferences, against which he wanted to set off his own standpoint.

There are two possible ways out of the dilemma. One, which is usually chosen by writers in similar straits, is to distort one's own communication strategically and diplomatically, anticipating the most dangerous reactions to it and attempting to modify and mollify them in advance by means of compromises and conciliatory manoeuvres, even though a good deal of objectively established truth may go by the board in the process. The other way is to state the truth without regard for its reception, to winter one's truths as it were until the spring sun dispels the fog with which they will inevitably be surrounded. If the observer in question happens to be a psychologist as well as a musician, thus able, may be, to offer a few scraps of truth about the unconscious which, by its very nature, is damp and productive of fog, it will be a lengthy winter indeed. However, after ages of elaborate theories of cognition, it is time that we embarked upon its indiscreet practice.

III

In our tabular survey of first performances (MR, Feb., 1954), I have pointed to the fact that 'the most strikingly new technical feature' of Stravinsky's Cantata of 1952 was 'the (tonal) adoption of serial technique' in the tenor's *Ricercar* II and, half a year later in the same feature (MR, Aug., 1954), Erwin Stein[6] has drawn attention to 'bitonal serial technique producing the closest contrapuntal thematicism' in Stravinsky's Septet of 1953. It must be

[6] The Vienna-born Erwin Stein (1885–1958) was a student of Schoenberg from 1906 to 1910 and from 1920 to 1923 director of performances for Schoenberg's *Verein für Musikalische Privataufführungen* ('Society for Private Musical Performances'). Editor of the journal *Pult und Tackstock* from 1924 to 1930, he was then on the staff of Universal Edition, a connection which proved useful when the Jewish Stein had to flee Vienna for London after the *Anschluss*: he became an editor at Boosey & Hawkes, working especially on scores by Mahler, Schoenberg and Britten (all of them personal acquaintances). One of the founders of the periodical *Tempo*, he also edited the first collection of Schoenberg's letters (*Arnold Schoenberg: Ausgewählte Briefe*, B. Schotts Söhne, Mainz, 1958; translated by Eithne Wilkins and Ernst Kaiser as *Letters of Schoenberg*, Faber, London, 1964) .

emphasized that these adoptions of Schoenberg's technique are obvious analytical *data*, not a matter of opinion at all; the fact that there has been some controversy about the matter is merely due to the fact that the anti-Schoenbergians don't know anything about the application of the serial method. On the other hand, the Schoenbergians who do, tend to note Stravinsky's new departure with infantile glee, as if a new victory had been won in party politics. The only point in which their feelings may, in fact, be based on a correct evaluation is that Schoenberg's historical significance is herewith increased – in proportion, indeed, as Stravinsky's tonal and polytonal versions of serialism prove of musical value (a corollary which the Schoenbergians may not feel inclined to heed).

Musically unimportant, but psychologically of the concretest interest is the fact that Stravinsky's 'Schoenbergisms' started after Schoenberg's death.[7] Unconscious incorporation is a reaction, well-known psychologically, to the death of a person, often an actual or potential parent figure, whose image within the reactor's mind had been charged with intense, and often highly ambivalent emotion. For me, the causal connection between Schoenberg's death and his method's rebirth in Stravinsky (which I first suspected in view of the Cantata) was clinched by two objective symptoms, i.e. (1) that in the Septet, the composer gave, quite unnecessarily, the title 'row' to scalic basses which have nothing whatever to do with his serial technique and are used to confirm tonality, and (2) that in an interview with Arthur Jacobs,[8] he reacted strongly against the latter's somewhat inquisitive query about the sometimes-mentioned Schoenbergian influence upon the Septet, remembering, upon this occasion, that the Russian equivalent of 'row' was used for the concept of the scale, and pointing to the tonal function of his 'rows'. For the psychoanalytically trained musician, the situation now seems crystal-clear. The incorporation of Schoenberg's method has, of course, developed on an unconscious, i.e. repressed level. Its rationalization may take the form of Stravinsky's probable belief that he 'has it' from the old contrapuntists. What is known as 'the return of the repressed' manifests itself in his – musically purposeless – employment of the word 'row' in the score of the Septet. As always, this 'return' results in a 'compromise formation' between the repressed and the repressing agencies: by way of the unconscious mechanism of 'displacement', the word 'row', whose atonal implications are not tolerated, is transferred from the composition's actual note-rows to the basic confirmation of tonality. The associative channel which makes this operation possible is given by the Russian meaning of 'row' which, in fact, turns up as rationalization in defence against Jacobs' (psychologically speaking)

[7] Schoenberg died on 13 July 1951, at the age of 76.

[8] Arthur Jacobs, 'Talking with Igor Stravinsky', *Radio Times*, Vol. 123, No. 1593, 21 May 1954, p. 8.

dangerous attack upon Stravinsky's unconscious: our friend put his foot into it, as one might easily have told him in advance; in addition, there are two further possible associations which, on the basis of the Russian identity of 'row' and 'scale', may well have furthered the process. One is a very legitimate association between 'row' and 'scale': in pre-twelve-tonal, serial days, the chromatic scale was called the 'twelve-tone row', a fact of which Stravinsky is probably aware; secondly, when the twelve-tone row proper had emerged, critics of dodecaphony continued to identify the 'tone-row' with the chromatic scale. Sure enough, the role of Stravinsky's so-called 'rows' in the Septet corresponds to that of the chromatic scale in a twelve-tone composition. If my interpretation is correct, a second 'return of the repressed' is involved: the original meaning of the term 'row' lurks in the background, suggesting that we are not so far removed from Schoenberg as the overt application of the term would have it.

If, then, we may characterize the latest Stravinsky as, partially, an even intenser unconscious Schoenbergian than his adoption of Schoenberg's method indicates *per se,* we have to emphasize, at the same time, that no evaluation whatsoever emerges from our psychological analysis; we hope it is not necessary to point out that questions of musical value can only be decided on intra-musical evidence, without reference to either history or psychology. What our analysis does suggest is that musical history, by which I mean, not the chronology of styles but the evolution of techniques, can profit greatly by the application of psychoanalysis. As long as musicology takes no more than amateur notice of the clinically established results of depth psychology and, for the rest, chiefly concerns itself with *textual criticism* on the one hand and the *history of music* on the other, it has no right to its bombastic title, its fields of competence being adequately described by the italicized concepts. 'Musicology' is a translation of the French *musicologie* which in its turn derives from the German *Musikwissenchaft* (science of music), first introduced by F. Chrysander in 1863;[9] but in 1954, the majority of 'musicologists' are entirely ignorant of scientific method and have never done an honest piece of scientific work in their lives.

IV

In the interests of neat symmetry, our essay would, at this point, welcome the discovery that Schoenberg was an unconscious Stravinskyian. Some support

[9] Friedrich Chrysander (1836–1901) was the first scholar to approach Handel's music systematically, co-founding the Händel-Gesellschaft in 1856 with a view to publishing a collected edition. He spent two periods (1868–71 and 1875–82) as editor of the *Allgemeine musikalische Zeitung* and edited two collections of essays that were instrumental in the establishment of musicology as a discipline, the *Jahrbuch für musikalische Wissenschaft*, published in 1863 and 1867. With two other founding fathers of musicology, Guido Adler and the Bach scholar Philipp Spitta, he launched the quarterly *Vierteljahrsschrift für Musikwissenschaft* in 1885. It survived only until 1894 but set a precedent that influences writing about music to this day.

for such a suggestion would indeed seem to be forthcoming: one or two critics maintain that the 'Dance round the Golden Calf' from the opera, *Moses und Aron* (reviewed by Erwin Stein in our last tabular survey, Aug., 1954) is strongly influenced by *The Rite of Spring*. However, this view does not bear the most cursory technical examination – and here a comparative evaluation is quite in order; in fact, if ever two pieces were comparable, these are the two. They are, musically speaking, 'about' the same ideas and emotions, and avail themselves of the same formal and textural categories of expression; the simple question arises which of the two expresses itself better and more fully. In drastic view of the 'Dance round the Golden Calf', I consider *The Rite of Spring*, whatever its historical role may have been, a musical failure and cannot see that it has any chance of survival, except as a museum piece. Emotionally it is all too sophisticated, whereas compositionally it employs the most primitive methods. With the 'Dance', it is exactly the other way round. Emotionally it dives into the most frighteningly primitive depths which no music had hitherto touched (we remember Erwin Stein's observation, '… range of expression from utmost tenderness to the most brutal violence'), whereas in musical thought and development it is a marvel of the clearest, yet extremest and subtlest complexity which make[s] it possible for the composer to express heaven and hell, as well as the prose-poetic future and the rhyming past, in one and the same piece, and even at one and the same time.

There is a psychological possibility, perhaps even a probability, of the *Rite*'s having influenced the *Dance* in an extra-musical way: Schoenberg's unconscious or preconscious may well have thought, 'I'll show him how to do this sort of thing'. (Our unconscious minds demean themselves like that.) If such should have been the case, we should again be confronted with a somewhat hostile identification, and Schoenberg would have been, after all, a temporary and unconscious Stravinskyian, but only sub-musically, nowise in musical terms. As a matter of musical fact I submit, in any case, that the *Rite* is a dance and the *Dance* a rite.

It might, of course, be pointed out that it is unfair to compare a work of the 31-year-old Stravinsky with a work of the 58-year-old Schoenberg, but my comparison between the two pieces is not concerned with fairness – i.e. with a comparison between their respective composers – at all. If we wish to attempt an evaluating comparison between the two poles of the contemporary musical situation (or may we say, on the basis of this article, the ex-poles?), we must compare, *inter alia*, in developmental terms, and consider where, and how far, either composer has developed. If we are not careful, we shall thus land ourselves in Wiesengrund-Adorno.

V

Just as there is, in my submission, a *psychological* causal connection between Schoenberg's death and the birth of Stravinsky's serial techniques, there is a *musical* causal connection between Stravinsky's emergence as a pure contrapuntist and chamber musician and his employment of serialism. Schoenberg had always been a contrapuntist and a chamber-musician – even in the *Verklärte Nacht* and the *Gurrelieder*: unfortunately, our critics are more adept in reading the first page of a score (the one where the instrumentation is given in letter type) than in deciphering the subsequent pages of music type which, in the case of the *Gurrelieder*, would give them some chamber-musical surprises if they could read them – or if they would listen to the textures instead of staring at the orchestra. It was in fact his contrapuntal character which drove Schoenberg towards solo instrumentation and which, later, came to be responsible, amongst other factors, for the development of serial technique. All serial methods, twelve-tonal or tonal, are basically polyphonic; their harmonic aspects, however, obtrusive in certain special instances (e.g. the opening of Schoenberg's own 4th String Quartet), are secondary phenomena, and every essentially harmonic mind known to me that has dabbled in serial techniques has come to musical grief. Now, there can no longer be any doubt that a new contrapuntal age is on the way; it is only because most of our music critics, with their homophonic ears, cannot follow the new polyphony at all, that this fact is not yet 'officially' recognized. (In this connection, it is relevant to remember that Frank Howes buried Stravinsky along with Schoenberg,[10] whereupon Peter Pears – neither a Schoenbergian nor a Stravinskyian – proposed to confer upon him the honorary title of the 'Grand Undertaker of Music'.[11] Some considerable time later, on 18th November, 1953, Mr. Howes exhumed the body in view of the Cantata, in order to subject it to the following *post mortem*: 'Stravinsky may, if he pleases, knit with chattering inexpressive wind instruments, but let him keep his doctrinaire hands off English poetry, for which … he has no ear'. – See our tabular survey of Feb., 1954). There can likewise be no doubt that owing to the progressive weakening of diatonic cadential functions, the new counterpoint will become increasingly serial, both in its atonal and in its tonal spheres. With Stravinsky's becoming a Schoenbergian in matters contrapuntal, this prognosis is changing into wisdom after the event. Stravinsky is ceasing to be Schoenberg's counter-pole and is turning into what we might call Schoenberg's counterpoint.

[10] *Cf.* 'Two Revolutionaries: Schönberg and Stravinsky', *The Times*, 5 October 1951.

[11] Pears, 'writing from lively rehearsals of *Oedipus Rex* with the composer', sent a note from Cologne dated 6 October 1951, which was published in *Music Survey*, Vol. IV, No. 2, February 1952, p. 437.

VII
A Serial Masterpiece

The Music Review, Vol. 16, No. 4, November 1955, pp. 342–44

Igor Stravinsky. *In Memoriam Dylan Thomas* for tenor, string quartet, and 4 trombones.

Full score obtainable. Vocal score: 3s. 6d. (Boosey & Hawkes.)

Not since the Mass of 1947 (published 1948) for mixed chorus and double woodwind quintet has Stravinsky written a similarly perfect masterpiece. Its length is hardly more than a third of the former work, but its depth is greater than that of the Cantata (published 1952) and its breath is more continuous than that of the Septet (written and published in 1953).[1]

The sub-title, 'Dirge-Canons and Song', refers to the formal design. A central setting, for tenor and string quartet, of the poem which Dylan Thomas wrote in memory[2] of his father ('Do not go gentle into that good night') is enclosed by a prelude and postlude, both called 'Dirge-Canons' and alternating between the four trombones and the string quartet. In itself canonic, the song was written first, while the antiphonal outer sections were added as inevitable afterthoughts; if I may, very relevantly, avail myself of the language of logic – the prelude became a prosyllogism and the epilogue an episyllogism. The work was completed in the spring of 1954, about a year after Stravinsky first met the poet.

The musical interpretation of Thomas' double refrain is by no means automatic. It is a model of how to respect the form of a self-sufficient text and yet follow the demands of autonomous musical form. Within the space at my

[1] An earlier Keller article furnishes a description of the context into which this 'serial masterpiece' was born:

> The audience at the recent first English performance of this new Stravinsky work – a major event by any standards which do not altogether refuse to take the development of new music into account consisted of twenty people. Four of these were critics and the rest included a composer and his wife, a prominent promoter of 'contemporary' music, and a representative of Stravinsky's publisher, leaving just twelve representatives of the general public.
>
> *Cf.* Hans Keller, 'Contemporary Music', *The Musical Times*, Vol. 96, No. 1345, March 1955, pp. 131–32.

[2] Keller here follows Stravinsky's prefatory note in the miniature score; in fact, the poem was composed in summer–autumn 1951, and Thomas' father, D. J. Thomas, did not die until 16 December 1952.

disposal, it is impossible to deal with the astounding complexities and multiple variations of the structure; its barest outlines are complex enough:

Stanza No.	*POEM* *Lines and Refrains* *(I) & (II)*	*MUSIC* *Instrial ritornello (A)* *amd Refrains (B) & (C)*
	. . . .	(A)
(1)	— — — — . . . (I)	(B)
	— — — —	
	— — — — . . . (II)	(C)
	. . . .	(A^1)
(2)	— — — —	
	— — — —	
	— — — — . . . (I)	(B)
	. . . .	(A^2)
(3)	— — — —	
	— — — —	
	— — — — . . . (I)	(C^1)
	. . . .	(A^3)
(4)	— — — —	
	— — — —	
	— — — — . . . (I)	(B^2)
	. . . .	(A^4)
(5)	— — — —	
	— — — —	
	— — — — . . . (I)	(C^2)
	no interlude	
(6)	— — — —	(A^5)
	— — — —	
	— — — — . . . (I)	(B^3)
	— — — — . . . (II)	(C^3)
	. . . .	(A^6)

Not many words are needed if this scheme is really studied with reference to the score. The function of 'A' is pre-, inter-, and post-ludial, but as the structure closes up and becomes recapitulatory, the instrumental *ritornello* emerges, for once, together with the voice (first line of last stanza), in a formal context (C→A) which we have already heard twice and will hear again at the end and which thus assumes rondo-thematic significance. The vocal line over A^5 reverts, in its turn, to the corresponding (first) line of the fourth stanza, both starting with the same transposed inversion of the tone-row on which the entire work is based. The first line of the fifth stanza gives the same version of the row untransposed, thus reverting to the first line of the first stanza which, of course, is 'B'. The other two first lines are not so closely related to 'B' because they develop at what may fancifully be called the second-subject level of tension; one gives the retrograde form followed by the retrograde inversion, the other the retrograde inversion followed by the retrograde form. Since, however, the basic set is E–E♭–C–C♯–D, and since each first line starts with a complete form of the row, their mutual integration is established through the first semitone with which each has to begin. Unlike the rondo-like C→A, the combination A→B is itself twice reversed.

As for the basic method of unification, Stravinsky employs, for the first time, Schoenberg's method in the strictest fashion, although only horizontally. I have given a *complete* serial analysis of the song (the pre- and postlude analyse themselves) in this year's Spring issue of *Tempo.*[3] I hope my analysis may be taken as authoritative, since Stravinsky reacted to it with unqualified enthusiasm, which was particularly welcome in view of various problematic points in my article and analysis, above all my doubly serial interpretation of bars 16/4*f.* – the most complicated passage in the score from the point of view of the tone-row's behaviour.

Towards the end of my article, I remarked that the row was rhythmically committed in the outer sections, i.e. overtly thematic; 'yet Strawinsky[4] marks the "Theme" "Inversion" and so on throughout the Prelude. In the song itself, on the other hand, i.e. at the very moment when the old contrapuntal technique crystallizes into the new serial method, where the theme becomes a row and will not therefore be heard or seen as a matter of course, Strawinsky's brackets cease. Why, in that case, he has bothered to analyse the first section is incomprehensible'. In case the reader has asked himself a similar question, here is Stravinsky's marginal reply:

> Mr. Keller is absolutely right. *Explanation*: in correcting the proofs I forgot to erase in the prelude these brackets left over from my final sketches where they were put *throughout the work.** I. Str.
>
> *[Stravinsky's footnote:] this – complicating the reading of the instr. and vocal score.

A comparison between the full score and the pocket and vocal scores shows minor corrections in both the latter two; also, there are repeated down-bows in B–B[3] in the pocket score that are not shown in the full score.

[3] '*In Memoriam Dylan Thomas*: Strawinsky's Schoenbergian Technique', published in *Tempo*, No. 35, 1955, pp. 13–20. This was the article subsumed into 'Stravinsky Heard' and reproduced on pp. 133–41, below.

[4] Keller here respects the spelling used in the source.

VIII
Towards the Psychology of Stravinsky's Genius

The Listener, Vol. 56, No. 1444, 29 November 1956, p. 897

In his penetrating though often fallacious *Philosophie der neuen Musik* (Tübingen, 1949), Theodor W. Adorno plays off Schoenberg against Stravinsky whom he calls a death-mask of the past. Professor Adorno usually knows what he is talking about, but his talk is not always equal to his knowledge, chiefly because it is not inspired by that respect for a great genius without which the truest observation on him lacks perspective.

The fact remains that Stravinsky's creative character in general, and his attitude to the past in particular, has proved a headache to most musicians and critics, for the simple reason that we have never encountered this kind of great composer before. All good composers start out from the past; most bad composers remain stuck in it; but Stravinsky is the first great creator who speaks through it.

Where history fails, psychology must take its place. The problem of Stravinsky's creative character is that of our time – the problem of aggression. But the problem of his aggression is, paradoxically enough, the problem of his love.

Apropos of his treatment of Pergolesi's melodies[1] in the ballet *Pulcinella* (1919–20), Stravinsky asked: 'Should my line of action be dominated by my love or by my respect for Pergolesi's music? Is it love or respect that urges us to possess a woman? Is it not by love alone that we succeed in penetrating to the very essence of a being? But then, does love diminish respect? Respect alone remains barren and can never serve as a productive or creative factor. In order to create, there must be a dynamic force, and what force is more potent than love?'[2] He felt his 'conscience to be innocent of sacrilege' and moreover considered that his attitude towards Pergolesi was 'the only possible one

[1] In 1956 scholarship was still discovering the extent to which the music appropriated by Stravinsky was drawn from works written by composers other than Giovanni Battista Pergolesi (1710–36); *cf.* F. Walker, 'Two Centuries of Pergolesi Forgeries and Misattributions', *Music & Letters*, XXX, October 1949, pp. 297–320.

[2] Derived from Igor Stravinsky, *Chronicle of My Life, Gollancz, London*, 1936, p. 136; Keller is quoting the paraphrase printed in White's *Stravinsky: A Critical Survey*, *op. cit.*, p. 86. *Cf.* also note 4 on p. 83, below.

towards the music of earlier ages'.[3] Less known, but equally relevant, is Stravinsky's suggestion that 'rape may be justified by the creation of a child'.[4] Paul Valéry changed the metaphor: 'A lion consists of digested lambs'.[5]

Psychoanalysis recognises two basic types of love, self-love apart. Genetically the more primitive is identification, which stems from the earliest, sucking stage of infancy and whose prototype is oral incorporation: hence the technical term 'introjection' for the 'absorption of the environment into the personality' (Ernest Jones[6]); hence, too, Valéry's metaphor. The other type, 'object love', is what we commonly understand by love. In monosyllables, identification is based on the need to *be* someone. Identification is the more ambivalent of the two, not only because you destroy what you eat, but also because you want to replace the person you want to be.

Ordinary artistic development always starts with identification: while the composer's own creative ego is still weak, he identifies himself with his teachers and with older masters and proceeds to imitate them. As his originality grows, these father figures recede or are absorbed by his conscience and, if nothing drastic happens (such as the Bach crisis in Mozart's life), his creative 'love relations' with the music of other composers amount to no more than sporadic flirtations resulting in, say, variations on another composer's theme, which will be children of 'object love' rather than of identification.

Alone amongst geniuses, with the possible exception of Picasso, Stravinsky has actually developed his capacity for identification together with the unfolding of his intense originality. At the same time, as his commentary on 'Pulcinella' indicates, his creative mind also employs a good deal of highly aggressive 'object love': he makes the aggressive best of both love worlds, though identification remains the basic 'dynamic force'. No previous composer has shown any desire to compose his way 'into the very essence of a being'.

And all men kill the thing they love,
By all let this be heard,

[3] Derived from *ibid.*, p. 137.

[4] Frank Onnen (in *Stravinsky*, Continental Book Company, Stockholm, 1948, p. 25) gives a source for this remark: '"Il est permis de violer à condition de faire un enfant" ("Rape may be justified by the creation of a child") said Stravinsky once at – I believe – a press interview'. Stravinsky seems to have been paraphrasing an adage of Alexandre Dumas: 'Il est permis de violer l'histoire, à condition de lui faire de beaux enfants'.

[5] 'Le lion est fait de mouton assimilé', in Valéry's *Tel Quel I*, NRF Gallimard, Paris, 1941, p. 19.

[6] Ernest Jones (1879–1958) was Freud's first biographer (*Sigmund Freud: Life and Work*, three vols., Hogarth Press, London, 1953, 1955 and 1957) and a major figure in psychoanalysis in his own right: founder of the British Psychoanalytical Society in 1919 and of the *International Journal of Psychoanalysis* a year later, twice (1920–24 and 1932–49) President of the International Psychoanalytical Association. The definition quoted can be found in Jones' *Papers on Psycho-Analysis*, Baillière, Tindall and Cox, London, 3rd edn., 1923, p. 707.

> Some do it with a bitter look,
> Some with a flattering word,
> The coward does it with a kiss,
> The brave man with a sword! [7]

There is some special pleading here, but there is a truth too. Stravinsky has in fact himself employed the bitter look, the flattering word, and the sword, but he has never killed the past by kissing it, as so many of his followers and other neo-classicists have done.

The two symphonies which he will conduct twice next week are extremely healthy children of his ambivalent identification with more than one past, and if the first movement of the *Symphony in C* (1939–40) is a little uneasy about its synthesis of Stravinsky's characteristic, undeveloping *ostinato* technique and classical sonata development, the resultant formal friction turns out to be as valid a part of the structure as is, for instance, Beethoven's un-operatic attitude in *Fidelio.*

The *Symphony of Psalms* (1930), on the other hand, does not even evince such seeming imperfections: it is a spotless and gigantic masterpiece, profoundly expressive in its very suppression of expressionism, its in-turned, self-castigating aggression. Identifications with the past span a wide field, stretching back into the archaic, and when the opening four-part fugue of the second movement (with the answer in the dominant) raises its voice through what we might call the life-mask of Bach, we realise that the term 'neo-classicism' is just not good enough.

The severe limitations which Stravinsky's identifications impose upon his intense imagination are precisely what he wants. His urge towards formal stringency and simplicity goes beyond the requirements of unity and clarity: he does not discipline his inspiration; rather, he is more lavishly inspired by self-discipline than any other composer. Again, his love, this time his artistic self-love or self-respect, is unlike the usual artist's: again it is vehemently ambivalent, combined with, perhaps even outweighed by, aggression turned inward.

Symbolic of this self-restrictive, form-conscious simplicity is the fact that all three major works in next week's programme show cyclic devices on the one hand, and recognise C as their home tonality on the other (though two of them do not start out from home): no doubt the first concert programme of this kind in our entire history.

After Schoenberg's death, and too late for Professor Adorno to revise his theory about the antithesis of Stravinsky's and Schoenberg's attitudes, Stravinsky embarked on his serial period which has now culminated in his

[7] The source, of course, is Oscar Wilde's *The Ballad of Reading Gaol* (1897).

first twelve-tone music – the three middle movements of the *Canticum Sacrum* (1955), whose first and fifth movements, moreover, mirror each other in self-restrictive retrograde motion. My own little hypothesis, on the other hand, here seems to receive its final confirmation. The 'identification of the ego with the lost object' (Freud, *Mourning and Melancholia*, 1916)[8] is no news to the psychoanalyst, who will see in the previous ambivalent relation between the two musical leaders of our time an ideal foundation for Stravinsky's 'introjection' of Schoenberg's method: by way of creative mourning, Stravinsky identified himself with Schoenberg's serialism as soon as it had become a thing of the past. In justice to Professor Adorno, we must remind ourselves that his 'death mask of the past' now assumes a new significance, but we must continue to reject the negative evaluation implied in, or insinuated by, his formulation.

For the rest, great geniuses are few and far between, and we cannot afford to miss them when they come.

[8] The 'official' English translations of Freud's *Trauer und Melancholie* (written in 1915 and published in 1917) speak of 'an *identification* of the ego with the abandoned object'; *cf.* Sigmund Freud, *Collected Papers*, Vol. 4 (trans. Joan Riviere), Hogarth Press, London, 1924, p. 159, and *The Standard Edition of the Complete Psychological Works of Sigmund Freud*, Vol. XIV (trans. James Strachey), Hogarth Press and the Institute of Psycho-Analysis, London, 1957, p. 249.

IX
Rhythm: Gershwin and Stravinsky

The Score and I.M.A. Magazine, No. 20, June 1957, pp. 19–31

Rhythm is the ultimate source of music. True, the new-born screams before he rhythmically sucks, but his sucking does something about his screaming: it is his first constructive, pre-artistic act. When he has grown up and stands on the operatic stage, he is not allowed to scream without remembering rhythm; whereas if he has become a composer, aboriginal or ultra-modern, he is allowed to create a percussion piece without remembering pitch. In other words, there is rhythm without melody, but there is no melody or harmony or counterpoint without rhythm.

We can go further and say that rhythm, being so deep as to be pre-musical and indeed pre-acoustic, is the one element of music which can musically manifest itself outside the aural sphere. Stravinsky, characteristically enough, likes to watch an orchestra: he does not believe in closed eyes. His visual satisfaction is obviously rhythmical. The reason why most musicians loathe most ballets (except when they compose them) is that they get an anti-musical impression from the dancers' movements, as painful, in kind if not in degree, as the experience of someone playing out of time. For the musician, the distinctly musical experience of watching Fred Astaire dancing a Gershwin tune written for him is far more artistic than the spectacle of what, according to the ballet experts, is a profound ballet, sublimely danced. The musician's mind is physically committed to temporal sense. I don't think I am alone in my musical irritation at watching two Belisha beacons on either side of a zebra crossing disregarding each other. Like Astaire, they are visual percussion instruments, but unlike him they play a bad piece: it is a polymetric composition without rhythm. Each is in time by itself, but the relation they establish between themselves is arbitrary – unmotivated though not undetermined, inevitable without being necessary. Instead of a rhythmic impression, the burning questions 'why?' and 'what for?' arise – just as in the case of many rhythmic series: the trouble about these is, not that they are over-determined,[1]

[1] Keller usually employs this term in its non-evaluative, psychoanalytic sense, in which it refers to the idea that products of the unconscious will be condensations of a number of impulses and experiences; *cf.* also note 17 on p. 135.

but that they aren't half as determined as any rhythmic relation in a Mozart or Schoenberg work: they replace rhythm by what, in essence, is metrical *cliché*, itself undetermined.

That every work of art establishes its own rules, rhythmically and otherwise, is a dangerous half-truth. There is no communication without a minimum of pre-established terms of reference. Brand-new rules of the game are only possible where there is no communication – in a game. Delight in pseudo-artistic games, a sophisticated regression to childhood play, is the chief danger at any stage of artistic frustration.

The American neo-twelve-toners talk a great deal about 'pre-compositional' elements. By these they mean, not any pre-established common terms of reference, but rows constructed before they are submitted to the actual compositorial process, the creative act. Confusing analytical and creative order, they thus turn Schoenberg's own dodecaphony upside down. Even in his elementary essay on the principles of his method, Schoenberg says that

> sometimes a set [i.e. tone row] will not fit every condition an experienced composer can foresee, especially in those *ideal cases where the set appears at once in the form, character and phrasing of a theme.*[2]

In other words, the row is abstracted from a concrete basic idea. In a private letter to Josef Rufer (February 5, 1951), where he is able to be more personal, Schoenberg makes this point far more apodeictically:

> The original idea of a row invariably emerges in the form of a thematic character.[3]

The rules which the Schoenbergian tone row establishes, then, are subject to a concrete inventive ruling which is partly melodic and basically rhythmic. This original creative act ensures a solid basis of communication, for since it is the cause rather than the effect of the row, it must be partly determined by pre-dodecaphonic rules or conditions of expression. Thus, Schoenberg's rhythmic backgrounds are always firmly rooted in quasi-physical rhythmic

[2] *Composition with Twelve Tones*, in *Style and Idea* ([Philosophical Library,] New York, 1950; [Williams & Norgate,] London, 1951), p. 114; italics mine. –HK

[3] Quoted in Rufer's *Die Komposition mit zwölf Tönen* (Berlin, 1952), p. 86; translation mine. Humphrey Searle's translation (*Composition with Twelve Notes Related Only to One Another*, London, 1954, p. 92), though partly more literal, does not altogether hit the mark: 'The first conception of a series always takes place in the form of a thematic character'. Schoenberg's original German runs thus: 'Der erste Einfall einer Reihe erfolgt immer in Form eines thematischen Charakters'. –HK

Rufer (1893–1985) studied with Zemlinsky and Schoenberg in his native Vienna, following the latter to Berlin as his assistant when he took over Busoni's masterclass in composition at the Prussian Academy of the Arts. Rufer's direct involvement with Schoenberg during the development of serialism gave his later book on the subject especial authority: *Die Komposition mit Zwölf Tönen*, Max Hesses Verlag, Berlin, 1952; translated by Humphrey Searle as *Composition with Twelve Notes*, Barrie and Rockliff, London/Macmillan, New York, 1954. Keller reviewed the German version in *Music Review*, Vol. 15, No. 1, February 1954, pp. 84–86.

sense, which makes his foregrounds comprehensible to the musician and old-fashioned to the dodecaphoneys[4] – who, however, praise the 'advancedness' of the String Trio, without apparently noticing this passage:

Ex. 1

– one of the few instances in Schoenberg's entire output where he lets the rhythmic background, *against* which he composes, emerge to the fore, because otherwise the complex foreground itself would not become sufficiently comprehensible. Rhythmically, this passage could hardly be more primitive; if you displace the bar-lines by a half-bar, you get a perfectly square, even sequential four-bar structure, the scheme being that of a dance rhythm. Thus behaves one of the most anti-symmetrical composers in our musical history. In fact, I do not think a western composer can, at this historical juncture, honestly compose without reference, positive or negative, to the dance schemes which dominated, *inter alia*, the Austro-German tradition up to Brahms. The sometimes so-called 'measured' (as distinct from metrical) rhythms of Stravinsky, Bartók or Hindemith are by no means unrelated to these metrical backgrounds, which in fact, serve as implied, if suppressed, terms of reference. What seems a syncopation is a syncopation, though it may be much more than that.

The two great composers who have developed the art of syncopation – of meaningfully, comprehensibly and consistently contradicting one of the Belisha beacons – in sufficient isolation from other means of structuralization to be recognized as 'rhythmic' composers by music critics and popular music fans respectively, are Stravinsky, who is seventy-five, and Gershwin who, though sixteen years younger, died twenty years ago. They are no 'more rhythmic' than Schoenberg (no great composer is more rhythmic than any other great composer); but while Schoenberg, who comes from the sonata which sings as well as dances, 'builds a lofty Rhythm, that shall outlast the insolence of time',[5] Gershwin and Stravinsky beat time with its own weapon: they beat time against time; they do not sing against the dance, but dance on top of it and against it. Nevertheless, the two are as different as they are similar.

[4] Keller applied this term to composers and critics who espoused a 'serial technique' that was based on visual or mathematical manipulations rather than on concrete musical thought; *cf.* 'First Performances: Dodecaphoneys', *The Music Review* , Vol. 16, No. 4, November 1955, pp. 323–39.

[5] The quotation is from Joshua Poole's poem 'Proeme', published in his collection *The English Parnassus* in 1657.

How does Gershwin deal, for instance, with a rhythmic model like Ex. 1's – in his case four instead of eight equal notes which, again, starting at the full $\frac{4}{4}$ – bar, 'beat up' to the half-bar (Ex. 2(a))? He defines an implied, square background (Ex. 2(b)) by way of an harmonic *ostinato* rhythm (see Ex2(c)) and, compressing the melodic background while retaining the metrical 4-bar scheme, achieves a highly asymmetrical rhythmic structure within the symmetrical frame that is required for a popular tune, thus making a strictly functional virtue out of the necessity of immediate comprehensibility:

Ex.2

(a)

(b)

(c)

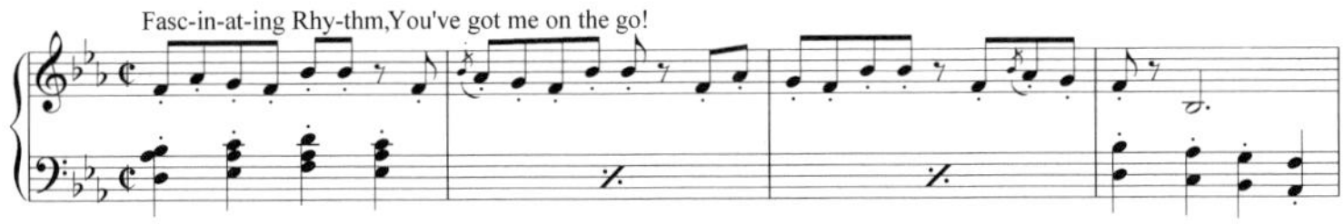

'You've got me on the go' indeed: every upbeat is an upbeat to an upbeat, thus confirming Riemann's theory which, if I may simplify, says just that.[6]

It is, however, a very sweeping theory, and none is better fitted to keep it in its place than Stravinsky. We readily identify the composer of this rhythm –

Ex. 3

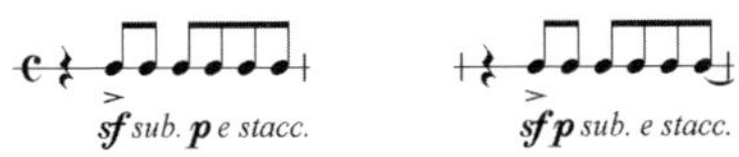

– which turns Ex. 2(a) upside down or, to be precise, right side left, rear side front: it is the strict retrograde version of a perfectly straightforward upbeat model, resulting in what is, for western pre-Stravinskyian ears, an unprecedented rhythmic structure, an extended, unprepared, pure downbeat consisting of equal metrical units which are normally used to confirm the regular metre by way of such up-beat phrases as Ex. 2(b), and falling on a weak beat of the bar into the bargain. Stravinsky knows full well that he is contradicting Ex. 2(a) with this rhythm from the *Symphony of Psalms*; in fact, the tension

[6] Hugo Riemann, *Musikalische Dynamik und Agogik* (Leipzig [*recte* Hamburg], 1884). Ironically enough, there is a Russian, but no English, translation. –HK

(The publisher of Riemann's book was Daniel Rahter (1828–91), who established his publishing house in Hamburg in 1879. From 1869 to 1890 he was also manager of the music-publisher A. Büttner in St Petersburg.)

created by the contradiction is part of the composition. The reason why he writes an accent as well as '*sf sub. p*' is the same as that which made Riemann formulate his up-beat theory,[7] the same too as the reason why so penetrating an observer as Theodor W. Adorno tears Stravinsky to shreds with the intellectual power of (though with less consistency than) a philosopher and the subterranean passion of a religious fanatic:[8] this reason is simply the upbeat tendency of our central-European musical tradition which, for Adorno, is identical with music, whereas Stravinsky flies into its face, his dynamics making sure that there should be no half-heartedness about the attack, that it be clear that nothing but the clean opposite of an upbeat phrase will do. Adorno, whose use of psychology, psychoanalysis and psychiatry is somewhat more extensive than his knowledge of these disciplines, thinks that Stravinsky's 'rhythmic attitude comes extremely close to the schema of catatonic conditions';[9] he regards this kind of rhythm as schizophrenic, its repetitive 'shocks' as arbitrary, and even its most 'restless activity' as, basically, psychotic passivity. All of which amounts to no more than the fact that he doesn't know an unmitigated, unprepared, unresolved downbeat phrase when he hears one: the shock of Ex. 3's accent is too great for him to absorb. He cannot identify the 'grain' – Ex. 2(a) – against which he feels it goes Belisha-beacon-like, and is thus unable to recognize its strict motivation, the strictly 'retrograde' tension it produces, the suspension and suspense which he mistakes for passivity because it is anti-active in the sense of anti-forward-urging.

Every well-composed passage, every articulated idea, makes two kinds of sense – local and total. Its local sense develops against the background of implied terms of reference shared by composer and listener; its total sense develops against the background of the composer's own premises – ultimately his basic idea. Having demonstrated the elements of Ex. 3's local significance, it next behoves us to give the lie to Adorno's charge of arbitrariness from the point of view of the *Symphony of Psalms*' total structure. In the last resort, Ex. 3 derives from the opening, fundamental thought, both metrically and rhythmically (Ex. 4):

Ex. 4

[7] Riemann (1849–1919) articulated – most extensively in his *System der musikalischen Rhythmik und Metrik* of 1903 – the theory of *Auftaktigkeit* ('upbeatness'), in which all metrical units proceed from a weak upbeat (*Auftakt*) to a strong downbeat.

[8] Theodor W. Adorno, *Philosophie der neuen Musik* ([Mohr,] Tübingen, 1949). The subsequent translations are mine. –HK

[9] *Ibid.*, p. 117. –HK

The metrical derivation from the evenly distributed semiquavers is obvious, but it is the rhythmic derivation that constitutes the characteristic creative act. Like Ex. 3, the work itself starts with what Adorno would call a 'shock' that is the contradictory opposite of an upbeat, and which together with the ensuing semiquaver movement yields the basic idea, of whose extraordinary rhythm Ex. 3 (which does not occur until the 3rd movement) turns out to be a well-defined compression, i.e. an exact diminution. Here it is again (*cf.* Ex. 3), superimposed upon the basic idea (*cf.* Ex. 4), with the latter in proportionately smaller note-values:

Ex. 5

Unable clearly to perceive either the local or the total structural motivation of any Stravinskyan syncopation, Adorno, though an outstanding musician, thinks Stravinsky's music mad: 'Just as catatonic actions are rigid and at the same time bizarre, so Stravinsky's repetitions combine conventionalism and damage, the former recalling the mask-like, ceremonial politeness of certain schizophrenics'.[10]

Nevertheless, even in his most unbalanced diagnoses, Adorno has 'got something'. Remembering the word 'bizarre' in his characterization, we turn to Stravinsky's earliest musical memories, which he described in his autobiography,[11] and which Markevitch, who recounted them in his *causerie* introducing his Brussels performances of *The Rite of Spring* early in 1949, rightly found intensely significant.[12] As a child, Stravinsky liked to visit an old peasant who used to sing to him, if singing was the word: he incessantly repeated two syllables 'in the most bizarre rhythms', providing, moreover, a percussive accompaniment by placing his right hand in his left arm-pit and, quickly beating his arm against his body, producing 'very rhythmic', comic sounds. When I read Adorno about Stravinsky, it often seems to me as if he were talking about that peasant rather than about the composer, and the 'something' he usually 'gets' is by no means always a superficial truth: often it is, on the contrary, too deep (as distinct from profound) to be artistically true, in that he seems to evaluate Stravinsky's psychological incentives and unconscious or preconscious stimuli rather than the finished work of art – a common fallacy at the root of wrong but sensitive criticism. What is obvious

[10] *Ibid.* –HK

[11] *Chroniques de ma Vie* ([Denoël et Steele,] Paris, 1935) . –HK

[12] Igor Markevitch, *Une Messe Naturelle,* the last and relevant section republished in the *Strawinsky* issue of *Musik der Zeit* ([Boosey & Hawkes,] Bonn, 1952) . –HK

is that the old peasant produced repetitive 'bizarre' rhythms against a metrically repetitive basic rhythm, not the arbitrary polymetre of the Belisha beacons on the one hand, nor the highly organized polyrhythmic syncopations of a Stravinsky on the other. But one thing the peasant seems to have had in common with both: his antipathy to upbeat structures.

Gershwin's childhood memories are equally illuminating. His unsentimental, masculine, 'rhythmic' attitude towards the most sentimental of *genres*, i.e. that of the American popular song, must actually have been promoted by the unmusicality of his early environment. He was a pretty wild boy, and

> ... by the mores of the city streets, anybody who studied music was a 'sissy' or 'Maggie', and George accepted the values of his comrades. In his early childhood music meant little to him ...[13]

At the ages of six and ten, however – at the beginning and in the middle of what the psychoanalyst calls the 'latency period', when the oedipal crisis (particularly fruitful in Gershwin's case) is over and sublimations develop – he underwent some musical experiences which had a profound influence on his creative growth.

> He was about six years old when, strolling along 125th Street, he stopped outside a penny arcade and heard Anton Rubinstein's *Melody in F* on an automatic piano. 'The peculiar jumps in the music held me rooted,' he later recalled ...
>
> One day, during the same period, while roller-skating in Harlem, he heard jazz music outside the Baron Wilkins Club where Jim Europe and his band performed regularly. The exciting rhythms and raucous tunes made such an impression on him that he never forgot them. From then on he often skated up to the club and sat down on the pavement outside to listen to the music.[14]

What David Ewen calls 'the most significant of George's musical adventures' occurred when, at the age of ten,

> he was playing ball outside P.S.25... Through the open window, he heard the strains of Dvořák's *Humoresque* played on a violin. The performer was one of his fellow students, an eight-year old prodigy by the name of Maxie Rosenzweig [now Max Rosen]...

Ewen goes on to quote Gershwin's recollection direct: 'It was, to me, a flashing revelation of beauty ...'.[15]

[13] David Ewen, *A Journey to Greatness: The Life and Music of George Gershwin* ([W. H. Allen,] London 1956), p. 29. –HK

[14] *Ibid.*, p. 30. –HK

[15] *Ibid.* –HK

When I suggest that these experiences influenced the growth of Gershwin's creative mind, I do not overlook the fact that his budding personality chose its experiences – one eminently rhythmic, the other two pre-eminently melodic, yet both characterized by rhythmic figures constantly recurring. The experiences are symptomatic either way, as causes and as effects, and their causative significance clearly emerges as soon as we realize that the structural outlines of the Rubinstein and the Dvořák are remembered in virtually every Gershwin song, whose rhythmic and harmonic vigour precludes, at the same time, any risk of 'sissyness', of which the *Humoresque*, at any rate, is not, in all conscience, entirely free. What is more, the unobtrusively pentatonic opening of the Dvořák with its subsequent diatonic assimilation, and the momentarily flattened third followed by the cadentially gapped seventh, are an unmistakable basis for Gershwin's melodic style with its subtle interplay of a more or less hidden tonal penta-scale (often gapped by a further degree, as in Ex. 7 below, or in ''Swonderful', 'I love your funny face' and 'How long has this been going on'[16]), of hexachords and 'blue' notes on the one hand, and diatonic implications, rejoinders, and contradictions on the other. 'There's a somebody I'm longing to see', like the rhythmically more complex 'Clap-a yo' hand' (see footnote 13), unfolds the full tonal penta-scale, the opening phrase being in fact a virtual variation of the opening of the *Humoresque*, though rhythmicized beyond superficial recognition. The entertainment industry has promptly de-rhythmicized and re-sentimentalized it: many readers will be surprised to learn that Gershwin directs *scherzando*, and that the theme is in sharply dotted rhythm. Thus the world of popular music regresses along the path of Gershwin's own development, approaching the sentimental occasional product of a 'serious' composer instead of adhering to the meaningful, rhythmic zest of a 'light' composer!

The 'peculiar jumps' of Rubinstein's *Melody* must have contributed their own share towards stimulating Gershwin's leaping tendency on the one hand, and, diatonic as they are, warning it against schematic, folkish, primitively jazzy uses of gapped scales on the other. Sure enough, the *Melody* 'jumps' to the dominant's minor ('blue') third (the tonic's 'blue' seventh), and descends to the dominant *via* its Neapolitan sixth, which we might call

[16] I have chosen the latter three examples because these songs can be heard in the new Paramount picture *Funny Face*, which is likely to remain current for quite some time. There are three more Gershwin songs in this film, 'He loves and she loves', 'Let's kiss and make up' and 'Clap-a yo' hand', the latter taken, not from the original *Funny Face* (1927), but from *Oh Kay!* (1926). Likewise, 'How long has this been going on' has been taken from another musical, i.e. *Rosalie* (1928), for which Gershwin only wrote seven numbers, Sigmund Romberg being responsible for the other eight. On the other hand, two leading numbers from the original *Funny Face* have not been included in the film, i.e. 'The Babbitt and the Bromide' and 'My one and only' ('What am I gonna do'), the latter a masterpiece which, fantastically enough, is out of print and received no mention in David Ewen's book (*op. cit.*). The remaining songs in the film are by another composer and of no musical value. –HK

its 'blue second' – following, on the terminological level, Gershwin's fruitful mix-up of diatonicism and jazz modality.

These, then, were the stimuli offered by Gershwin's early models: flowing melody with repeated, upbeating rhythmic figures; jazz syncopations; melodic leaps and gaps; and the possibility of combining the seven-note scale with, or playing it off against, all sorts of others, which in his case came to mean a wide range of possibilities, from four-note scales to 'blue' nine-note scales. With his unfailing sense of form (though, like Chopin and Webern, only of small form), he developed a degree of integration between melodic and rhythmic gaps (i.e. syncopations: see Ex. 7 below) which many of our rhythmic serialists would envy him, if they had developed their spontaneous musicianship sufficiently to recognize the melodic gaps in the first place.[17]

'Rhuthmós' means about the same as 'rhythm', but 'rheîn' – the verb is always older than the noun – means 'to flow'. When, say, Mahler writes 'fliessend, aber ohne Hast' (flowing, but without haste) in the development of his Fourth Symphony's opening movement, he announces the approach of our time's rhythmic crises, due to the return of counterpoint and the simultaneous 'emancipation of the dissonance'. In traditional Italian terminology, the direction would have been tautological: song flows anyway, and the Italian instruments have to sing, even when they are dancing. The direction *scorrevole* is no pleonasm because it adds an element which Mahler expressly excludes – that of haste.

The music of the central-European tradition flows. It is developmental music, and the square, metrical dance schemes against which its unfolding melodies are thrown into relief make sure that the supremacy of time, in both its psychological and its musico-technical sense, is never endangered, even though it may be questioned by sundry healthy opposition motions across the bar-lines. It is all very well, and of course quite true, to say that bar-lines should be seen but not played, yet the simple and important fact remains that they are always heard: even when you listen to the best, rhythmic rather than metrical interpretation of a pre-modern piece, you know what time it is in.

This complex marriage of song and dance, with the dance doing all the dirty work and the song therefore able to enjoy itself, is the whole strength of the Austro-German masterpieces. In fact, while developmental music readily develops into the opposite of drum music, it can't do without the drum's implications, even though it may silence its regular beat. The upbeat is development in germ. You don't beat a drum up, but down. Yet you have to

[17] I drew the attention of a young, highly serially minded composer, who had formed the conventional 'highbrow' opinion that Gershwin was *Kitsch*, to the diatonic 'naturalization' of the pentatonic scale in 'There's a somebody I'm longing to see', which he happened to be whistling; I shall never forget his startled face as he woke up to the fact that the opening 7-note ascent was nothing but the pentatonic scale driving up to the higher octave of the supertonic. –HK

raise your hands before and in between the drum beats. True, anacrusis does derive from song and speech, but song and speech are themselves determined by the rhythms of infantile sexuality, from the moment 'go' – the first sucking experience, which contains as many 'upbeats' as 'downbeats'. The raising of the drummer's hand thus is not merely a practical necessity, but the silent part of a body rhythm which can be *voiced.* The flow of music is impossible without upbeats, but the relative structural importance of upbeat and downbeat may vary enormously. Even within the sonata, which beats up and up to an unprecedented degree, there are such extremes as Mendelssohn's *Midsummer Night's Dream* Overture, which is so downbeating, so static a masterpiece that it came to be Toscanini's best sonata,[18] and the opening of Schoenberg's second Quartet, with its tempo direction 'etwas langsamer anfangen' (start a little more slowly). More slowly than what? We haven't heard or seen anything yet! More slowly than the main tempo announced by the first main beat – 12 bars further along! It was Schoenberg rather than Riemann who brought the upbeat to its ultimate triumph, extending its field of structural action on the one hand while refusing to indulge in any but the most urgently needed cadential downbeats on the other – refusing to 'wrap things up like the classics, which is no longer necessary', as, I gather, he once said in class.[19] Congenital contrapuntist that he was, and owing loyalty to the sonata at the same time, he attacked the rhythmic crisis by freeing the role of the voice (natural or instrumentalized) from regular metre and exploiting its forward-urging, developing capacity to what has so far proved the limit. No other composer's music 'is' so little and 'becomes' so much: the flow has become a torrent.

Stravinsky on the other hand – and this is an achievement as overpowering as the discovery of the diatonic scale or the tone row – swims up-stream. He moves against time, he annihilates the rhythmic crisis by leading it to an unforeseeable conclusion: if I can't swim smoothly down, I shall swim up. The retrograde version of the upbeat which we have noted is merely a tiny symptom of this large-scale reversal of musical 'time'. The creative strength that is needed to counter the physically natural movement of music – the simple, primitive, regular rhythmic flow – must be as elemental as is the primitive, sexual impulse itself. Time must, of course, go on, and music must continue to proceed. In fact, Stravinsky never forgets to define, by overt or hidden implication, the flow (undiscovered by Adorno) against which he moves. Count $\frac{3}{16}$ across the constantly changing time signatures in the first

[18] *Sic*, though Keller's meaning may reasonably be judged obscure. Both Adorno and Furtwängler referred to Toscanini as a 'Taktschläger' ('time-beater'), and so Keller's point may be that the Overture lent itself to Toscanini's approach.

[19] Keller was acquainted with a number of people – such as Dika Newlin and Egon Wellesz – who had studied with Schoenberg and may have heard this phrase from them.

section of the *Sinfonia* from the Octet; or (see Ex. 6) count $\frac{3}{4}$ from Ex. 4 to the contralto entry and indeed beyond, until you get to the syncopations of *Et deprecationem meam,* where the metre emerges to the fore and, resubmerged, again 'works' without remainder at the contralto re-entry – and what may be left of Adorno's theory of arbitrary rhythmic shocks evaporates into thin air.

Ex. 6

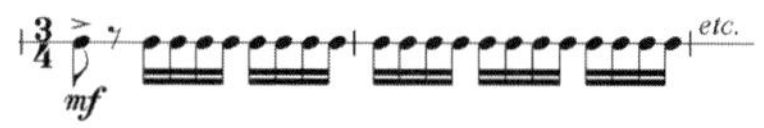

Quite independently of one another, Adorno[20] and I[21] have drawn attention to the strong sado-masochistic element in Stravinsky's creative character, his observation following mine within a matter of weeks: 'A sado-masochistic trait accompanies Stravinsky's music through all its phases'. When two musicians arrive at the same, rather complex characterization, one as a detractor, the other as an admirer, there is likely to be something in it. I seem to remember that in a Third Programme talk the Editor of this journal[22] was troubled by a later reference of mine[23] to the historical role of Stravinsky's creative sado-masochism. Perhaps he had the impression that an unfavourable evaluation was implied; but from my writings on Stravinsky[24] it should be evident that unlike Adorno, I should never have dreamt of evaluating a creative character trait as such, negatively or positively. The fact

[20] *Op. cit.* (1949), p. 104. –HK

[21] *The Music Review*, vol. x, No. 1 (February, 1949), p. 42. –HK

[22] *The Score* was founded in 1949 by William Glock, who remained its editor until it ceased publication in 1961. For twelve issues, from No. 10 (1954) until No. 22 (1957), its full title was *The Score and I.M.A. Magazine*; it then reverted to its original name. On Glock, *cf.* note 4 on p. 110, below.

[23] In *Benjamin Britten* (London, 1952), Donald Mitchell and Hans Keller (eds.), p. 339. –HK

[24] Far be it from me to suggest that they are required reading; all I would ask is that they should be read before an opinion on my critical attitude towards this towering genius is formed. A few months ago in *The Musical Times*, a writer suggested that I had positively changed my mind about Stravinsky in view of his serial works. In point of fact, while I have qualified my admiration for two of these, my praise of such masterpieces as the *Mass* or the *Symphony of Psalms* was at once intense and unreserved. I have never said, suggested or implied that serial technique has made a better composer of Stravinsky, and I have never used idiom, style or technique as a criterion for the evaluation of any work of any composer. –HK

The writer was Anthony Milner, in whose article 'The Lunatic Fringe Combed' (*The Musical Times*, Vol. 97, No. 1364, October 1956, pp. 516–18) is found the following: 'It is not very long since Stravinsky's adoption of serial techniques earned him the ecstatic eulogies of two London critics who had previously been lukewarm in their appreciation. One of these has recently hailed Mozart as an unconscious serialist'. Milner obviously had in mind Keller's article 'Strict Serial Technique in Classical Music', *Tempo*, No. 37, pp. 12–24, Autumn 1955, and/or his chapter 'The Chamber Music', in Robbins Landon and Mitchell (eds.), *The Mozart Companion, op. cit.*, pp. 90–137. Milner's argument that Keller had changed his mind may have been occasioned by an essay of Keller's from four years earlier ('The Musical Character', in *Benjamin Britten: A Commentary on his Works op. cit.*, p. 335), where he described *The Rake's Progress* and Strauss' *Die Liebe der Danae* as 'sham creations' which

> at no previous time [...] would have been written by good composers. [...] On even the most cursory inspection [...] *The Rake*'s and *Danae*'s 'beauty' and 'melody' will be found to be pale and defective copies of their easily recognizable models, so that there is not the faintest reason why one should not rather listen to the models themselves, e.g. *Così fan tutte* (more than *Don Giovanni*) in the case of *The Rake*, or Wagner and the earlier Strauss himself in the case of *Danae.*

as I see it is that Stravinsky's genius has utilized its sado-masochism, i.e. both its aggression turned inwards[25] and its enjoyment of such self-attack, towards his unique, tense, meaning-laden suppressionism. His anti-expressiveness does not, as Adorno thinks, result in emptiness, but in fullness fully opposed, in a state of statically intense tension which, on the deepest level, is achieved through his opposing the flow of rhythm by rhythm itself. In terms of the later Freudian instinct theory,[26] Stravinsky wages war against the musical expression of 'Eros', which is what leads to 'expressionism', by employing the instinct's own aim, the satisfaction through rhythm, in the service of 'Thanatos'. It is an endopsychic nuclear war if ever there was one, with the nuclear weapon of rhythm on either side, and if in the end there is equilibrium and peace, it only tends to show that the war to end all wars, if ever it happens, will have to be fought within.

Thus considered, Stravinsky's dynamic staticism is no longer a riddle, nor is his 'unmelodic' melodism: the rhythmic fight against rhythm, the reversal of the melodic impulse inevitably results in a new type of melody, the exact opposite of Wagner's, which is as erotic (in the Freudian sense) as Stravinsky's is sado-masochistic. The spatial impression, too, which Stravinsky's music has so often conveyed, loses its mystery, for if the struggle against time is to be successful, it cannot do without the illusion of a spatial aspect. We cannot imagine time moving against time except in terms of space, as when we run up a downward-moving escalator, or contradict the movement of a train by walking to the dining-car; in fact, a psychological suspension of time automatically produces space. Stravinsky does not close his eyes like the straightforwardly expressive musician: perhaps he knows that in order to express the rhythmic suppression of rhythm, one of the profoundest possible conflicts, he has to call space and pre-musical rhythm to his aid, that he has to break down the barriers between the dimensions and summon up synæsthesia. Even his, for a musician, unusual interest in the danced dance (as distinct from the composed dance) seems to become explainable: there is nothing

[25] In *The Message of Igor Strawinsky* ([Boosey & Hawkes,] London, 1953), Theodore Stravinsky, without any psychological knowledge and as it were inadvertently, gives a sensitive description of this gradual introversion of aggression, from the still extraverted 'aggressiveness [of *The Rite of Spring*] which gives it the cataclysmic character one knows' (p. 15) to the point where 'Strawinsky's evolution led him to simplify his language by scrapping his "aggressive" … side' (p. 18); except that one does not, of course, 'scrap' an instinctual force: if it is no longer visible or audible, it has turned inward. –HK

[26] Sigmund Freud, *Jenseits des Lustprinzips* ([Internationaler Psychoanalytischer Verlag,] Vienna, 1920). Third edition: Vienna, 1924. English translation by C. J. M. Hubback: *Beyond the Pleasure Principle* ([The International Psycho-analytical Press,] London, 1922). A new English translation is in preparation. –HK

Keller's closing remark here is mysterious: James Strachey's 'new translation' had been published by The Hogarth Press/The International Psycho-Analytical Library, London, in 1950 and five years later a 'somewhat modified' version had appeared in Vol. 18 of the *Standard Edition.* Although Keller, with his connections to the world of psychoanalysis, may have had advance knowledge of the 'corrected reprint' of the latter that appeared in 1961, it is possible that he knew of a project that did not come to fruition.

musical in a dance that cannot be expressed in music, but the movement of music against music may well have to call back into play the dance from, or through, which music has grown.

The difference between the two syncopators, the two dancers against the dance, is finally crystallizing. On the surface level, we have distinguished Gershwin and Stravinsky on the one hand from Schoenberg, our *tertium comparationis*, on the other; but in rhythmic essence Gershwin really stands between Stravinsky and Schoenberg, in fact nearer to Schoenberg.

Like Stravinsky, Gershwin's parents, the Gershovitzes, came from St. Petersburg. Gershwin's own pronounced American folklorism and his disobedient attitude to 'straight rhythm' may have benefited from his un-central-European background; perhaps it is not even a coincidence that his two early models, Dvořák and Rubinstein, were both Easterners, though both strongly Westernized. Like Schoenberg and Rubinstein, however, Gershwin was also a Jew, and as a musical race the Jews are erotic rather than aggressive, 'lyric' rather than 'rhythmic'.[27] The synthesis of the two elements in Gershwin's creative character is obvious. It is a synthesis under the primacy of the upbeating melodic flow: Jim Europe and his band have to heed the demands of Rubinstein and Dvořák. On July 11 twenty years ago, American radio listeners heard the announcement, 'The man who said he had more tunes in his head than he could put down on paper in a hundred years is dead today in Hollywood'. Gershwin has written songs in 'straight rhythm', but he never wrote a rhythm, however 'fascinating', that was not a forward-urging tune at the same time: *pace* his rhythm, what he wrote was songs. If Stravinsky's 'Eros' serves his 'Thanatos', Gershwin's 'Thanatos', his aggression, serves his 'Eros'.

When Gershwin dances against the dance, then, the contradiction always serves the ultimate end of up- and onward-beating motion. His syncopations are either anticipations or anticipatory suspensions: when he stems the flow, the effect is that of a floodgate, in that an all the intenser forward-motion is anticipated. He never moves up-stream, never suspends time. Nowhere is this fundamental character difference between him and Stravinsky more striking than where Stravinsky might be thought to meet him on his own ground, in the *Ebony Concerto*, whose every upbeat serves its own opposition, serves to be beaten back or beat itself back. Neither the *Ebony Concerto* nor the *Rhapsody in Blue* are what both have been described as – 'symphonic jazz'; at the same time, they move away from what *could* be thus described in opposite directions: one up-stream, the other down.[28]

[27] Starting with Joachim, the Jews have come to occupy most front places among violinists. Their success as pianists, on the other hand, has by no means been so disproportionate. –HK

[28] In his *Stravinsky* (Stockholm, 1948, pp. 42ff), Frank Onnen likewise objects to the term 'symphonic jazz', but since he goes on to say that 'Stravinsky's *Ebony Concerto* … is, in the first place, a deeply

Gershwin's interest in the danced dance is naive, personal, almost pleonastic – the overflow of the rhythmic energy he puts into his music anyway:

> His fine muscular co-ordination that made him such a splendid pianist (and frequently without practising), and so good an athlete, also made him an excellent dancer. He used feet, body, and hands with the limpid grace of a trained performer. He sometimes gave strikingly effective imitations of Fred Astaire, even in some of his more adroit steps; and during the rehearsals of *Lady Be Good* he gave Astaire a valuable suggestion for an exit step for *Fascinating Rhythm*.[29]

Astaire becomes an optional percussion instrument in Gershwin's scoring, directly so with his step-dancing, and synæsthetically, visually, with his movements, which underline certain features of the music but are not, of course, really necessary.

Throughout the preceding investigation, I have, needless to say, isolated outstanding creative character traits and achievements. Naturally, there is much more to Stravinsky than his sado-masochistic downbeats, while Schoenberg has written his static music which suspends time, pre-eminently in the third of the *Five Pieces for Orchestra*, the only one with a 'spatial' title (*Summer Morning by a Lake*). My outline of Gershwin's character, however rough, is completer, because his is not a universal genius like Schoenberg's or Stravinsky's. Within its circumscribed limits, however, it is extremely complex, as is his simply-clad music. Leibowitz[30] needs about three pages to analyze the thirty-year-old Webern's 12-bar orchestral piece that opens Op. 10; if I were to analyze the thirty-year-old Gershwin's 32-bar[31] 'Embraceable You' on precisely the same level, it would take me about six pages; as for the compression of rhythmic structure that is 'The Man I Love', it would require an extended article.

What these three composers – my two title figures and the one I have chosen to 'produce' them – have in common is their incorruptible allegiance to that elemental rhythmic source which is in all of us inasmuch as we are musical, and which makes us understand each other's music. Whether they follow it or contradict it, they always draw on it, and their rules of procedure always acknowledge it. In this they differ from a considerable number of

---

moving piece of music, over which lies the sadness and the melancholy of the blues, the old laments of a race that was from generation to generation oppressed and down-trodden', a description that could literally be applied to more than one of Gershwin's works for the concert hall, his clarification does not seem to get us much further. –HK

[29] David Ewen, *op. cit.*, p. 136. –HK

[30] René Leibowitz, *Schoenberg et son école* ([J. B. Janin,] Paris, 1947). English translation by Dika Newlin: *Schoenberg and his School* ([Philosophical Library,] New York, 1949), pp. 199ff. –HK
Cf. also note 2 on p. 35, above.

[31] Perhaps '16-bar' would be a more musical description. –HK

contemporary composers whose rhythmic source is but a trickle, and who waste their time devising means to replace it, *inter alia*, by what they call 'static' music. There is all the difference in the world between the dynamic staticism of a Stravinsky and the rhythm-less, empty immobility of those who misinterpret Webern, that ascetic but nowise impotent expressionist, for their own purposes of neurotic non-expression.[32] Ira Gershwin, the brother of the composer whose lyrics form a powerful contribution to some of the greatest rhythmic structures of our time, has really put our art's *condition sine qua non* in a nutshell:

Ex. 7

Sequitur.

[32] By no means all neo-Webernites are included in this condemnation. –HK

X
Symphony of Psalms

Programme note for a performance in Leeds Town Hall on 17 October 1958, as part of the Leeds Centenary Music Festival, in which Kenneth Leighton's Cello Concerto (soloist Maurice Gendron) was sandwiched between Charpentier's *Te Deum* (in its first performance in England, some 260 years after its composition, the soloists being the sopranos Jennifer Vyvyan and Honor Sheppard, contralto Norma Procter, tenor William McAlpine and baritone Geraint Evans) and the Stravinsky; the BBC Symphony Orchestra and Festival Chorus was conducted by Rudolf Schwarz.

Stravinsky is the greatest mystery of our century, if not of our musical history. Schoenberg is a mystery to those who don't understand him; Stravinsky is a mystery to those who understand him. As for those who don't, though there are fewer of them than in the case of Schoenberg, they are ruder. Take Theodor Wiesengrund Adorno, the German music philosopher-in-chief, the man from whom Thomas Mann took twelve-tone lessons before he wrote *Doctor Faustus.*[1] Talking about the unbearability of *Oedipus Rex* and the *Symphony of Psalms* in his *magnum opus*, *The Philosophy of New Music*, Adorno diagnoses a 'contradiction between the pretence to grandness and sublimity, and the obstinately meagre musical content'.[2] The trouble is not that Prof. Adorno is obviously mistaken, but that even those of us who understand the greatness of the *Symphony of Psalms* feel that he has something there; only, he somehow got it wrong.

Our clue is Adorno's long but meaningful phrase, 'the obstinately meagre content'. Stravinsky's mystery is his suppressionism – the way he says things, expresses emotions, by suppressing them, by imposing upon himself the severest possible limitations, including, of course, other composers' styles as well as ideas. The content is not 'obstinately meagre'; it is obstinately – indeed, if I may say so, ostinately – suppressed and yet communicated by way

[1] On Adorno, *cf.* Keller's comments and note 3 on p. 35, above.

[2] *Philosophie der neuen Musik, op. cit.* Since an English version of this book did not appear until 1973, Keller's quotations from the work before that time must be presumed to be his own translations.

of the tension which this continuous suppression produces. You can't suppress without having something to suppress, which is what distinguishes Stravinsky from the Stravinskyians.

His suppressionism radiates in every dimension. Horizontally, it results in such tunes as the one with which the choir introduces itself in the first movement – a tune of two notes:

Ex. 1

Vertically, it produces Stravinsky's so-called wrong-note technique, his so-called unfunctional harmony. The functions, however, are there – underground. At crucial junctures they even emerge. Could anyone deny the carefully prepared feeling of a dominant G major chord at the end of the first movement, as this gives way to the C minor fugue of the second? (The music is continuous.)

Texturally, one merely has to quote the scoring in order to show that the repressive tendency manifests itself in the very sound of things. Ideally, the mixed chorus is all male. It should 'contain children's voices, which may be replaced by female voices (soprano and alto) if a children's choir is not available'.[3] The orchestra comprises 5 flutes, 4 oboes, 1 cor anglais, 3 bassoons, 1 double bassoon, 4 horns, 5 trumpets, 3 trombones, 1 tuba; timpani and bass drum; harp and 2 pianos; cellos and double basses. It is indeed almost amusing to find that in a work commissioned by Kussevitsky to celebrate the fiftieth anniversary of the Boston Symphony Orchestra, there are no parts for clarinets, none even for violins and violas! Stravinsky's expressive, or rather suppressive, needs were stronger than the demands of the occasion.

Trying to describe these needs by way of metaphor or simile, we discover that the best extra-musical illustration is to be found in the work itself – Stravinsky's predilection for Latin. 'The words of the Psalms are those of the Vulgate,' he reminds us in his introductory observations, 'and should be sung in Latin.'[4] Why? When Schoenberg wrote the 130th Psalm in Hebrew he did so for emotional reasons. When Stravinsky wrote this Psalm Symphony in Latin he did so for anti-emotional reasons. What is the difference between 'O praise God in his holiness' and *Laudate Dominum in sanctis ejus*? The latter suppresses the emotion it contains.

But the straightest way down to the very nature of Stravinsky's suppressionism is through his rhythm. Rhythm is the ultimate source of music;

[3] Prefatory note in the published score.

[4] *Ibid.*

'by their rhythms shall ye know them!', as Josef Rufer rightly exclaims in his book on twelve-tone composition.[5]

Stravinsky's rhythms have wrongly been described as static. It is Adorno's misunderstanding all over again. If they are static, they are as static as when you swim up-stream. Stravinsky suppresses time itself: he moves against it. The creative strength that is needed to counter the physically natural movement of music – the simple, primitive, regular rhythmic flow – must be as elemental as is the primitive rhythmic impulse itself.

Music which moves with time, which gives you a temporal, 'dynamic' feeling, is essentially upbeat music: one thing leading to the next. The Central-European tradition might be called the apotheosis of the upbeat, and hence of development. Stravinsky composes against this whole tradition, all the more so when he uses its material. His music is primarily downbeat music. This is why a man like Adorno, so profoundly steeped in Austro-German music, misunderstands Stravinsky equally profoundly. This is also why we, who think that we understand Stravinsky, are still mystified: it hasn't happened before, certainly not with such 'obstinate' consistency. And in any case, it is easier to follow a temporal movement than an anti-temporal one which, after all, must needs take place in time, too. Adorno watches the up-stream swimmer and finds him pathetic: he doesn't notice that the river is flowing. We do, and this is exactly what mystifies us. What is he doing? Or rather – how do we know what he is doing, even though we have no direct experience of the strength of the current? But the strength can be felt, and the feeling can be intellectually determined. A simple example from the *Symphony*'s last movement:

Ex. 2

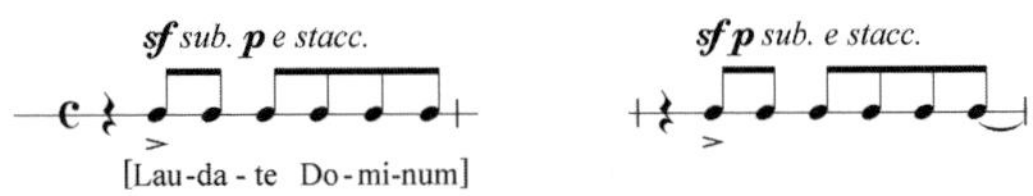

This basic rhythm, first given out by horns and bassoons and later emerging as *Laudate Dominum*, is literally unprecedented in pre-Stravinskyan music, an extended, unprepared, pure downbeat consisting of equal metrical units which are normally used to confirm the regular metre by way of such upbeat rhythms as those in Ex. 3 (a) or (b):

The resultant at the back of one's own mind as well as Stravinsky's, of all these upbeats from our musical culture is a measure of the rhythmic current against which he swims; his downbeat phrase would lose much of its significance if it were not an upbeat phrase turned upside down or, to be precise,

[5] *Cf.* note 1 on p. 50, above. The quotation here is from p. 64, although there 'rhythm' is singular and there is no exclamation mark.

Ex. 3

right side left, rear side front. By their very presence his accent and the *sf sub. p* on top of it show you what would happen without them: the players and we would slip back, in the direction of the current, rather than swim against it.

We said that this downbeat phrase was unprepared. It is not preceded by an upbeat; it seems to come from nowhere. Is Adorno right, then, when he writes of Stravinsky's arbitrary rhythmic 'shocks'? We have had a glance at what we might call the local sense of the phrase; is it without total sense? To be sure, the rhythm forms the basis of much that is to come, but is it itself without foundation? It is not. In fact, it springs from the basic idea, the very first announcement (Ex. 4):

Ex. 4

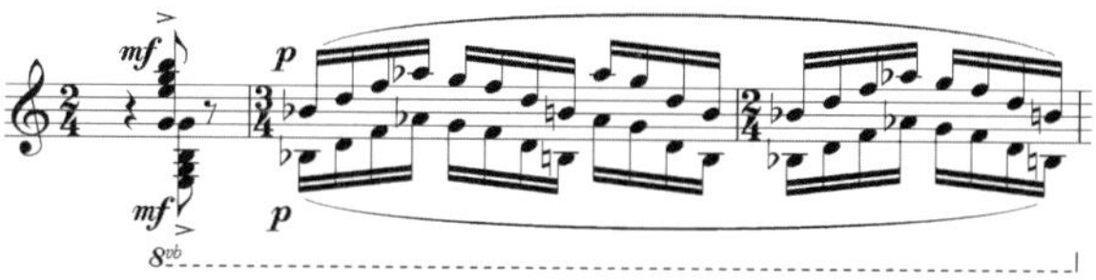

The metrical derivation from the evenly distributed semiquavers is obvious, but it is the unambiguous rhythmic derivation that constitutes the characteristic creative act. Like Ex. 2, the work itself starts with what Adorno would call a 'shock' that is the contradictory opposite of an upbeat, and which together with the ensuing semiquaver movement yields the basic idea, of whose extraordinary rhythm Ex. 2 turns out to be a well-defined compression , i.e., an exact diminution. Here it is again (*cf.* Ex. 2), superimposed upon the basic idea (*cf.* Ex. 4), with the latter in proportionally smaller note-values:

Ex. 5

This is how, from the outset, Stravinsky stems his straight, forward-driving emotion – and this is how the most diverse themes hang together in a supreme masterpiece.

The *Symphonie de Psaumes* was begun in the early part of 1930. Stravinsky's European concert tours made uninterrupted work on it impossible;

nevertheless, he finished it on August 15th of the same year. The orchestration was completed a few months later. The score bears the French inscription, 'composed to the glory of God and dedicated to the Boston Symphony on the occasion of the fiftieth anniversary of its existence'. The three movements into which the continuous structure falls show no tempo indications in the conventional sense, but only metronome marks.[6] In the main, the thematic material is unified, in the background, by two interlinking ascending thirds (of which more below) and, in the foreground, by the third movement's cyclic references to the first.

The text of the first movement (crotchet equals 92) would be Verses 12–13 of Psalm 39 in the Authorized Version. An accompanied chorale is preceded by an introduction which centres on Stravinsky's characteristic downbeat 'shock' – the opening E minor chord in Ex. 4, whose punctuations stretch into the body of the movement. When the altos enter with the prayer or lamentation of Ex. 1 (anticipated in the orchestra), it may be fruitful to remind oneself that this theme is basic enough to be repeated in the last movement. The accompanying ostinato, moreover, throws the basic thirds into relief, which Ex. 6 reduces to one line (and simplifies enharmonically):

Ex. 6

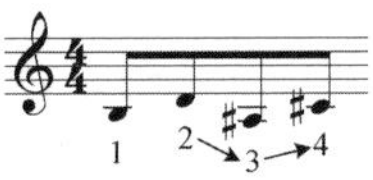

The theme of the middle section (*Quoniam advena*) shows, for Stravinsky, unusual breadth.

The text of the second movement (quaver equals 60) corresponds to Verses 1, 2 and 3 of the Authorized Version's Psalm 40. The music is a gigantic double fugue. Nicolas Slonimsky describes the movement as 'a four-part fugue with a subject of four principal notes within the range of a major seventh, the *comes* being in the dominant'.[7] But where do these four notes come from, and what is it that makes us immediately agree with Stravinsky to invest the range of the motif with special significance?

Ex. 7

The fact is that we are here confronted with a creative procedure which foreshadows Stravinsky's development, some twenty years later, towards

[6] One might observe that Stravinsky's 'suppressionism' further shows itself in this way.

[7] Nicolas Slonimsky, *Music Since 1900*, Coleman-Ross Company Inc., New York, Third Edition, 1949, p. 325.

Schoenberg's twelve-tone technique. Ex. 7, that is to say, treats Ex. 6 like a tone-row, and the quasi-dodecaphonic octave transposition of note 3 produces the motif's new range of a major seventh. In addition, the octave transposition yields two new melodic intervals which, logically, are given preferential treatment over the old-established minor third. For the rest, when this opening C minor fugue raises its voice through what we might call the life-mask of Bach, we realize that the term 'neo-classicism' is just not good enough for such a creation.

The second four-part fugue enters with the chorus while the first subject (*cf.* Ex. 7) is heard on what there are of strings in the orchestra. In his valuable book, *Stravinsky*, Eric Walter White, misled perhaps by the key signature of 3 flats, describes the choral fugue as being in E flat major; actually it is in E flat minor.[8]

The third movement (crotchet equals 48), on the 150th Psalm, is by far the most extended. It derives its opening and closing *Alleluia* from Ex. 1, which also returns, more manifestly, on the horns as the chorus sings the first verse. The tempo changes for the substantial middle section (minim equals 80) which begins with Ex. 2. After an orchestral introduction to the second verse, Ex. 1 assumes a new guise at *Laudate eum in virtutibus ejus.* In the middle of the middle section, which is constructed against a symmetrical background, the introductory *Alleluia* returns axis-like, an interjected recapitulation which, from the standpoint of the total structure, sounds like a rondo return. The middle section is the only part of the symphony which evinces appreciable symphonic development.

A slow version of Ex. 2 leads back to the original tempo, where an Italianate melody (*Laudate eum in timpani et choro*) builds up a fugato that starts in strict canonic imitation at the fifth below and at a bar's distance and eventually introduces, by way of a sudden change to E flat major, the sublimely hypnotic coda, which still derives ultimately from Ex. 1. The movement finishes as it began.

[8] *Stravinsky: A Critical Survey, op. cit.*, p. 136. *Cf.* note 2 on p. 27, above.

XI
Strawinsky's Performance of *Agon*: A Report

Tempo, No. 50, Winter 1958, pp. 22–25;
republished in *Tempo*, No. 100, Spring 1972, pp. 19–22

There is criticism and there is reporting, or at any rate there ought to be. I do not mean the kind of thing we read in the newspapers, where writers criticize things they have heard and report things they haven't, in order to conceal the fact. Thus, as criticism and reportage are understood today, the former is the more responsible task, but it should really be the other way round whenever the facts are more important than the critic's opinions, which is not seldom. At the same time, opinions do enjoy greater popularity with both the reader and the critic himself: they are easier to get for either. The unpopular truth is that while any fool can opine and indeed perchance opine rightly, only a qualified observer can report, and only a qualified reader is interested in facts, plenty of them and nothing but them.

True musical reportage, none the less, is not entirely unknown. When we read Eduard Hanslick's description of Wagner conducting Beethoven, for instance, we get a fairly concrete idea of the facts of the interpretations, despite the circumstance that Hanslick loathed them; he even offers us a chance to love them through his hate. Hanslick has been much and justly maligned (there is some danger at the moment of an excessive revaluation at Wagner's and Bruckner's expense), but he did get his facts far straighter than his opinions.

Wagner's Beethoven, though doubtless a true artistic sensation, is not of the same basic interest as Beethoven's Beethoven or Strawinsky's Strawinsky.[1] The great contemporary master's recent performances of *Agon* (a work which a previous experience at the Royal Festival Hall[2] has shown to be by no means easy to interpret) impose the duty upon the critic to report such details of execution as may shed light on performing problems and thus help the living future of the work.

[1] *Cf.* the Editorial Introduction, p. 22, above.

[2] Keller presumably refers to the performance given in what *The Times* described as the 'special late evening concert to be given by Collegium Musicum Londinii' on 21 May 1958 (*cf.* 'New Ballet With Music By Stravinsky', *The Times*, 7 May 1958, p. 5).

My observations are based on attendance at the penultimate rehearsal and at the first of the two performances;[3] one or two remarks will also take the second performance (which I heard over the radio) into account. At the rehearsal, from a considerable distance, I did not always understand what Strawinsky said but I did always hear (and see) the effect of his instructions; I would thus submit my report as authentic.

Pas-de-Quatre. Owing chiefly to the sustained C against which the B's clash, the octave unisons between cellos and double basses always tend to be out of tune, both here and, of course, at the end (bars 568 *f.* etc.). In my presence, Strawinsky did not attempt to remedy the distonations, presumably because too much time would have had to be sacrificed. His zest nevertheless carried off the passages in question, but any lesser musician will have to more pedantic at these points if the listener's perception is not to be distracted.

In bars 30 *f.* and 590 *f.*, the clarinet staccatos could not have been more incisive; *staccatissimo* would really be the word. As for the tempo, here as elsewhere Strawinsky seemed to adhere to his own metronome marks pretty strictly, with the result that the present movement (♪ = 156) took 1' 39".

The cautiously serial *Double Pas-de-Quatre* lasted 1' 28".

In the ensuing coda (*Triple Pas-de-Quatre*), which played 1' 3", the second violins will probably always be inclined to overdo bars 113 *ff.* Strawinsky restrained them; the line makes itself heard without any special exertions.

The tempo of the *Pre-* or *Interlude* varied imperceptibly and logically in its three occurrences, despite the identical metronome marks (♩ = 126). The modifications were sufficiently infinitesimal to be attributable to unconscious rather than conscious intention. The first time round was the slowest, plausibly so: the first time is the newest. An immediate warning: such minute tempo shadings are inevitably exaggerated as soon as they are materialized rather than inwardly realized.

All trained hearts went out to the leader in his violin solos;[4] he faced his difficult task with heroic calm and determination. It should not be necessary to point out that criticisms I may seem to imply in the following remarks are no reflection on his abilities; my sole concern is the future.

First, the beginning of the saraband (*First Pas-de-Trois*). Very tentatively – too much so in my opinion – Strawinsky suggested two downbows for the *vigoroso* basic motif:

[3] Stravinsky conducted the work in two concerts of his own music, given on 10 and 12 December 1958 in the Royal Festival Hall and played by the BBC Symphony Orchestra. Both concerts also featured *Apollon musagète* and the *Symphony in Three Movements*; the first also included three pieces from the 1945 *Firebird Suite*. Most of the first concert has been released on CD: BBC Legends BBCL42532.

[4] Paul Beard (1901–89), the leader of the BBC Symphony Orchestra from 1936 until his retirement in 1962.

Ex. 1

The leader did not seem to consider this approach advisable, and the project was abandoned – to the detriment of the motif's character. It is a pity that Strawinsky does not play the violin: he would speak with greater apparent authority in instances of this kind. (Needless to add, he knew what he was talking about, and his cautious manner was sheer modesty.)[5] In many cases, the musically real difference between up- and downbows is exaggerated, but Ex. 1 is certainly not one of them. On the other hand, one can understand, and indeed sympathize, with the leader's preference, at any rate on the psychological level: especially in modern music, it does not happen all too often that two closely successive double- or triple-stoppings can be linked so smoothly, with no left-hand labours intervening, so why not make the most of the occasion when it comes? But here precisely lies the danger for future interpretations. The passage is really *too well* written from the instrumental point of view, thus making for too uninhibited a progress from the snap to the long note. (It could even be slurred without the slightest difficulty.) Thus dies character. Let us stress, then, that once the characterization of the motif is uppermost in our minds, there is no conceivable violinistic objection to Strawinsky's original suggestion. It ought to be executed on every future occasion; beauty of sound must take second place.

At the end of the movement, the leader played Ex. 2 *à la* Ex. 3,

Ex. 2

Ex. 3

though here the very opposite characterization from that of the opening would seem to be intended. If your hands are not too small, it is possible to tie the *f*″ without breaking the snap downwards (which would be musically wrong), though it must be admitted that as it stands the motif is unplayable

[5] *Cf.* notes 1 and 2 on p. 96, below.

unless you break downwards and thus play the slur. It is true, too, that if you bow in the way suggested, you will tend to find yourself with a fraction of a lonely *f''* on your hands before the *a* ensues, but this can be made to imply the *diminuendo*, whereas in Ex. 3 there is no chance of any *diminuendo*, implied or expressed – only a *ffp*. Again I must remind the reader that I am not reproaching the leader, who played Ex. 3 itself splendidly. He may merely have been carrying out the composer's instructions which, in that case, would appear to have been based on considerations too considerate. In any event, I would suggest that the last bar be re-notated in order to exclude any misunderstandings produced by the strictly unplayable Ex. 2. The movement took 1' 12".

In the galliard (1' 15"), after the first double-bar with its change of canonic roles, a tricky texture is reached in bar 175, where the mandoline easily finds itself at loggerheads with the first flute. Once again, no doubt, for reasons of temporal economy, Strawinsky did not do anything about the problem, which remained evident both at the first performance and, to a lesser extent, at the second; and again, any future interpretation of less than gigantic stature will have to concern itself with this danger spot. (The flute's parallel entry in bar 173 is easier because the mandoline gives a quaver's warning, whereas in bar 157 the flute has to jump in after the mandoline's tie.)

In the violin solo of the subsequent twelve-tonal coda (A–G–G♯–F♯–F–E♭–D–C–C♯–B–E–B♭), the leader gave an impressive performance of consistent on-the-string bowing, but I am not sure whether a less consistent and in fact less tone-conscious approach might not be preferable; the general swing and particular cross-accents (bars 196–7!) might become more audible if the bow were allowed to leave the string. Strawinsky emphasized the need for articulation in the first trumpet's bar 229; he really wanted slight accents (*cf.* the staccatos in the mandoline's preceding bar). This movement lasted 1' 39", the *Second Pas-de-Trois* (half-row: D–E–F–G–F♯–B) 52". In *Bransle Gay*, for sensitive or possibly over-sensitive ears, the castanets sounded like a pedal on a slightly sharp B, which was most disturbing. I have no doubt they were abetted – physically so – by the actual B's, but something must have been wrong with the construction of the instrument: its pitch was certainly not sufficiently indeterminate.

In *Bransle de Poitou* (1' 38"), which completes and transposes the last-quoted row (see the violins' first 4 bars), there is a tendency towards an early violin entry on the last crotchet of bar 342; I think it is enough for the players to be conscious of the danger to avoid it.

In the coda of the *Pas-de-Deux* (row: F–G♭–A–A♭–G–B♭–C♭–D–D♭–E–E♭–C), Strawinsky seems to have made a definite change in the score: in bar 505, Ex. 4 is not slurred (see Ex. 5).

Ex. 4

Ex. 5

In the fugato that opens the concluding *Four Trios*, the accents are supposed to help towards producing a sound 'like trumpets'; the contextual reasons are obvious.

Agon was written between 1954 and 1957.

XII
'Conversations with Igor Stravinsky'

Tempo, No. 52, Autumn 1959, pp. 16 and 21–25

A critic and friend, rare combination, has suggested that there are, in principle, two ways of dealing with Stravinsky's latest book.[1] One is to fall flat on one's face and exclaim, 'A great man's book, a great book!' The other was to review it simply as a book on music.

To my mind, either course of action is fallacious. The awed approach is a nineteenth-century fallacy, the rationalistic approach a twentieth-century fallacy. At the same time, the romantic, irrationalistic approach is the more objective, the more rational. The truth, *quod licet Jovi, non licet bovi*, became a truism long before the birth of the romantic genius-hero, and to treat the book of a genius like that of any old ass (as virtually all my colleagues did in the case of Schoenberg's *Style and Idea*) is to start with a wrong fact and remove oneself from the level of artistic reality for the duration of one's review.

The purely romantic approach, on the other hand, though it starts with the most realistic basic motif, the fact of genius, tends to inhibit understanding through sentimentality. Understanding: that is our supreme duty towards genius. I am not obliged to understand an ass unless he happens to be my pupil, but I am obliged to be any genius's pupil whom I am capable of understanding.

Stravinsky hates the term 'genius', but I am certainly not obliged to follow his hates, which are part of his anti-romantic confusion. They have proved highly fruitful creatively and quite fruitless critically. But we have to distinguish between confusions which spring from his aversions and those which spring from what we might call a faulty conceptual technique. Stravinsky says that he is not a conceptual thinker, that he 'lacks words'.[2] The common critical reaction is to say: 'If you are using words, you have to be judged by the laws of terms, and if you contradict yourself you are talking nonsense like everybody else'. The twentieth-century fallacy again. It is supported by a

[1] Igor Stravinsky and Robert Craft, *Conversations with Igor Stravinsky*, Doubleday, Garden City, N.Y., 1959/Faber and Faber, London, 1959.

[2] *Ibid.*, p. 14.

hangover from analytic philosophy which, though it has cleared the air from romanticized philosophy as Stravinsky has cleared the air from Strauss, remains an institutionalized obsessional neurosis, a supremely rationalized fear of, and refusal to understand, what the other person means. (Not surprisingly, linguistic analysis has achieved its broadest success in cultures where the normally educated person has no philosophical background and no training in classical logic.) If we merely analyse Stravinsky's contradictions we get out where he came in. If we try to understand them, we walk in with him, discover what he has discovered, and maybe, if our own conceptual technique is developed, eventually resolve them by being able to walk just that little way further along, until we arrive at the point where the truth of a contradiction can be expressed logically.

One such contradiction concerns this very question of technique. 'Technique is the whole man', says Stravinsky. 'A technique or a style for saying something original does not exist *a priori*, it is created by the original saying itself … "Thought" is not one thing and "technique" another, namely, the ability to transfer, "express" or develop thoughts … Technique is not a teachable science, neither is it learning, nor scholarship, nor even the knowledge of how to do something.'[3] But towards the other end of the book, Stravinsky says, with equal justification, that the critics 'are incompetent in the technique of the contemporary musical language'.[4] It would take one of our many average linguistic analysts pages to expose this contradiction which we may assume to be obvious; and to demonstrate that Stravinsky's utterances were meaningless and 'emotive'.[5]

In reality, they are so full of meaning that they cannot altogether comprehend it; whence it is easy for us not to comprehend them. Alternatively, we must attempt to 'know what he means'. Technique is not a static thing; it develops from what Stravinsky says it isn't into what he says it is. Nor is this the whole truth. The most primitive, impersonal stage of a technique already evinces a personal element and, conversely, technique at its most developed must needs retain an impersonal aspect, 'the technique of the contemporary musical language', without which that language would be nothing but private lunacy. 'In the case of my own music', says Stravinsky, 'I know that my first works, the *Faune et Bergère* and the Symphony in E flat, lack personality while at the same time they demonstrate definite technical ability with the musical materials.'[6] Within a page and a half of the book, we seem to have come a far

[3] *Ibid.*, p. 25.

[4] *Ibid.*, p. 119.

[5] 'Emotive' has itself become a subtly emotive term applied to every logical implication illogically expressed. –HK

[6] *Ibid.*, p. 26.

way from technique being 'the whole man', but actually we have only gone a far way back, to the stage where Stravinsky had to avail himself of the (then) 'contemporary musical language'.

Stravinsky involves himself in what is basically the same meaningful confusion at different levels of the creative process. 'My statement in my grammar will be clear to the musician who has followed music up to where my contemporaries and I have brought it.'[7] The confusion is brewing: 'my grammar' *versus* 'music up to where my contemporaries and I have brought it'. And when he is asked, 'What is theory in musical composition?', he replies: 'Hindsight. It doesn't exist. There are compositions from which it is deduced. Or, if this isn't quite true, it has a by-product existence that is powerless to create or even to justify. Nevertheless, composition involves a deep intuition of theory'.[8] So composition involves a deep intuition of something which doesn't exist, or, 'if this isn't quite true', of something that is powerless to create or even to justify. Yet again, Stravinsky suggests quite justly that the critics 'are not even equipped to judge one's grammar. They do not see how a musical phrase is constructed, do not know how music is written'.[9] Once more, then, the objective and the subjective are uneasily confused: the construction of 'a musical phrase' on the one hand, 'one's grammar' on the other. What is more, 'one's grammar', 'my grammar', harbours a contradiction in itself, for grammar is objective; in fact, it is part and parcel of the theory of language, the theory which 'doesn't exist'.

Considered, as before, dynamically rather than statically, the contradiction is easily resolved, its full meaning readily comprehensible. Intuitive theory is foresight of the future's hindsight on the one hand (Schoenberg's twelve-note theorizing!), and the instinctive aspect of present hindsight on the other (letting the seventh in a $^{4}_{3}$ rise without knowing why). All consistency obeys an implicit system which is called 'theory' when it becomes explicit. 'Musical form', Stravinsky says, 'is the result of the "logical discussion" of musical materials.' There is no logical discussion without the alternative of illogical discussion, and there is no possibility of illogical discussion without terms of reference, without a system, an at least potential theory against which such illogicality would offend. Now, creativity consistently breaks that system – 'consistently' in both senses, for every break-away means, at the same time, a new systematization, which is why 'composition involves a deep intuition of theory'.[10] Moreover, the break-away itself is determined, if only negatively, by the system against which it offends; otherwise it is destined to remain

[7] *Ibid.*, p. 14.

[8] *Ibid.*, p. 12.

[9] *Ibid.*, p. 119.

[10] *Ibid.*, p. 13.

incomprehensible or, at best, illogical in Stravinsky's sense. In short, if one is a creator, 'one's grammar' at once follows and contradicts and contradictingly follows 'the contemporary (or just-past) musical language' which is the basis of communication – the language whose grammar provides the terms of reference which creator and actual or potential understander have in common before a note is heard.

So far, I have put my conceptual technique at the service of Stravinsky's thought. As soon as we arrive at what is perhaps the most complex as well as the most fruitful aspect of his confusion, however, I shall have to abandon the attempt to 'explain what he means'. For while hitherto he seems to me to have solved the relevant problems without quite being able to express the solution in words, at this forthcoming stage he has, I think, failed to solve [them] altogether. I thus feel compelled to go beyond even his implied thought, to cease reviewing *Conversations with Stravinsky* and enter into a conversation with him myself. My thoughts, which are reflections from, or rather of, part of the theory of my functional analysis, will have to be simplified and expressed somewhat dogmatically; no other procedure is feasible within the available space.

Stravinsky has often said that 'an artist must avoid symmetry but he may construct in parallelisms'.[11] Enlarging on this observation in the present book, he says he does not know 'whether or not the suggestion of symmetry is avoidable in the art of architecture, whether it is natural to architecture. However, painters who paint architectural subject matter and borrow architectural designs are often guilty of it. And only the master musicians have managed to avoid it in periods whose architecture has embodied aesthetic idealisms, i.e., when architecture was symmetry and symmetry was confused with form itself. Of all the musicians of his age Haydn was the most aware, I think, that to be perfectly symmetrical is to be perfectly dead. We are some of us still divided by an illusory compulsion towards "classical" symmetry on the one hand, and by the desire to compose as purely non-symmetrically as the Incas, on the other'.[12]

This 'division', this conflicting attitude towards symmetry remains unexplained. And while we all agree that to be perfectly symmetrical is to be perfectly dead, we are all the more mystified by this compulsion towards symmetry, which, by implication, is of the liveliest kind. Nor do we feel altogether comfortable when Stravinsky plays off Haydn against the other composers of his time. Of course, we all 'know what he means'; but does that make Haydn any 'better' than Mozart? Absurd suggestion; yet, along the lines of Stravinsky's argument, it seems inescapable. Schoenberg before him, while

[11] *Ibid.*, p. 16.

[12] *Ibid.*

taking in Mozart with Haydn, played the two off against Beethoven in precisely the same sense: 'Deviation from regularity and symmetry does not necessarily endanger comprehensibility. One might accordingly wonder why in Haydn's and Mozart's forms irregularity is more frequently present than in Beethoven's' (*Style and Idea*[13]). And so it goes on; I have been asked by more than one composing student why Schoenberg's own Fourth Quartet is so 'square', and even as I write this article, I am again confronted with the same question by a young composer: one might say that because of its seemingly easy accessibility, the Quartet (as opposed to, say, the string Trio or violin Phantasy) is proving the most incomprehensible of Schoenberg's twelve-note works to the youngest generation of musicians.

Once more we have to approach the problem dynamically, developmentally. Musical symmetry, which incidentally does not derive from architecture but from the dance, is not altogether the same at different times, nor with different composers at the same time, nor with the same composer at different stages in his development. The ease with which we are able to analyse a symmetrical structure according to the homophonic rhythmic feeling of the classical era makes us forget that musical symmetry does not exist in the abstract; indeed, *perfect symmetry in music is non-existent.* What we choose to call perfect symmetry takes one or the other kind of elementary asymmetry for granted. A temporal form cannot be symmetrical because what comes before influences what comes after, even when to the static axis one side looks like the other. What we intuitively accept as symmetries are, of course, the regular rhythmic structures of 4 bars, 8 bars, etc., perfect examples of which are – if I may respectfully pull the master's leg for a moment – the basic, principal themes from the following great, mature Haydn quartets: Op. 20, No. 1; Op. 33, No. 2; Op. 33, No. 6; Op. 42; Op. 50, No 3; Op. 50, No. 5; Op. 54, No. 3; Op. 55, No. 1; Op. 55, No. 2; Op. 55, No 3; Op. 64, No. 1; Op. 64, No. 4; Op. 64, No. 5; Op. 64, No. 6; Op. 74, No. 1; Op. 74, No. 2; Op. 74, No. 3; Op. 76, No. 1; Op. 76, No. 3; Op. 76, No. 5; Op. 77, No. 2.[14] At the same time, it is quite true that as against the 4-bar, 8-bar scheme, Haydn will prove more often violently anti-symmetrical than either Mozart or Beethoven. But the scheme remains an abstraction, and as soon as we take concrete instances by any of the masters, we will find asymmetries galore within and/or immediately outside the structure we are inspecting. Moreover, symmetry has more than one dimension, and where Haydn seems more conscious of the need for asymmetry than Mozart, it will be found that he

[13] *Op. cit.*, p. 409.

[14] In fact, as I have shown elsewhere [*cf.*, for example, 'The Interpretation of the Haydn Quartets', *The Score*, No. 24, November 1958, pp. 14–35], what makes a great Haydn quartet 'celebrated' is nothing more mysterious than square rhythmic structures. –HK

XIII
No Bridge to Nowhere: An Introduction to Stravinsky's *Movements* and Schoenberg's Violin Concerto

The Musical Times, Vol. 102, No. 1417, March 1961, pp. 156–58

On March 22, Schoenberg's Violin Concerto and Stravinsky's *Movements* for piano and orchestra will be heard over the radio from a BBC concert at the Royal Festival Hall, and I have gladly accepted the impossible task of introducing these works to those who don't know them – which means to everybody, including, of course, myself.[1] I would never pretend to 'know' the Schoenberg work, on which I am supposed to be an expert, if 'knowing' means what you and I know it to mean: the kind of experience you and I have of Beethoven's Fifth Symphony. Nothing less is good enough, and if we think it is, we don't yet know Beethoven's Fifth. But at least I may be said to have started on the road towards knowing Schoenberg's instinctively recognizable masterpiece, which is more than can be granted so far as my insight into the Stravinsky *Movements* (1958–59) is concerned. They have not yet been performed in this country, and while I did hear the first European performance (and the last rehearsal) at the ISCM Festival in Cologne last year, I doubt whether it could be called a performance at all. At any rate, some of the tempo relations were clearer to me on the printed page than in the Cologne interpretation; and since tempo plays an all-important role in this work, I decided, after my suspicions had been aroused at the rehearsal, to time the performance. The result, 7 mins 49 secs, compared mysteriously with the ten minutes given as official duration in the score – not to speak of Stravinsky's revised duration of twelve minutes, which he found through practical experience, when he conducted the work in New York.[2]

At the same time, when Stravinsky says that 'the movements are related more by tempo than by contrasts of such things as timbre, "mood",

[1] Keller's programme note for the concert follows, on pp. 87–88.

[2] Stravinsky refers to 'a span of only twelve minutes' in Igor Stravinsky and Robert Craft, *Memories and Commentaries*, University of California Press, Berkeley and Los Angeles/Faber and Faber, London 1960, p. 107. (*Cf.* p. 111, below, for details of the six books of 'conversations' between Stravinsky and Craft.)

character',[3] he is, I think, deceiving himself in his usual manner. It is usual for him to deny 'expression' because, quite unnecessarily, he associates expressiveness with extra-musical meaning; and the very fact that he puts 'mood' in inverted commas seems to indicate that once again, he is trying to prove himself as purely musical as he can, without allowing for the possibility of purely musical moods.[4] Perhaps it is Stravinsky's own description of the *Movements* that has led the reviewer of the work in the current issue of *Music & Letters* to the observation that 'with the exception of the fourth movement it is non-thematic'.[5] There are many things in this immensely compelling score which I would not be able to explain, but nothing in it is quite so obscure to me as this assertion of partial non-thematicism, which I would ask the listener to disregard: otherwise, he may run the risk of not hearing this music as music – and as great music at that, for as such it reveals itself long before one gets to know it.

The work comprises five movements which – dare I say it? – are contrasted in rhythm and texture. They are linked by four interludes, the last of which leads without a break from the fourth movement into the fifth.

At the first hearing, two aspects of the music strike one immediately and with great force, one expected, the other unexpected. Expected is the downright uncanny textural clarity and the sharp characterization, both horizontal and vertical – whatever the composer may say about the absence of contrasting characters: perhaps the concept of 'character' is, for him, pregnant with extra-musical associations too, since he grew up at a time when the romantic 'character piece' was much the vogue.

The unexpected aspect of the *Movements* is their unprecedented rhythmic complexity. Stravinsky has often been complicated rhythmically, but never, until now, really complex: the wealth of the work's rhythmic relations and polyrhythmic combinations is, undoubtedly, the newest contribution of Stravinsky's ever younger creative mind – ever younger because with each

[3] *Ibid.*.

[4] Years earlier, Stravinsky had famously released a declaration that music was incapable of expressing anything but itself:

> I consider that music is, by its very nature, essentially powerless to *express* anything at all, whether a feeling, an attitude of mind, a psychological mood, a phenomenon of nature, etc. ... *Expression* has never been an inherent property of music. That is by no means the purpose of its existence. If, as is nearly always the case, music appears to express something, this is only an illusion and not a reality. It is simply an additional attribute which, by tacit and inveterate agreement, we have lent it, thrust upon it, as a label, a convention – in short, an aspect which, unconsciously or by force of habit, we have come to confuse with its essential being.

The original (French) text appeared in *Chroniques de ma vie* (2 vols, Denoël & Steele, Paris, 1935, 1936), written with an unknown degree of unacknowledged involvement by Walter Nouvel. An anonymous and incomplete English translation was published as *Chronicle of My Life* (Gollancz, London, 1936) and *An Autobiography* (Simon and Schuster, New York, 1936); the above quotation is from pp. 91–92 of the Gollancz edition.

[5] *Cf.* Colin Mason, 'Reviews of Music', *Music & Letters*, Vol. XLII, No. 1, January 1961, p. 93.

work, he seems to become more adventurous. It is through the rhythmic dimension, too, that one first feels and discovers the thematic build-up of the *Movements*: maybe our afore-quoted colleague concentrated too much on the melodic dimension.

Another novel aspect of the work, though in itself a negative one, is its stressed atonality, which contradicts much that Stravinsky has said and almost all he has done in the past. This is not a criticism, on the contrary: every composer who remains true to himself, to his own development, becomes unfaithful to his past, whereas the so-called 'consistent' composers all end up in self-imitation, sometimes at an early stage (especially nowadays, when theoretical consistency is at a premium). There is an intriguing positive side, again immediately audible, to this atonality of the *Movements*: the vertical note combinations and progressions remain as characteristically Stravinskyian as before, whereas previously one might have thought – I did, anyway – that even in his serial works, Stravinsky's profoundly individual harmony had something to do with his tonal implications.

The music's twelve-note technique itself I propose to leave on one side. It has not yet helped me towards a better understanding, and it is unrealistic to suppose that it would help anybody else upon first acquaintance. The row rotates very much in the background of the work, and it will be through our better knowledge of its foreground that we shall eventually come to feel this constructive background – if we are so inclined. I have already seen frantic and pathetic attempts to unravel the serial mysteries of this work, attempts which remind me of a remark Schoenberg made to me in a letter half a year before his death: writing of one of the world's acknowledged twelve-note authorities, he said that the man was 'one of those non-musicians, who look in my music only for the twelve notes – not realizing in the least its musical contents, expression and merits'.[6] (The English is Schoenberg's.)

Yet, when we come to Schoenberg's own Violin Concerto of 1936, an awareness of the note-row need not be altogether useless. The row moves much more in the foreground than in the case of the Stravinsky; it is indeed quite obviously abstracted from Schoenberg's concrete thematic thought, from his melodic invention. If I may speak from teaching experience, for those who are at all interested, the ability to whistle such a note-row and its mirror forms from memory proves a help towards a quicker perception of what happens in the actual music. At the same time, it cannot be sufficiently stressed that you can understand any good twelve-note piece without in the least bothering about its row, just as you can understand a diatonic work

[6] Quoted in Keller's 'Schoenberg and the Men of the Press', *Music Survey* (*New Series*), Vol. III, No. 3, March 1951, pp.160–68, where the last word is given as 'merit' (p. 164). The letter itself (with the word 'merits') is reproduced and transcribed in Keller's 'Unpublished Schoenberg Letters: Early, Middle and Late', *Music Survey* (*New Series*), Vol. IV, No. 3, June 1952, pp. 449–71.

without tracing the triad which, with its derivatives, rotates throughout the music. Now, at the beginning of the Concerto, the row is distributed between the violin and the accompanying lower strings, but as soon as the violin leaves the G-string, it has the twelve notes all to itself, and they can thus clearly be heard: A-B♭-E♭-B-E-F♯-C-C♯-G-A♭-D-F. (In the orchestra at the same time, there is the less easily audible inversion of the row at the fifth below.)

Schoenberg played all stringed instruments of the orchestra except for the double bass, and when he wrote this Violin Concerto, which I regard as the greatest since Mendelssohn's, his attitude was one of intimate sympathy for, of empathy with the solo part: in spite of its enormous difficulties, which prompted him to suggest that it called for a six-fingered violinist, the music is never written against the instrument, even though it may sometimes seem to go beyond its present capacities. Yet, for the player, it is always a question of coping with violinistic difficulties; whereas in the Brahms Concerto, *pace* Joachim's help, it is occasionally a question of coping with unviolinistic ones. Schoenberg's very opening on the G-string convinces us at once that here is a fiddle concerto in the most intrinsic sense.

The formal scheme of the three-movement work is based on firm classical foundations and so helps us to understand all those many highly original thoughts and developments which are thrown into relief against the traditional background. Essentially, the first movement is, in fact, a sonata form, and the second a relatively simple ternary form. The third movement is a rondo which eventually, in the cadenza before the end, rounds off the whole work in cyclic fashion. The development of this finale is far more dynamic than that of the usual rondo. Its rhythmic character, for instance, emerges but gradually: it is only with the first return of the theme that the movement openly declares its allegiance to the march.

Before last year's European première of Stravinsky's *Movements*, I got hold of a learned journal containing an introductory article on the work.[7] I had to read it twice before I understood that it was incomprehensible, and it was not until some time after the performance that I discovered its wrong analytic facts. We all know about the cleft between contemporary music and its audiences, but compared with the kind of writing that is supposed to bridge it, the music itself is easy. The reason for this paradoxical state of affairs is obvious. Everybody is part of this crisis, even composers themselves: nobody is really at home yet in another man's difficult music. Yet the writers on music, be they critics or composers, have to pretend that they are. They even have to pretend to themselves, for otherwise they would feel that they play

[7] Keller's reference is probably to Colin Mason's 'Stravinsky's Newest Works', *Tempo*, No. 53/54, Spring/Summer 1960, pp. 2–10.

into the mistrusting public's hands: if we don't know this music inside out, what will the public (not to speak of the fellow critics) think? Won't they feel justified in turning away from the music altogether?

As a matter of fact, they won't. The crisis is there, but so is the music, and some of us know that some of it is great before we know it as well as one should know great music. We can honestly communicate our beginning understanding, our experience of inspiration, without building bridges to nowhere, without trying to write introductions which cannot yet be written, and could not yet be understood. That is why I said at the outset that I gladly accepted an impossible task. When the task becomes possible it will cease to be necessary.

XIV
Movements

Programme note for a concert of the BBC Symphony Orchestra conducted by Hans Rosbaud, in the Royal Festival Hall on 22 March 1961. *Movements* was played twice (with Aloys Kontarsky as soloist in its first British performance), preceded in the first half by Blacher's *Orchester-Ornament*, Op. 44, and followed by Webern's *Six Pieces*, Op. 6, and Hindemith's Concerto for Orchestra, Op. 38; a repeat performance in the second half was followed by Schoenberg's Violin Concerto, Op. 36 (soloist Tibor Varga).

These five movements, with interludes between (whose last runs straight from the fourth into the fifth movement), are perhaps the most difficult work Stravinsky has yet written. I hope this realistic observation will not have a deterrent effect. One smells a great work before one grasps it, and each of these experiences brings its own joys. At the I.S.C.M. Festival in Cologne last year, hardened by days of incomprehensibility and all-too-comprehensibility, I heard the first European performance of the *Movements* (1958–59). Even at first hearing, the inadequacy of the interpretation was only too obvious, but nevertheless, and despite the fact that I hardly experienced a single moment of real understanding, the difference between the incomprehensible and the uncomprehended struck me like a revelation. Confronted by the incomprehensible, one tries to move closer, only to see it vanish in the distance; the uncomprehended, as soon as you make a move towards it, starts to move towards you, propelled by its own expressive power (with apologies to the composer's aversion to the term 'expression'[1]).

Stravinsky himself has drawn attention to the unprecedented serial complexity of the work. This aspect, however, need not detain us on the present occasion: complexity can be so great that you do not notice it at all, at any rate to begin with. More to the present point is his remark that the work's 'rhythmic language is also the most advanced I have so far employed':[2] in this field, one feels the multitude of meaningful interrelations long before one is able to come to grips with them. Where is the Stravinsky of whom Theodor

[1] *Cf.* note 4 on p. 83, above.

[2] *Memories and Commentaries*, *op. cit.*, p. 106.

Wiesengrund Adorno, in his *Philosophy of New Music* (1949),[3] could say that he 'renounces whatever could produce intrinsic temporal relations'?[4] While, says Stravinsky, 'each section of the piece is confined to a certain range of instrumental timbre ... the movements are related more by tempo than by contrasts of such things as timbre, "mood", character';[5] indeed, the very essence of the work seems to me to lie in its temporal relations, with all the melodic and harmonic implications that flow from them. It is true that Stravinsky lays the greatest stress on the complicated rotations of his tone-row, but these may themselves prove to be rhythmically determined; or that is what I divine.

Where, again, is the Stravinsky of whose principle of 'damaged tonality' the furious Adorno was trying to make so much, or so little? For the first time here, Stravinsky marries his serial technique to what he describes as 'anti-tonality', a tendency which he calls 'perhaps the most significant development in the *Movements*'. It will surprise Adorno, but then, it does Stravinsky too: 'I am amazed at this myself, in view of the fact that in *Threni*[6] simple triadic references occur in every bar'. What I find still more amazing is how in these atonal circumstances, he retains his characteristic harmony which, as it were, can still be spotted in the dark.

No, the *Philosophy of New Music*, would have to be thoroughly revised after each new Stravinsky work. He is the one great composer who, again and again, sheds his most individual traits in order to become ever more characteristic.

[3] *Cf.* p. 35, above.

[4] As before, this translation is presumably Keller's own – *cf.* note 2 on p. 64, above.

[5] *Memories and Commentaries*, *op. cit.*, p. 107.

[6] *Threni* (1958), scored for six soloists (soprano, alto, two tenors and two basses) and orchestra, sets passages from the Lamentations of Jeremiah (in the Latin of the Vulgate), as its subtitle ('id est Lamentationes Jeremiae Prophetae') makes clear.

XV
The Note-Row on May 31

The Musical Times, Vol. 103, No. 1431, May 1962, pp. 315–16

For the opening concert of this year's festival of the International Society for Contemporary Music, at the Festival Hall on May 31 (also being broadcast), two contemporary classics have been chosen in addition to the new works picked from the national submissions to the international jury. The two represent the first and the latest steps in orchestral 12-note technique – Schoenberg's *Variations* for orchestra, op 31, written 34 years ago, and Stravinsky's *A Sermon, a Narrative and a Prayer* for contralto and tenor, speaker, chorus and orchestra, the master's latest published work, which will now receive its first performance in this country. It may seem absurd to call a work a 'classic' which nobody has yet heard except for those who attended its premiere at Basle on February 23 this year. But any work Stravinsky writes nowadays is bound to become a classic; indeed, even the most cursory examination of the new 16-minute score confirms such a trustful prognosis. The clarity of thought, of structure and texture, is once again that of a mature master-mind inspired by genius; what is yet more, there is a new melodic distinction, achieved with the help of words on the one hand and, more profoundly, of the 12-note method on the other. For the first time, perhaps, we realize that had Stravinsky not been born and bred into a melodic crisis, the charge of melodic poverty might never have been levelled against him. True, it always was an exaggerated criticism, but at more than one previous stage in his development one could see how it arose.

Now, once one recognizes the enormous help 12-note technique offers a composer towards getting him out of the melodic rut produced by the ageing of the diatonic cadence, one's mind turns back to the state of Schoenberg's own melodism between the break-up of tonality (or rather, of his own tonalities) and his discovery of 12-note technique. What happened then? Schoenberg was no doubt more of a born melodist than is Stravinsky; how did he cope with the crisis? The conventional view, quite right so far as it goes (and indeed based on Schoenberg's own observations), is that during that period of so-called 'free' atonality, he found himself unable to write extended forms except when supported by a text. Extended form is one thing, extended melody another (as the first movement of Beethoven's Fifth shows), and it has never been made clear that melodically, too, Schoenberg's creativity underwent a crisis in those crucial years: in his purely instrumental works of the time, nothing approaching the breadth of, say, the tune that is the theme of the orchestral *Variations* can be found; in fact, never have small form and small-scale melody been so closely allied. (In Chopin, on the contrary, small forms and extended melodies depend on each other.)

If this melodic potential of 12-note technique, of which Stravinsky's latest work is perhaps the most drastic, the most sudden proof to date, is accepted as a creative fact, Peter Stadlen's anti-serial crusade, which is still limping along happily, may well be brought to a standstill. ('Serial connections ... have no correlate in sound, however diligently we may stare at them on paper' is his latest formulation for the newspaper reader.)[1]

For how else can the row have a sub-thematic, and hence sub-melodic effect but through its audibility, whether potential or actual? For most of us, let me hasten to add, this controversy has grown into one of the most tedious sights of our musical scene. Yet we must take it seriously, not only because Mr Stadlen's views still prove marketable, but also because they have a fraction of a point. It behoves us, in other words, to establish a differential diagnosis, in simple, straight words. Where is Mr Stadlen right, where wrong? He is right where note-rows are used without aural conscience, and hence without direct musical (as distinct from psychological) significance. Of course there is such a thing as visual serialism, but that doesn't make all serialism visual – certainly not Schoenberg's or Stravinsky's.

Every now and again, Mr Stadlen reminds us that Webern refused to tell him all about his rows, because they were of no importance to the player. Well, are they or aren't they?–Mr Stadlen rightly asks. If they aren't, they can't have any constructive meaning in sound (as distinct from their possible indirect, psychological significance); if they are of help to the player, why didn't Webern tell him?

However, the alternative is not quite so straight-forward. In art, there is such a thing as secret science – and don't think I mean anything vague. A real secret is not something which shuns the light of day, but something which needs a special, clear mental sunlight in order to be unambiguously perceptible; it is what, for Pythagoras, was esoteric as opposed to exoteric knowledge. Webern may well have doubted whether Stadlen could be expected to adopt,

[1] The Vienna-born Peter Stadlen (1910–96) was a music critic for *The Daily Telegraph* from 1959, succeeding Martin Cooper as Chief Critic in 1977 and retiring in 1986. Before a problem with one of his hands forced him to leave the stage, Stadlen had been a prominent pianist, giving the first performance of Webern's *Variations* for piano, Op. 27, and the first European performance of Schoenberg's Piano Concerto. Though a former student of Webern, he had developed misgivings about the audibility and musical realism of serial technique, and published an article, 'Serialism Reconsidered', in *The Score* of February 1958, setting off a debate which rumbled on for several years.

spontaneously, an aural attitude towards the note-row – a doubt which the critic's subsequent development appears to have justified. If an aurally conceived row is perceived visually rather than aurally, it tends to do more harm than good, for the simple reason that the sound is knocked out of the music – some of it, anyway. On the other hand, Schoenberg himself has given an example of a fruitful disclosure of the 12-note secret:

> The main advantage of this method of composing with twelve notes is its unifying effect. In a very convincing way, I experienced the satisfaction of having been right about this when I once prepared the singers of my opera *Von Heute auf Morgen* for a performance. The technique, rhythm and intonation of all these parts were tremendously difficult for them, though they all possessed absolute pitch. But suddenly one of the singers came and told me that since he had become familiar with the basic set [the original form of the note-row], everything seemed easier for him. At short intervals all the other singers told me the same thing independently. I was very pleased with this ...[2]

Almost two generations stand between Schoenberg's *Variations* and Stravinsky's latest work. Time is said to move very fast in our century, and indeed, between these two classics, whole eras have come and gone – that of so-called 'total serialism', for instance, in its phoneyness a gift to Mr Stadlen's debunking urges.[3] At the same time, however, the evolution of genuinely creative techniques is as slow as ever – if not a little slower, because the techniques, musically applied, have become more difficult; the easier it is to cheat, the more difficult it is to compose. Who, examining the serial techniques of the *Variations* and the *Sermon*, could guess that decades lay between them? Far from moving fast, the development of sub-thematic 12-note technique has proved a very gradual affair – in itself a sign of its musical realism. The truth is that not only Mr Stadlen, but the rest of us, creators as well as recipients, need time to assimilate. One day – who knows, perhaps on May 31? – we shall all wake up and realize that we needn't worry.

[2] Arnold Schoenberg, 'Composition With Twelve Tones' (lecture-article, 1941), published in *Style and Idea*, *op. cit.*, p. 143; expanded 1975 version ed. Leonard Stein, St. Martin's Press, New York/Faber & Faber, London, p. 244.

[3] In his *1975* (*1984 minus 9*), *op. cit.*, p. 192, Keller wrote:

> Total serialism was, in the fifties, a creative world-view which, like Hitler's Third Reich, was expected to last a thousand years, and to which most leaders of the Continental avant-garde owed allegiance at some stage or other. Schoenberg's serialisation of pitches – the tone-row – was complemented by the serialisation of everything else – rhythm, dynamics, tone-colour, form, and even time itself [...].

XVI
Me about Us and Stravinsky

Music and Musicians, Vol. 10, No. 10, 10 June 1962, p. 23

It took me two seconds to accept the Editor's invitation to write an introduction to this book,[1] which is chiefly my wife's and partly my own. One second I devoted to recollections of many instructive 'self-reviews' – quite a feature in some Continental journals – which told me more about the works under review than could be gathered from the evaluations of critics who hadn't read them. The other second I remembered various press interviews I had given on things I had done or was supposed to have done. 'Right', I thought, 'if anybody is going to distort the truth this time, I'm going to do it myself.'

Q: What exactly is the idea of this book?

A: There isn't any. Milein did not draw Stravinsky because she expected him to be 80 one day. I did not think about Stravinsky because Milein drew him. The drawings were there; the thoughts were there; the eightieth birthday approached – and, most important, the publisher was interested.

Q: Does Milein Cosman only draw musicians?

A: She's been asked that stupid question so often she's forgotten the answer. She's interested in people in general and character and movement in particular; besides, she's musical.

Q: What, then, made her concentrate on Stravinsky?

A: She never concentrates. It isn't in her nature. All visual artists are loafers. Picasso, for instance ...

Q: Never mind about Picasso. How did all these Stravinsky drawings come into existence?

A: By way of a traumatic neurosis. Milein started drawing Stravinsky at Venice, on the occasion of the premiere of *The Rake's Progress*.[2] Carl Ebert,

[1] *Stravinsky at Rehearsal: A Sketchbook by Milein Cosman with text by Hans Keller* (Dobson, 15s.) –HK

[2] The first performance of *The Rake's Progress* was given at the Teatro La Fenice on 11 September 1951, conducted by the composer. Elisabeth Schwarzkopf created the role of Anne Trulove, Robert Rounseville that of Tom Bakewell; Otakar Kraus was Nick Shadow, Jennie Tourel Baba the Turk and Hugues Cuénod the Auctioneer Sellem.

who is big, got in between.[3] Stravinsky remained half-finished. She's been in Faustian search of the other half ever since.[4]

Q: Is the other half in the book?

A: She'd be too modest to say so. I'm not.

Q: Did Stravinsky ever sit for her?

A: No, not after Venice. It seemed to her a contradiction of his character to have him sit. Literally all the drawings in the book, including the heads, were done while he was moving about at rehearsal. You don't ask a dancer to sit for you.

Q: The drawing reproduced here, when was that done?

[3] A student of Max Reinhardt, Ebert (1887–1980) was 'Operndirektor und -Intendant' at the Stadtstheater in Darmstadt from 1927 and from 1931 filled the same position at the Städtische Oper (now the Deutsche Oper) in Berlin. Blacklisted by the Nazis as a 'Musik-Bolschewist', Ebert made his international reputation as producer of a series of Mozart operas, and Verdi's *Macbeth*, at Glyndebourne, from 1934 onwards (the conductor was Fritz Busch who, like his violinist brother, Adolf, refused to perform in Nazi Germany). At the time of this first production of *The Rake's Progress*, Ebert was head of the Institute for Opera of the University of Southern California at Los Angeles; in 1954 he rejoined the Städtische Oper in Berlin.

[4] Milein Cosman writes about these circumstances in more detail on pp. 173–75, below.

A: At a rehearsal for *Persephone* at the Festival Hall last year.

Q: Is there any connection between the drawings and your text?

A: I thought it was about time you got on to the text. Both Milein and I hate abstract twaddle, she in her art, I in mine. That's where the connection lies. She brings out Stravinsky's character, so do I.

Q: Can't you be a little more concrete yourself? What is your text about?

A: The concrete reasons for Stravinsky's concrete change-over to serial technique, amongst other, related things.

Q: That sounds pretty boring to me.

A: It's a tough piece, but it isn't boring. Besides, I haven't asked you to read it. All the same, you ought to be ashamed of yourself. Here is the greatest surprise in the history of music, of art, of anything.

Q: Well, there's always Ipswich Town making the League Championship.[5]

A: That's a good answer which gives me a good question. On the positive side, Ipswich at least had Crawford and Phil[l]ips;[6] on the negative side, Tottenham were pre-occupied with the European Cup and Burnley were getting worried about the double because Spurs had made it last year. No comparable circumstances surrounded Stravinsky's championing serialism: in the whole world, you wouldn't have found a single musician betting on it.[7] Stravinsky had hated the twelve-note technique for decades, from the moment go. He may always have changed his style, but he never before changed it towards something he had hated. Yet, after the initial shock, everybody took it all as a matter of course. It's irresponsible, artistically and intellectually.

Q: What is?

A: Not being surprised.

Q: Do you yourself consider Stravinsky at Rehearsal *a good book?*

A: There are four distinct answers to this complicated question: (a) I think Milein's drawings are marvellous. (b) She thinks my text is marvellous. (c) I think my text is marvellous. The fourth answer I leave to your imagination.

Q: Do you think everybody who buys the book is going to enjoy it?

A: You are begging your own question.

Q: Which?

A: That anybody is going to buy it.

[5] Under the management of Alf Ramsey from 1955, Ipswich Town F.C. had moved steadily up from Division Three, through Division Two, until on 28 April 1962 it won the League Championship after its very first season in Division One – the first time any English club had done so. In 1963 Ramsey left Ipswich to manage the English national team, leading it to victory in the 1966 World Cup.

[6] Ray Crawford (b. 1936) played for Ipswich Town from 1958 to 1963, scoring 143 goals during his 197 appearances for the club; Edward ('Ted') Phillips (b. 1933) scored 161 goals in 269 appearances during his eleven years (1953–64) with Ipswich.

[7] Keller may have meant the term literally as much as metaphorically: his betting on football results was so successful that he was banned from his local bookies.

Q: If it's all that marvellous, why shouldn't they?

A: Because people who are interested in drawings do not tend to be interested in music criticism (my kind of criticism anyway), and *vice versa.*

Q: Are you suggesting that you have done the wrong kind of book?

A: On the contrary, the outstanding virtue of the book is that it doesn't care about people's failings. There's so much phoney *rapprochement* between the arts nowadays – 'visual' scores, 'musical' painting, one painter even experimenting in electronic sound – that a bit of modest, but honest integration could do something towards clearing the air. Milein and I are converging on the nature of Stravinsky's creative personality from two opposite sides.

Q: Finally, do you think he is a genius?

A: I know he is, even so[8] he doesn't accept the term. All geniuses are unique, but some are uniquer than others, and he may be the uniquest of them all. That's why he still raises doubt: uniqueness is not readily acceptable if it doesn't contradict its own meaning – if it isn't precedented.

[8] Printed as published, syntax notwithstanding.

XVII
Stravinsky's Violin Concerto

Radio Times, Vol. 161, No. 2091, 5 December 1963, p. 6

Like most tonal violin concertos which respect the solo instrument, Stravinsky's (1931) is in D major, the violin's most brilliant key, as well as its most natural. His knowledge of the instrument is not an insider's (neither was Brahms's for that matter, nor Tchaikovsky's, nor Schumann's as opposed to Mendelssohn's),[1] but his outside knowledge is complete: it is ridiculous to suggest, as has quite often been done, that the work is written against the instrument.[2]

On the contrary, Stravinsky took enormous care to remain violinistic despite the wealth of unusual sounds in his mind that clamoured for realisation. The neo-classical style of the four-movement work enables him to throw his new sharp sonorities into relief against classical models, and indeed to use and re-shape such classical turns of phrase as are, unmistakably, among the violin's character traits.

What is true is that Stravinsky, the self-disciplinarian *par excellence*, limits himself to a certain sector of the violin's expressive field – to what I would call 'down-beat', if not in fact 'down-bow' music. To breathe out is more important to him than to breathe in: the whole of this violin concerto contains hardly a single crucial phrase that could be described as an upbeat phrase,

[1] In his *Chronicle of My Life* (*op. cit.*, p. 268), Stravinsky is frank about his 'outsider' status:

> I hesitated at first, because I am not a violinist and I was afraid that my slight knowledge of that instrument would not be sufficient to enable me to solve the many problems which would necessarily arise in the course of a major work specially composed for it.

[2] Samuel Dushkin (1891–1976), for whom the Violin Concerto was composed, later recalled:

> One day when we were lunching in a restaurant, Stravinsky took out a piece of paper and wrote down this chord [d′, e′′, a′′′] and asked me if it could be played. I had never seen a chord with such an enormous stretch, from the E to the top A, and I said, 'No.' Stravinsky said sadly, '*Quel dommage*' ('What a pity'). After I got home, I tried it, and, to my astonishment, I found that in that register, the stretch of the eleventh was relatively easy to play, and the sound fascinated me. I telephoned Stravinsky at once to tell him that it could be done. When the Concerto was finished, more than six months later, I understood his disappointment when I first said, 'No.' This chord, in a different dress, begins each of the four movements. Stravinsky himself calls it his 'passport' to that Concerto.

Cf. 'Working with Stravinsky', in *Stravinsky*, ed. E. Corle, Duell, Sloane and Pearce, New York, 1949, p. 182.

and only one or two which start with an upbeat. The bowed instruments, more than any other like to differentiate between up- and down-beats; but for the duration of this masterpiece, the violin has to get used to exhaling without having inhaled, to fall without having risen. Stravinsky's characteristic rhythms depend on one's breathing in, as it were, behind everybody's back.

XVIII
Stravinsky Eats

The Sunday Times, 11 December 1966, p. 43

Let me start on a point of pedantry; you won't regret it. I am not talking about the ordinary type of misprint, of which not even Eric Walter White's new and conscientious Stravinsky tome[1] is free: I suppose we have to put up with such things as *Weltschermz*, because not only are foreign languages funny – they have to be seen to be funny. Come to think of it, what I am talking about is nothing less than how music history is made.

The birth of that ambivalence between Schoenberg and Stravinsky which continues to dominate the history of contemporary music is to be found in Schoenberg's forty-year-old *Three Satires*, Op. 28. In the second of these, called, 'Versatility', he hit out at Stravinsky's neo-classicism with a joyful lack of subtlety in his text:

> Ja, wer tommerlt denn da?
> Das ist ja der kleine Modernsky!

Eric Walter White and/or his publisher approached the first line with musicological caution. Take nothing for granted. What's this, 'tommerlt'? There's no such word in the dictionary – not even in Duden, the German O.E.D. Ha! It's a misprint. The word must be 'trommelt' (drums). Of course, Schoenberg would object to Stravinsky's percussiveness. So it's 'trommelt' that goes into White's complete reprint of the German text,[2] and indeed into his translation:

> But who's this beating the drum?
> It's little Modernsky![3]

The evidence has been critically examined; musicology emerges, once again, the thoughtful victor over misleading if printed appearances. And now let me give you the truth. 'Ja, wer tommerlt denn da?' is conventional Viennese baby

[1] *Stravinsky: The Composer and His Works*, by Eric Walter White. Faber 6 gns. –HK

[2] *Ibid.*, p. 282 (1966 edn.)

[3] *Ibid.*

language as used by adults and tolerated by children, 'tommerlt' being a diminutive corruption of 'kommt' (comes). The correct translation, therefore, is –

> Why, look who's coming here!
> If it isn't little Modernsky!

Just imagine the Sunday Times hadn't sent me the book: it would have taken another half-century to clear that one up.[4]

In the course of the decades, Stravinsky has proved the more genuinely ambivalent – the hate-lover pure and complex. Schoenberg's attitude seems to have remained one of musical aversion which came to be mixed with cool respect as he (and Stravinsky) grew older. Stravinsky, on the other hand, turned his ambivalence into creativity. 'It is significant', says White, 'that this important move [towards serialism] occurred only after the death in 1951 of Schoenberg, the pioneer and founder of the "Method".' My theory is that it's a case of creative mourning. For the past fifty years, ever since Freud published his *Mourning and Melancholia*, we have known that what he called the 'identification of the ego with the lost object'[5] is at the root of all mourning. Since Stravinsky's is an identifying creative character anyhow, he naturally avails himself of the mourning mechanisms as soon as a hate-love object is dead: 'He is constitutionally incapable of reacting in this way to the work of any of his living contemporaries – to do so would be a form of aesthetic cannibalism ... Even in his apprentice days, the composition that most clearly showed his attachment to his master (*The Firebird*) was written not under Rimsky-Korsakov's direct supervision but after his death'.[6]

That bit about aesthetic cannibalism, though, is psychologically misleading: introjection, incorporation of the lost object is, after all, an oral process. But it is the dead composers whom Stravinsky lovingly consumes; the living ones he tries to keep out of his works if not his thoughts. Schoenberg, so long as he was alive, seemed a simple object of rejection.

Now, in case you think that Stravinsky was merely being a-atonal, remember that the violence of his remarks about Britten's *War Requiem* has proved too savage to reach public print in this country;[7] in fact, throughout the 608

[4] In the second edition of White's book, the German original has been corrected and the translation modified to say: 'Why, who's coming here?'; *cf.* White, *Stravinsky: The Composer and His Works*, 2nd edn., Faber and Faber, London, 1979, p. 320.

[5] *Cf.* note 8 on p. 48, above.

[6] White, *Stravinsky: The Composer and His Works*, 1966 edn., p. 514; the original has 'esthetic'

[7] Keller presumably refers to a passage in the Stravinsky-Craft *Themes and Episodes* (Alfred A. Knopf, New York, 1966, pp. 13–14) which was considerably truncated when it re-appeared as part of the volume *Themes and Conclusions* released in the UK (Faber and Faber, London 1972, pp. 26–27), where an Introduction warns that the texts have been 'revised – corrected, cut, expanded':

> The tide of applause virtually packaged along with the *War Requiem* is so loud and the

pages of his comprehensive book, White remains tactfully unaware of one of the most interesting fields of tension in the history of modern music. Yet less than virginal readers will not fail to notice that *The Flood*[8] uses the same succession of twelve notes as *The Turn of the Screw*,[9] and that it was composed after Britten's own *Noye's Fludde*,[10] just as Stravinsky's *Abraham and Isaac*[11] succeeded Britten's work of the same title[12]… Does one need clearer symptoms of hostile identification? But since Britten is alive, Stravinsky is kicking rather than assimilating.

What does it all amount to? Ordinary artistic development has always started with identification: while the composer's own creative ego was still weak, he identified himself with his teachers and with older masters and proceeded to imitate them. But in this retrospective and circumspect age, at the end of one culture and the beginning of another, it is possible for a genius like Stravinsky's or Picasso's to retain and develop his capacity for identification together with the unfolding of his intense originality. Nobody is independent today, because everybody is insecure. One cannot but ask oneself, with a shudder, whether there were identifying geniuses in the past for whom the time was not ripe. Genius will out, we say. How do we know if some didn't?

Battle-of-Britten sentiment is so thick that these phenomena, and the national inferiority feeling in music they expose, are at least as absorbing as the music. Behold the critics as they vie in abasement before the wonder of native-born genius. […]

Kleenex at the ready, then, and feeling as though one has failed to stand up for 'God Save the Queen,' one goes from the critics to the music, to find (a) a Honegger-type cinemascope epic in an idiom derived in part from Boulanger-period Stravinsky (the 'shifting' major-minor thirds at [96], the 'shifting' accents of the 9/8 rhythm in the 'Offertorium'); (b) patterns rather than inventions (the timpani figure at [49], for example, is a good invention but a poor pattern); (c) one very effective dramatic idea, that of casting the chorus in Latin in and the male soloists in English; (d) an absence of real counterpoint; (e) a bounteous presence of literalisms ('The drums of Time,' sings the baritone, and 'boom, boom, boom' go the obedient timpani); of cinema music (the fanfares before [111], and the strings-and-drum music at [95]; and of organ-point (the sedative in C at [74]).

[8] 1961–62

[9] 1954

[10] 1957–58

[11] 1962–63

[12] 1952

XIX
Stravinsky the Downbeater

The Listener, Vol. 78, No. 2012, 19 October 1967, p. 509

When God created man in his own image, male and female created he them, he also created upbeat music and downbeat music, likewise in his own image, as evident from the moment go in the music of the spheres. The reasons why there is no mention of it in Genesis are three. First, the chronicler didn't think it was much of a story at the time: he wanted to confine himself to what he thought were essentials, and he happened to be unmusical. Secondly and laudably, he thought that people would immediately identify upbeat with female and downbeat with male (or vice versa) in order to keep their world view tidy, and not being musical, he didn't know whether there was any point in that. As a matter of fact, there isn't: the two distinctions cut across each other, and there has been enough trouble about the differential diagnosis between male and female anyway. Thirdly, the terms 'upbeat music' and 'downbeat music' did not then exist: all the chronicler knew was that there was something basic in music corresponding to breathing in and out.

To be precise, the two terms started their written existence a few minutes ago, and they won't be allowed to die if I can help it. And now, let me start; not at the beginning, but at the end.

When Schoenberg objected to the English musical term 'development', to which he came rather late in life, he said that all music, not just a middle section in a sonata form, was development.[1] He was wrong: Stravinsky's fiddle concerto (1931), for instance, isn't. But then, Schoenberg wasn't thinking of Stravinsky's fiddle concerto: nothing could have been further from his mind than Stravinsky's neo-classical period, which he had ridiculed in a musical satire about 'the little Modernsky'.[2] In fact, the little Modernsky had a hard time at the hands of the Central Europeans in general and the Austro-Germans in particular – right up to the time when, punctually upon Schoenberg's death (1951), he turned 12-tone. But in 1949 Theodor Adorno, our

[1] *Structural Functions of Harmony*, Williams and Norgate, London, 1954 (rev. edn. Norton, New York/Faber & Faber, London, 1969), p. 145.

[2] *Cf.* p. 98, above.

age's musical philosopher-in-chief, still based his whole *Philosophy of New Music* on the field of tension created by the polarity he postulated between Schoenberg and Stravinsky, playing off the one against the other. Stravinsky's music he then regarded as a death-mask of the past – which, mind you, is my metaphor: it took my friend Adorno several pages, or rather one sentence extending over several pages, to rid himself of his hostility with a sufficiently scholarly conscience. The violinist Rudolf Kolisch, Schoenberg's principal, heavily authorised interpreter, has described Stravinsky's neo-classical creations as 'music about music';[3] while their defenders have submitted, in equally general terms, that they reflect Stravinsky's 'own distinctive personality as much as his acute sense of the past' – that in the fiddle concerto, despite its memories of Vivaldi, Bach and Mozart, 'there is not a single bar that could have been written by any composer but Stravinsky' (Mosco Carner).[4] Why not? Answers usually concentrate on references to harmony and rhythm – to Stravinsky's characteristic wrong-note technique, and to his unmistakable rhythmic character. True enough, but what is it that makes the wrong notes and the rhythms characteristic?

Meaning, according to my theory of music, can invariably be defined in terms of demonstrable tensions, and indeed relations, between what you hear and what you had expected to hear – between manifest foreground and latent, well-implied background.[5] In his neo-classical period, Stravinsky chose to push his classical backgrounds very much to the fore, with the inevitable result that he had to contradict them all the more violently if he wanted to retain the tensions of which musical substance consists. The most

[3] In 'The Unpopularity of Mahler's Popularity', *The Listener*, Vol. 85, No. 2194, 5 April 1971, p. 491 (republished in *Hans Keller: Essays on Music, op. cit.*, pp. 68–70) Keller notes that Kolisch was 'quoted, with approval, by the late Theodor Adorno in his *Philosophy of Modern Music*'. In 'Drowning in *The River*', *Opera*, 27 (September 1976), pp. 817–21, Keller credits the elderly Kolisch ('eighty last July') with thus having coined 'an invaluable critical phrase, of central importance at our century's critical stage in the history of composition'; through Adorno it was 'perhaps rendered immortal'. Kolisch used the phrase also about Morton Gould (*cf.* 'Lecture on American Music', in Anne Schreffler and David Trippett (eds), *MusikTheorie*, Vol. 24, No. 3, 2009, p. 258). Felix Khuner (1906–91), the second violinist in the Kolisch String Quartet, made the same remark about Stravinsky, recalling it in interview with Caroline Crawford (*Felix Khuner: A Violinist's Journey from Vienna's Kolisch Quartet to the San Francisco Symphony and Opera Orchestras*, Regional Oral History Office, Bancroft Library, University of California, 1996; available online at www.khuner.com/history/in01.htm). Of course, it is more than likely that the two violinists discussed the idea during the fourteen years they played together, from Khuner's joining the Quartet in 1927 to its disbandment in 1941.

[4] Mosco Carner (*né* Cohen, 1904–85) was born in Vienna and studied musicology at the University there under Guido Adler. Initially he made his living as an operatic conductor, first in Opava (1929–30) and then in Danzig (1930–33). With the Nazis' accession to power he moved to London, his home for the rest of his life. Once again, he first made his mark as a conductor before becoming known as a writer, working as music-critic for *Time and Tide* (1949–62), *The Evening News* (1957–61) and a number of other publications. Among his several books *Puccini: A Critical Biography* (Duckworth, London, 1958) and *Alban Berg: The Man and his Work* (Duckworth, London, 1975) were especially well received. I have not been able to locate the source of this quotation.

[5] Keller presented a somewhat fuller exposition in 'Towards a Theory of Music', *The Listener*, Vol. 83, No. 2150, 11 June, 1970, pp. 795–96, and 'Closer Towards a Theory of Music', *The Listener*, Vol. 85, No. 2186, 18 February, 1971, pp. 218–19.

violent and consistent contradiction is one which strikes at the very root of that which is being contradicted, and which, at the same time, comes naturally to the composer's creative character.

Now, the root of classical structure is developmental thought, forward-urging, unfolding, dynamic: so far, Schoenberg was right. Without any oversimplification, the classical tradition, indeed the whole of Austro-German music, can be described as upbeat music: the upbeat, breathing in before breathing out, is the primal model for all musical unfolding and development, in which upbeat phrases will readily function like literal, single-beat upbeats. In German, significantly enough, the upbeat is called 'up-bar' (*Auftakt*): Austro-German thought has always been acutely conscious of weak (up-) and strong (down-) bars, as has classical invention in Italy. On the other hand, Stravinsky's life-long fascination with what I call suppressionism, with musical staticism, made him the downbeater *par excellence*, who – sado-masochistically – replaced upbeating shapes, where the main accent comes late in the phrase, by downbeats *cum* afterbeats, where – as in this example from the *Symphony of Psalms* – the sole stress comes first.

Functional harmony – prototypically the dominant seventh followed by the tonic or submediant – urges towards upbeat music; non-functional harmony, such as Debussy's, points the way forward and backwards to downbeat music. Here, then, lies the answer to Stravinsky's wrong-note harmonies and 'distorted' classical rhythms: they are so constructed as to serve his downbeat contradictions of the upbeat music he uses as implied and suppressed background.

Now the bowed instruments, which are the central sound of Europe's developmental, upbeating, symphonic tradition, are in fact the upbeating instruments κατ' ἐξοχηυ. A little thoughtlessly, to my mind, they have always been likened to, almost identified with, the human voice, because they can sing. But the voice cannot breathe in while it sings: the bow can. The up-bow is, in fact, the purest physical expression of both the elementary upbeat and the extended upbeat phrase. No wonder the violin is the queen of upbeat music – just as the drum, both primitive and sophisticated, i.e., sublimated into percussive patterns produced by other instruments, is the king of downbeat music – and don't be misled by the sex difference: England, under queens, has proved quite a masculine country.

Stravinsky's Violin Concerto thus emerges as the climax of the tension between 'neo' and 'classical', between downbeat foreground and upbeat background: there is hardly a single unambiguous upbeat or upbeat phrase introducing anything new in the entire work, which so stands alone in the vast literature for the instrument, creating an unexpected expressive field for it. *The Soldier's Tale* (1918) apart, Stravinsky had never before used the solo violin, but now he enlisted its help to challenge classicism at its base: meaningfully contradicting the instrument's character, he widened and indeed sharpened it. The concerto starts with no fewer than four down-beats and -bows, and soon the suppressed upbeats, now downbeats, are there for all to hear:

Where the upbeat background comes so much to the fore that the fiddler might actually be tempted to play it, Stravinsky makes sure of the contradiction by placing accents on the dethroned upbeats:

In essence the riddle of Stravinsky is, perhaps, solved. His is downbeat music about, and against, upbeat music – and that includes his every single seeming *volte-face*, right up to his adoption of Schoenberg's 12-tone method. For whereas, technically, his dodecaphony is closer to Schoenberg's than to Webern's, he uses this very affinity to contradict Schoenberg's developmental, upbeating invention. In this sense, Adorno's polarity remained realistic – beyond Schoenberg's death, when the philosopher may have thought that his philosophy had become outdated. But it is the Violin Concerto that is Stravinsky's most overt self-characterisation: throughout, it is obvious to the naked ear that the master is intent upon beating upbeats down.

XX
Concerto in D

Programme note for a concert of the Royal Philharmonic Society, with the English Chamber Orchestra conducted by Daniel Barenboim, in the Royal Festival Hall on 2 April 1969; the programme opened with the Elgar *Serenade* and Haydn's Cello Concerto in D major (soloist Jacqueline Du Pré) and closed, after the Stravinsky, with Haydn's Symphony No. 83

Also known as the 'Basle Concerto' because it was written (in 1946) for the twentieth anniversary of the Basle Chamber Orchestra and dedicated to its conductor, Paul Sacher, this concerto for string orchestra was one of Stravinsky's last neo-classical works. Much, perhaps too much, has been made of his surprising change of style; his switch to serial technique, in particular, shattered the musical world, giving rise to shouts of triumph and moans of dejection. I myself wrote that 'Stravinsky's absorption of Schoenberg's technique was arguably the profoundest surprise in the history of music'.[1] Well, it may have been, but the question remains whether we were justified in being all that surprised. Being wise after the event, which is a shade better than not being wise at all, it seems that Stravinsky has always remained a neo-classicist. His harmonies nowadays are more closely related to, say, the present Concerto than to the harmonies of the classical twelve-tone composers; and as for his melodies – well, he adopted twelve-tone technique as soon as it became 'classical' itself, in a contemporary sense: he found something new to be neo-classical about.

What is yet more striking, however, is that hindsight discloses seminal serial technique in Stravinsky's neo-classical works proper; in fact, one could go so far as to say that the Concerto in D, all three movements of it, is based on the tiniest possible tone-row – a series of two notes a minor second apart. From the moment go, i.e., the first melodic interval in bars 6/7,

Ex. 1

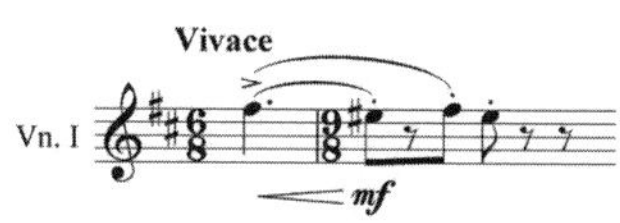

[1] In *Stravinsky at Rehearsal*, *op. cit.*,. p. 3, subsumed into 'Stravinsky Heard' in *Stravinsky Seen and Heard*; *cf.* p. 128, below.

this 'two-note row' dominates the material – in all dimensions, like a proper twelve-tone row. What is more, in the work's first harmonic bar (3), the 'row' has already appeared vertically, F natural clashing against the F sharp on top. And like a real tone-row (as opposed to a melodic motif), this mini-series soon turns out to be wholly independent of its initial rhythm (Example 1), as well as appearing upside down, back to front, and in so-called 'octave-transposition', i.e., disguised as a major seventh. Even the key-scheme is influenced by it: the first movement's *moderato* middle section is in D♭ major, a semitone below the home-key.

As a texture, the Concerto is one of the cleanest, clearest compositions of our age – and as music, it's one of the most accessible.

XXI
Perséphone

Programme note for a concert of the Royal Philharmonic Society, with the BBC Symphony Orchestra conducted by Colin Davis, in the Royal Festival Hall on 27 January 1971; the programme opened with Beethoven's overture *Namensfeier*, after which Norbert Brainin and Peter Schidlof – fellow internees of Keller's in the Onchan internment camp on the Isle of Man in 1940 – performed Mozart's *Sinfonia Concertante*, K364. The soloists in *Perséphone* were the Lithuanian-born British ballerina Svetlana Beriosova and Canadian tenor André Turp.

The work is a 'melodrama' for female reciter (Persephone, the goddess), tenor (Eumolpus, the Eleusinian Priest), mixed chorus and orchestra. André Gide's text, printed below with an English translation,[1] is based on the Greek myth in which Persephone (the daughter of Demeter, the goddess of fertility) is abducted into the underworld, whence she is reborn as the symbol of spring. Originally composed for production as a ballet, by Ida Rubinstein's company of dancers, at the Paris Opéra in April 1934, the score was revised, not very drastically so, in 1949. Gide held strong views about French prosody, Stravinsky even stronger ones about how to set words to music, not to speak of syllables. As a result, what had started as a cordial collaboration finished up with Gide going on holiday to Sicily as the rehearsals for the Paris production were starting. Paul Valéry supported Stravinsky and affirmed 'the musician's prerogative to treat loose and formless prosodies [a backhander at Gide, this] according to his musical ideas, even if the latter led to "distortion" of phrasing or to the breaking up, for purposes of syllabification, of the words themselves'.[2] Thus encouraged, Stravinsky, in his turn, published his famous manifesto in *Excelsior*[3] – on the eve of the first performance. It ended with what have become historic words: 'All this is in no way due to caprice on my

[1] The English translation was ascribed in the programme simply to Éditions Gallimard.

[2] Quoted in Eric Walter White, *Stravinsky: The Composer and His Works*, 2nd edn., *op. cit.*, p. 338.

[3] White (*ibid.*, p. 84) explains that

> Stravinsky seems to have felt the need for issuing an advance kind of public *apologia* that would clarify his particular way of setting syllables rather than words, his attitude to the vexed question of emotion in music, and his dislike of coruscating orchestral effects. [...] This appeared in *Excelsior* for 29 April.

part. I am on a perfectly sure road. There is nothing to discuss or criticise. One does not criticise anyone who is functioning. A nose is not manufactured – a nose just *is*. Thus, too, my art'. Two days after the first performance, Valéry wrote a note to Stravinsky, which ended in capital letters: 'LONG LIVE YOUR NOSE'.[4]

Longer, in fact, than Stravinsky himself might have wished at a later stage, when he described the use of melodrama (speech and music) in *Perséphone* as 'a sin that cannot be undone, only forgiven'.[5] All that has to be forgiven, in this writer's humble submission, is that he did not attach rhythmic values to the speech which, for the rest, is treated with such tender caution by the musical texture that it, in its turn, cannot help showing the same respect to the music itself.

As opposed to such choral works as the *Symphony of Psalms*, the *Mass*, the *Canticum sacrum* or *Tenebrae*, all of them sacred, *Perséphone* is in fact stressedly homophonic almost throughout. It is, moreover, strictly anti-developmental, showing Stravinsky's unceasing mastery of his many different arts of repetition, with *ostinato* figures, *ostinato* chords, and even single *ostinato* notes supporting a wide variety of thematic transformation within a stern tonal scheme. The texture alternates between the transparent (melodrama) and the translucent; the style is neo-classical, neo-preclassical, and even neo-archaic. Perhaps the only reason why the work is often regarded as problematic is that search as you will, you won't find any problems in it: they are all solved for you. If there is such a thing as hypnosis without its nasty side, spiritual hypnosis in fact, this is it. Stravinsky's gestures are none the less efficacious for being deliberately half-empty: half a cup of something does more to us than a full cup of something else. Or, to change the metaphor, Stravinsky provides us with one half because he wants us to provide the other. This, for once, is genuinely artistic audience participation: with crystalline clarity, the creator defines for us what we are participating in.

[4] Quoted in *ibid.*, p. 338.

[5] 'Sins cannot be undone, only forgiven', *Conversations with Igor Stravinsky, op. cit.*, p. 21. But as White (*Stravinsky: The Composer and His Works, op. cit.*, p. 84) observes,

> it should be noted that a few years later, with characteristic agility, Stravinsky had changed his mind and was using serial music to accompany declamation in *A Sermon, a Narrative, and a Prayer* [1960–61] and also in *The Flood* [1961–62].

XXII
Stravinsky v. Stravinsky

The article published under this title in *The Listener*, Vol. 86, No. 2212, 19 August 1971, pp. 250–51, was originally written for publication as one of a long-running series of 'Views' in the magazine; a galley proof in the Hans Keller Archive at Cambridge University Library reveals that the intended publication date was 6 May. Both this galley and the original typescript demonstrate that Keller's text was shortened for its eventual publication (when it was used to promote three forthcoming Stravinsky performances at the Proms); the version presented here restores the excised material (shown within square brackets) while respecting small changes made in the published text.

Stravinsky's death has left the honest amongst us disconsolate, disconcerted and any other dis- you might care to mention.[1] Indeed there has not been a comparably distorting genius in the history of music: he creatively distorted classical styles and Schoenberg's 12-tone technique with equal ease – anything, in fact, so long as it felt dead enough. Schoenberg, therefore, posed a bit of a problem; Stravinsky solved it by waiting, at least, until the composer himself was dead, whereupon he promptly turned to, and on, serial technique, which he had previously attacked. You might also say, he turned his sterile verbal attack into a productive sonic one – nor does attack mean lack of assimilation and identification: long before Wilde said that 'each man kills the thing he loves',[2] many a distinguished cannibal made a meal of his love-objects,[3] and Stravinsky was the most distinguished cannibal of them all.

As a result, there was this feeling of dissociation from him when he died, rather than one of mourning identification: [we didn't feel like eating him up in our turn. Even one of his best understanders and (hence) most unreserved

[1] Stravinsky died on 6 April 1971, at the age of 88.

[2] *Cf.* note 7 on p. 47, above.

[3] In *Criticism* (Faber & Faber, London, 1987, p. 92) Keller observed that incorporation, 'symbolically, is continuing [...] to be practised amongst the most civilized – in the Roman Catholic ritual'.

admirers, William Glock,[4] was anxious to point out that Stravinsky wasn't one of the very greatest – at the very moment when any admirer of any other genius would have felt, for the duration of the mourning period, that he was the greatest:] it was as if the only thing the dead Stravinsky would allow us wholly to identify with was his own ruthless, anti-emotional quest for aesthetic objectivity.

[The funeral, inasmuch as one could get the feel of it in front of the television set, was indeed as cool in atmosphere as the music performed at it, which included Stravinsky's own. If one compares what one knows about Beethoven's funeral, not to speak of Wagner's, and remembers that Stravinsky remains, after all, the most successful composer of our time (and indeed one of the most successful geniuses of all times), one gets a mystifying measure of our musical world's detachment.]

The problem of his position becomes the more fascinating when one considers that while few really loved him, nobody hated him – or, if they did, dared to say so, at any rate in the past decade or two. In Stravinsky's neo-classical period, Schoenberg was able to joke, a trifle crudely, about 'the little Modernsky';[5] and in 1949, the Schoenberg school had its last and highly intellectualised fling in the shape of Th. W. Adorno's *Philosophy of New Music*, which described Stravinsky's music, in dozens of pages with a new sentence on every other page, as a death mask of the past (my metaphor).[6] Since then, however, there's been a steady armistice in the guise of a peace treaty: whatever violent objections some outstanding musicians and composers have had to Stravinsky's music, they've muttered them, shamefacedly, in private; in public they have joined the chorus of respect, best sung at arm's length. They have thus contrasted themselves violently with Stravinsky's own verbal attitudes. For in the years of his ultimate wisdom, the master was not beyond descending to the level of uncomprehending gutter journalism when pronouncing upon the music of such dangerous rivals as Beethoven, Brahms, Schoenberg or, most savagely, Britten. [In fact, his tolerant conscience about his partial ignorance of the objects of his criticisms was colourfully independent of the unbending, clear-eared self-criticism he employed in the composing process.]

[4] Glock (1908–2000) was an organ scholar at Cambridge University, where he read history, before going to Berlin to study with Artur Schnabel (1930–33). The latter years of his time as a music-critic for *The Observer* (1934–45) overlapped with war service in the RAF. Glock's influence on British musical life was considerable: he founded *The Score* in 1949 and edited it until 1961; he founded the Dartington Summer School of Music in 1953, acting as its director until 1979; and was Director of the Bath Festival for eight years from 1976. But it was as 'Controller, Music' for the BBC from 1959 to 1972, in charge of programming the Proms from 1960 to 1973, that he had most effect, using his position to promote musical modernism, to the consternation of those who preferred more conservative fare. He was knighted in 1970.

[5] *Cf.* p. 98, above.

[6] On Adorno, *cf.* note 3 on p. 35, above.

Now, why every available knife into Britten? Ultimately, perhaps, because Britten is the only composer of stature who did eat up Stravinsky the way Stravinsky ate up others. In fact, while Adorno was right to identify Schoenberg and Stravinsky as the basic polarity of our age, while Glock was right in describing, twenty-odd years later, the two as our century's giants, there is this additional mystery – that whereas one of them influenced everybody (Stravinsky included) except for one or two, the other influenced nobody except for one or two: Britten apart, Stravinsky exerted his influence almost exclusively on musical monkeys. Otherwise, the musical world's detachment was there long before the funeral. It seems that you have to be at least as great as Stravinsky in order to be able to eat and creatively digest him – or anybody else for that matter; and the nature of his music made any other kind of influence impossible, for the simple reason that he introduced no technical innovations; he just swallowed them.

What, then, is the nature of his music? Suppressionist, I have called it, and here lies the key to both the coolness and the universality of the musical world's admiration. For what Stravinsky suppresses is, to put it bluntly, *us* – our own musical experiences with their affective values. And his genius, which ultimately lies in this very suppressionism, makes us agree with him, share his sado-masochistic attitude, even though we cannot readily achieve whole-hearted identification where much of our heart serves him as material for his suppressions – our heart-beat, our very breathing being intriguingly distorted in the process: often we aren't even allowed to breathe in, only out. The fiddle is the in-breathing instrument *par excellence*, but Stravinsky's fiddle concerto only breathes out – insists on downbeat phrases to the exclusion of upbeat phrases: whenever something seems dangerously like an upbeat, Stravinsky puts an accent on it.

Our culture is compulsively retrospective, hence introspective. We are either preoccupied with the past – or when, like John Cage at his outpost, we try to rid ourselves of it altogether, we merely succeed in showing our preoccupation with our preoccupations. The very concept of an avant-garde is past-laden, proves our luggage-van to be overloaded: in Mozart's time, everybody was avant-garde and nobody had to say so.

Stravinsky made this compulsive retro- and introspection his own: all his material is past, remote or recent. And by eating up the past, with his musical backgrounds disclosing themselves to the naked ear the way other composers' foregrounds do, he reflects our own ambivalence towards our inheritance, so that when he suppresses the emotion which the past engenders in us, when he establishes, not an area without emotion, but a field of tension between intense emotion and its equally intense suppression, he reflects the whole of the contemporary mind, its guilty anti-expressionism, its compulsion to remember the past and its fear of being reminded of it, the nightmare of running away from something to which one is chained.

His sense for encompassing the contemporary mind, the whole of it and every seamy side of it, is all-comprehensive, all-comprehending; its artistic surety goes so far as to turn inartistic reaction to art into art, artistic stupidity into wisdom. The outstanding example is his assimilation of Webern, who was the ultimate expressionist and, by virtue of the very fact that he pumped a movement's expression into a phrase, rendered himself liable to irreparable misunderstanding. The expressive content, that is, was not easily felt at the reception end, the short phrase or motif heard – and, more often than not, played! – as something unemotional, anti-emotional, 'clean': an impression promoted by the uncompromising clarity of Webern's textures.

Right, said Stravinsky's unerring creative mind, I ought to know better but it is my artistic duty not to: Webern's music may be powerful, but so is its misunderstanding, and it is its misunderstanding that I'm going to make comprehensible; and off he went. Countless are the ears that now hear Webern in the light of Stravinsky's reinterpretation of their original mishearing – and if that seems a little hard on Webern, the fact remains that those ears have taken in Stravinsky's own lapidary creative substance on the way. Nor have we any aesthetic right to blame him: the developed, intelligent ear can understand and understandingly misunderstand at the same time [, and a genius has only one duty – to address himself to that kind of ear].

The mystery is shallowing. I mentioned the other week that Rudolph Kolisch called Stravinsky 'music about music'[7] – but I don't think my friend is aware of the magnitude of his compliment, which he no doubt meant as a subtle criticism. 'About': this is what our age has been about all along, and the frantic attempts at uncontrolled improvisation, random music, anti-art and isolated intellectual games unrelated to anything outside themselves[8] – all these symptoms are but the next best thing to shutting one's ears, including one's inner ears, which alas one can't.

Whatever we may find wrong with Stravinsky, then, we know jolly well why we keep it private. Our cowardice is profound, not superficial: what's wrong with him is wrong with us – and indeed only with us, not with him. He has, after all, turned it into creative discovery, into a statement of truth. He so emerges as *the* composer of our time, the diagnostician of the contemporary

[7] *Cf.* note 2 on p. 102, above.

[8] Such 'frantic attempts' were the target of Keller's famous spoof, *Mobile for tape and percussion*, by the non-existent composer 'Piotr Zak'. Keller and the pianist Susan Bradshaw went into a BBC studio, randomly hitting percussion instruments and whistling; at one point Keller had to point out to Bradshaw that she was making too much musical sense – the desired result was meaningless noise. Broadcast (twice) on 5 June 1961, in a performance ostensibly by 'Claude Tessier' and 'Anton Schmidt', the work was – as Keller had expected – taken seriously by the critics. An extract can be heard on YouTube at www.youtube.com/watch?v=6maWI85kSxU.

mind – whereas the other pole, Schoenberg, had so little to do with his own time that in the most crucial phase of his development, there were about five people who understood his music (Stravinsky not amongst them).

When Schoenberg died, Boulez wrote a rude article under the title, 'Schoenberg is dead'.[9] The title of my own rude article could well be 'Stravinsky is alive' – in fact, until further notice, there's nobody aliver. The discomfort we may feel at our experience of his music is not his problem, but ours; the displeasure with which we note our pleasure ought to please us: it shows that something so crucial has been said about us that it's worth our distaste of the very music which, in all its ever-changing styles, sternly insists on remaining tasteful.

[9] 'Schoenberg est mort', *The Score*, No. 6, February 1952, pp. 18–22; republished in Pierre Boulez, *Relevés d'apprenti*, Seuil, Paris, 1966, pp. 265–74 (English trans., as *Notes of an Apprenticeship*, by Herbert Weinstock, Alfred A. Knopf, New York, 1968; rev. edn., as *Stocktakings from an Apprenticeship*, by Paule Thévenin, trans. Stephen Walsh, Clarendon Press, Oxford, 1991).

XXIII
Words *v.* Music

The Listener, Vol. 88, No. 2274, 26 October 1972, pp. 547–49

Themes and Conclusions. By Igor Stravinsky. Faber £6
Stravinsky: The Chronicle of a Friendship, 1948–1971. By Robert Craft. Gollancz £4
And Music at the Close: Stravinsky's Last Years. By Lillian Libman. Macmillan £3.50 (to be published on 2 November)
Encounters with Stravinsky. By Paul Horgan. Bodley Head £3

Both psychologically and financially, people are cashing in on Stravinsky's death with due haste. You can't fairly find anything undue about it when the master is posthumously amongst them. 'I can now confess to the partly mercenary motive behind some of my prefaces, reviews, interviews. Bluntly, the balance between my income and my needs has, for a decade or more, rested on the "deductibility" ' of the latter. To write, in America, is to "write-off".' Much of it reads like it, too, and the spectacle of Stravinsky parasitising himself is hardly more savoury than are the other three books, even though they contain far less thought. Of Stravinsky's own collection of odds and un-thought-out beginnings, many first appeared in such learned journals as *Show*, *Harper's Magazine* and the *Los Angeles Times*. And many of these are now republished for the third time: the book which was 'seen through the press' (with plenty of German misprints) by Robert Craft is, largely, a rehash of *Themes and Episodes* (1966) and *Retrospectives and Conclusions* (1969).[1] Considering that these two volumes were the tail-end of a series of six (*Conversations with* [*Igor*] *Stravinsky*, *Memories and Commentaries*, *Expositions and Developments* and *Dialogues and a Diary* being the first four[2]), the degree of whose authenticity is not always worth discovering and won't ever be discovered anyway, there is conclusive support here for my often-suggested criminal Bill against books: the real, great criminals will write them nevertheless.

Inevitably, these 'squibs, programme notes, interviews, prefaces, reviews,

[1] Both published by Alfred A. Knopf, New York.

[2] Published, respectively, in 1959 (Doubleday, Garden City/Faber and Faber, London), 1960 (University of California Press, Berkeley and Los Angeles/Faber and Faber, London), 1962 (Doubleday, Garden City/Faber and Faber, London) and 1963 (Doubleday, Garden City/Faber and Faber, London). Keller's review of the first of them can be found on pp. 75–81, above.

columns' etc do contain the occasional explosion of Stravinsky's musical genius – deeply gratifying shocks in the context:

> University of Washington interviewer: 'To go back to the question of scope, Mr Stravinsky, do you consider Webern's to be too narrow?' 'Not for Webern. I cannot understand the word in musical terms. Webern's time-scale is tiny, his quantity minute, his variety limited; but are these the measurements of scope? If scope were concerned with depth, for example, and not merely with width and expanse, then Webern's can be very great.'

But unfortunately, not even all of Stravinsky's strictly musical observations are musical: he had put his musical conscience into music and left it there. On Beethoven, he is hardly more enlightening as a friend than he used to be as a foe, and unreservedly welcomes Joseph Kerman's book on the quartets,[3] which abounds with instinctive insight, infantile analytic mistakes, and insidious devaluations stemming from them: no doubt Kerman satisfies both sides of Stravinsky's ambivalence towards Beethoven.

Nevertheless, I'd rather read Stravinsky's book all over again than any chapter from the other three. There is little hope that Robert Craft has now squeezed the last ounce, 424 pages of it, out of his friendship with Stravinsky: after all, there's the threat of a biography. Let me declare my considered prejudice against Mr Craft's approach to truth at the outset. So far as I can perceive, he honestly thinks that there is a valid substitute for truth, and that the preferability of truth tends to be exaggerated, perhaps like that of butter to margarine. For me, the time-honoured, tedious Craft-Stravinsky issue is basically simple: as soon as you put something in inverted commas which somebody hasn't in fact written or said in those very words, you're lying. End of ethics. In Stravinsky's own *Themes and Conclusions*, there's a rather pathetic facsimile page from *Memories and Commentaries*, showing his 'deletions and one [*sic*] of his corrections' – which is supposed to show, no doubt, that he had actually seen what he was supposed to have said. Now it may well be that *The Chronicle of a Friendship* contains rather more authenticity than one or the other previous volume, that the very fact of a narrative discharged Craft of the duty to make things up a little. But the possible gain in authenticity does not result in increased interest: we've had it all – or rather, not much of what we haven't yet had is worth having. During the later acts of *Der Rosenkavalier*, he tells us, some of Stravinsky's comments were: 'Strauss holds his breath too long', 'Bad taste and vigour go well together', and 'If Richard, then Wagner, if Strauss, then Johann'. I first heard this joke when I was nine, and it wasn't Stravinsky either who made it, but my father, who told me it wasn't his.

One would take it all in one's stride, I suppose, if two conditions were fulfilled. For one thing, there would have to be more of the genuine article.

[3] *The Beethoven Quartets*, W. W. Norton, New York, 1966/Oxford University Press, London, 1967.

That paragraph about Strauss, for instance, while full of platitudinous quotations *à la* 'How can anybody swallow all of that *schlagsahne*?' also contains a gem about why Strauss does not move: 'He was never committed. He didn't give a damn'.[4] But there is little on that level of insight. For another thing, there would have to be less would-be memorable name-dropping – or at least, Mr Craft would have to renounce kicking them while he drops them. Here he is about one of our age's major minds: '[His][5] fists are milk-white, pudgy, hairless, but the fingers are stained with nicotine, and the nails are nibbled half-way to the moons'. And here on a likely genius: '[He is][6] a humourless,[7] limp, loose man, but with profound eyes'. If you want to know who these people are, you are as Sunday-paper-minded as Robert Craft seems to me:[8] buy yourself the book and you'll lap it all up.

The other two books are yet worse, but with humble respect to Vera Stravinsky I don't think that Lillian Libman's is the worst of them all. Miss Libman was Stravinsky's secretary, more and less. 'She was a very short time with us – about ten years', says Mrs Stravinsky. 'Her book is startlingly tactless and vulgar.' Craft, it is true, is startlingly tactful to Stravinsky and tactless about everybody else. Anyhow, after volumes of his and his master's taste, a little vulgarity doesn't come amiss, so long as the truth comes out that way: 'By the time Stravinsky stood up for the final run-through and the official take, the orchestra was thoroughly indoctrinated with Robert's tempo and his interpretation and would therefore have great difficulty adjusting. Add these circumstances to just time enough for a maximum of two takes and it is easy to understand the pointed questions raised in musical circles in the last five or six years about the authenticity of certain Stravinsky recordings made in the final decade,' especially as he 'did *not* listen to playbacks, at least not during any of the sessions I attended'. Then the final unintentional irony: 'He would never,

[4] In 'The Keller Column: Two and a Half Major Events', *Music and Musicians*, July 1985, p. 14, Keller offered what was probably his last published comment on Strauss:

> Strauss's early symphonic poems, as well as *Elektra*, *Salome* and *Metamorphosen*, are evidence of how great this composer could have become if he hadn't been such a convinced opportunist, intra- as well as extra-musically: his adjustment to the Nazis shows no difference from his adjustment to saleable styles; I always call him the only great composer who wasn't a great composer'.

Republished in Hans Keller, *Truth and Music: The Complete Writings from* Music and Musicians, ed. Mark Doran, Toccata Press, London, 2011.

[5] Editorial square brackets: the published text fails to make clear a change to the original.

[6] Editorial square brackets: again, the published text fails to make clear a change to the original.

[7] Keller or his editor has here anglicised the American spelling of the original.

[8] Editorial duty overrides fears of accusation of Sunday-paper-mindedness: Craft is describing, respectively, Auden and Messiaen (both on p. 71). In the 1963 *Dialogues and a Diary*, the first line had appeared as 'milk-white, pudgy, and hairless' (p. 112); in the 1966 *Themes and Episodes*, the second described 'a humorless man with a loose physique but profoundly preoccupied eyes' (p. 199). In Craft's 'revised and expanded' 1994 edition of *Stravinsky: Chronicle of a Friendship* (Vanderbilt University Press, Nashville), there are further differences: 'Auden's paws are pudgy, milk-white, hairless' (p. 182) and Messiaen is 'a limp, humorless man with profound eyes and no small talk' (p. 184).

when he knew of it (and once or twice he did not), permit the release under his name of a record containing none of his takes'.

After one has had to suffer, for years, Stravinsky's alleged opinion on every modern note under the clouded sky, it is mildly refreshing to hear that 'for the most part he did not listen to modern works at all, and there were very few with which he was thoroughly familiar'. If you ask me, he wasn't even familiar with the Beethoven works he thought he knew. But Miss Libman, however honourable her bad intentions, is not knowledgeable: in fact, in one or two places, her ignorance is quite shattering, as when she calls Schoenberg 'the German composer' (Schoenberg was slightly less German than Tommy Docherty is English[9]). Add to this that her approach and style are those of the other Sunday press, and you have to suspect the mask of the unmasker too.

But one of life's ultimate truths is that there's always something worse – especially when it's Paul Horgan's 'personal record', 52 pages of which elapse before he as much as meets his hero.[10] Within this introductory part, there is dramatic news: 'I need of that time only to mention Rouben Mamoulian, Vladimir Rosing, George Houston, Nicolas Slonimsky, Ernst Bacon, Otto Luening, Martha Graham, Anna Duncan, Guy Harrison, Lucile Johnson Bigelow and, most importantly for the final emphasis of this narrative, Eugene Goossens, to express what has never lost savour for me as a cherished debt to my elders and betters for taking me seriously on evidence which was not highly visible at the time, and for receiving the contributions of my energy and temperament as ardently as they were offered in the work of the newly-formed opera theatre in Rochester'. If you like that sort of single sentence, you're in for a treat, enlivened by exquisite neologisms: 'I thought he resembled Lenin, but this was heresy, for my "Russianism", like that of all my associates, under Rosing and Mamoulian, our Russian directors, was imperialist and white, not to say refugistic'.

The trouble is that the main amble isn't any better than the preamble. The last crumbs of Stravinsky's conceptual sagedom are duly picked up: 'The Japanese language is not a language – it is a habit'. If you try hard enough, you can make any great mind look an idiot, without trying. But it's nice to know that it was Mr Horgan, not Stravinsky, who was responsible for the inane title *Expositions and Developments*, Stravinsky never having written natural expositions and developments – a natural sonata form – in his life.

It's a long way back from all this sterile twaddle, about £16 worth of it, to the pregnant, sovereignly intelligent, crystal-clear music of a genius. I recommend a taxi: otherwise, you might be late.

[9] At the time Keller was writing, Tommy Docherty, born in Glasgow in 1928, was manager of the Scottish national football team.

[10] Keller's disdain may have been exacerbated by the standing Paul Horgan (1903–95) enjoyed as a writer: his first novel, *The Fault of Angels* (1933) won the Harper Prize, and two subsequent books – *Great River: The Rio Grande in North American History* (1954) and *Lamy of Santa Fe* (1975) – won Pulitzer Prizes for history.

XXIV
An Instrumental Problem in *Pulcinella*

Tempo, No. 105, June 1973, pp. 22–24

Stravinsky knew little about violin technique. It happens in the best circles. Schumann, on the evidence of his highly substantial string quartets, knew as much about string playing as I know about the cimbalom. Brahms and Tchaikovsky wrote great violin concertos against the violin. And Mahler's auditioning of violinists was a joke: 'He attached the greatest significance to the steadiest possible bowing in sustained notes', Carl Flesch[1] recounts,

> and therefore considered the beginning of the third act of *Siegfried* [Flesch means the beginning of Act III, Scene 3][2] a touchstone for the bowing technique of an orchestral violinist ... He first asked me to play a Mozart Adagio, and then set the *Siegfried* passage in front of me. As my bow glided over the strings with the phlegmatic calm of a world-weary philosopher, he seemed greatly pleased, wanted to nail me down to the post of leader at once, and accompanied me himself to the administration building ... .

Two dangers confront the composer unversed in any important instrumental respect. One is amateurism – which is the smaller danger. The real risk is professionalism – having his imagination curbed by wrong professional advice, be it lazily conventional or indeed concealedly amateurish itself: a string player's advice tends to spring from soloistic or chamber-musical feeling even where orchestral sound is concerned, and even when he is an experienced orchestral worker, because it is his individual playing that his sound-consciousness clings to in order not to lose identity – a psychologically realistic defence in all conscience.

I have, in these pages, specified one example of Stravinsky giving in to wrong professional advice – when, at a rehearsal and in my presence, he felt he had to withdraw a direction which, in technical reality, would have been

[1] *Memoirs*, [Rockliffe,] London, 1957, p. 87. –HK
Keller does not mention that he undertook the co-editing (with Carl F. Flesch, the violinist's son) and translation of Flesch's *Memoirs* himself. *Cf.* also Carl F. Flesch, *'And do you also play the violin?'*, Toccata Press, London, 1990, pp. 126–35.

[2] Keller's intercalation.

entirely justified.[3] I am convinced that there is another, far more important, and indeed dramatic example; more important because the wrong professional advice I am alleging has actually been perpetuated in the score, and because its effect is a major distortion and – in Stravinsky of all composers! – obscuration of the intended texture and rhythm.

I am referring to the passage indicated by my music example, i.e. the chief accompanimental figure in the 'Serenata' from *Pulcinella*, as it appears in the revised version of 1965. For years, I have been unhappy about this sound as it emerges in performance – *any* performance, including Stravinsky's own on CBS SBRG 72452 (if it is indeed Stravinsky's own). I well remember that when I first heard the work, not having seen the score, I was unable to hear what was happening, or to divine what was supposed to be happening: the texture was a mess and has remained one ever since, with the first few demisemiquavers just audible if you are lucky, and the rest merging into a vague supporting noise for the tenor's siciliana melody.

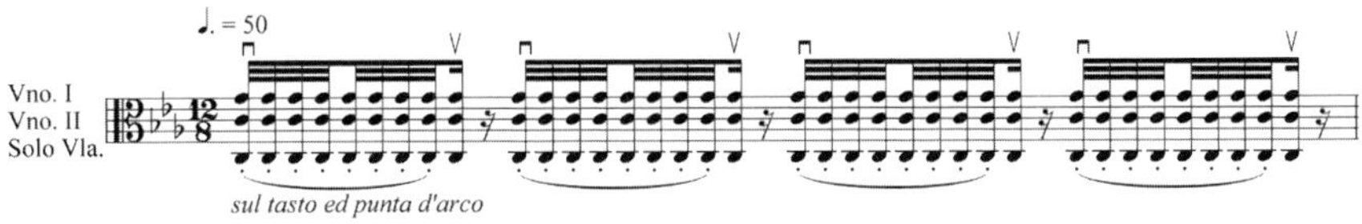

Perhaps because I was co-responsible for it, the European Broadcasting Union's recent performance of the work was, for me, the last straw: I decided I must try to do something about Stravinsky's miscalculation. The first question to ask is whether sharp rhythmic articulation or an indistinct noise – as, say, in the sextuplets at the beginning of Beethoven's Ninth – is intended; and there can, I submit, be only one answer: the total texture stands or falls with its rhythmic definition. The second question concerns the notated execution. Again, there can be no doubt. The downbow for the eight demisemiquavers followed by an upbow, the request to play near the point, and the staccato dots under the slur make only one bowing possible – a thrown virtuoso bowing known as *ricochet*[4] or as one variety of *saltato*,[5] and best remembered from such typical fiddler's pieces as the Paganini *Caprices*, or assorted encores by Wieniawski and other 'ki's. The point here is that even in the most auspicious soloistic circumstances, with a good fiddler on the one hand and a well-lying passage on the other, one does not easily get a great deal of precision from this kind of bowing: the magnanimous listener readily

[3] 'Strawinsky's Performance of 'Agon': a report', *Tempo* 100, Spring 1972. –HK
Cf. pp. 70–74, above, for this article as it first appeared in *Tempo*, No. 50, Winter 1958, pp. 22–25.

[4] See Ivan Galamian, *Principles of Violin Playing and Teaching*, [Prentice Hall, Englewood Cliffs,] New Jersey, 1962, pp. 81 ff. –HK

[5] See Carl Flesch, *The Art of Violin Playing*, [Carl Fischer,] New York, 1924, Vol. 1, p. 76. –HK

takes the approximate sound for the deed, since in such passages, the notes are guessable anyway, and can therefore be hallucinated by the listening ear. As a matter of fact, Carl Flesch, whom nobody can accuse of lack of pedantry, actually allows himself to record 'the slight degree of exactness demanded by this type of bowing'.

Now while it is true that in Stravinsky's accompaniment, at least the problem of co-ordination between left and right hand does not arise, since the left hand does not change notes, the idea that a string *chorus* could execute these thrown bowings with anything approaching rhythmic synchronization and clarity is so manifestly absurd that one is at a loss to explain the slavish adherence to Stravinsky's notation down the decades. It seems to me that a violinist's soloistic soul must have been responsible for Stravinsky's carefully notated bowing: the fiddler wanted to have, or wanted others to have, a bit of fun, and never mind what the total texture was going to sound like.

It might, of course, be suggested that if a more normal bowing is adopted, if the strings are asked to play down and up from note to note, the eight demisemiquavers might not easily and well-definedly be accommodated within Stravinsky's prescribed tempo either – but he himself has given the answer to that one: at the very beginning of the 'Serenata', where the cellos have to play fifths in natural harmonics which could not be made to sound at all if *ricochet* were employed, he notates the selfsame group with *staccato* dots but without a slur, merely directing the players to bow at the point – a task which has always been well accomplished in performance.

The solution? To adhere, throughout, to the mere staccato dots of the opening notation, which makes the required rhythmical sound-picture quite clear. And let us leave the decision how best to realize it to the conductor and the players: it is even conceivable that this quick rhythm could be achieved by slightly different bowings on the part of individual players, according to their own technical aptitudes and idiosyncracies, so that not everybody need automatically play at the point. Let us remember that Stokowski has, as a matter of ultra-realistic principle, abolished uniform bowings in his orchestras – and is there a more concretely sound-conscious conductor in the world?

For the rest, those of us who have to read plenty of less than masterly scores in their working lives have come to the slightly oversimplified conclusion that the less a composer knows about string technique, the more carefully will he notate the bowings in his string parts – to the point of disregarding the self-evident fact that what bows up must bow down, of meticulously marking successive up-and downbows as if there were any alternative; the naive intention, I suppose, is to prove one's instrumental expertise.[6] But in this

[6] Keller's views on the unnecessary and counter-productive nature of bowing marks are presented in detail in 'Composers of the World, De-bow!', *Tempo*, No. 137, June 1981, pp. 17–21.

illiterate age, when musicians can hardly be trusted with the ability to read music, great composers, too, have taken to over-notation – which, if they lack expertise in any particular instrumental field, is quite likely to result in the wrong notation for the very right sound they have in their minds – all the more so since, so far as the orchestra is concerned, there just is no such thing as expert advice, for the simple reason that there is no such artistic person as an orchestral player: it's a job, not a calling which develops more than the most elementary specific expertise. And a string section can't give collective expert advice because it can't hear itself in the total textural context anyway; it can't even hear its own exact sound as a whole.

XXV
Factual Orgy

A review of the second edition of Eric Walter White's *Stravinsky: The Composer and his Works* (Faber and Faber, London, 1979), published in *The Spectator* on 26 January 1980. White's book was also sold in a special limited edition to mark a Stravinsky festival given in London between autumn 1979 and summer 1981, mainly by the London Sinfonietta and London Symphony Orchestra.

There was a time when I objected to Eric Walter White, much as I liked him personally.[1] It was the time of *Benjamin Britten* (1948).[2] Maybe there was nothing wrong with it, but to my youthful mind, there wasn't enough right with it, and 'right' I meant almost judicially: what right did this musical amateur have to write about music? Without professional insight, what could he possibly offer?

A lot, I have meanwhile found out and in any case, the concept of 'professional insight' begs the question of how which truths are found and conveyed. In definable circumstances, amateur insight is irreplaceable, and the unconscious might still await discovery if Freud had been a professional psychologist or a professional philosopher: mind was 'professionally' identical with consciousness, and that was it. Nor is it only the lack of professional prejudice that sharpens the conscientious amateur's insight, but lack of professional boredom too: in the end, the whole-hearted amateur's amor of his subject can produce a more continual 'professionalism' than the all too normal professional is capable of. The outstanding amateur is a successful autodidact – and is there a better type of education for a good mind?

Such thoughts occurred to me, guiltily, as I read the first edition of *Stravinsky* 14 years ago: here was a book which, despite the circumstance that

[1] White (1905–85) read English at Oxford (1924–27) before working as a translator for the League of Nations in Geneva (1929–33) and for the National Council for Social Service in London (1935–42). He became assistant secretary to the Council for the Encouragement of Music and the Arts (which in 1946 became the Arts Council of Great Britain), retaining the post until 1971. Besides his work on Britten and Stravinsky, he wrote also on seventeenth- and eighteenth-century English opera.

[2] E. W. White, *Benjamin Britten: A Sketch of his Life and Works*, Boosey & Hawkes, London, 1948; revised 2nd edn., London, 1954; revised and enlarged (ed. John Evans) as *Benjamin Britten: His Life and Operas*, Faber & Faber, London, 1970; revised 2nd edn., 1983. Keller reviewed White's Britten book in the 'old series' of *Music Survey* (that is, before he became co-editor): Vol. 1, No. 6 (1949), p. 202. White was an occasional contributor to the Mitchell-Keller 'New Series' (1949–52).

too much had already been published about the composer, met a burning need for facts of deep musical relevance, which most of those other writings had neglected or ignored: all geniuses are unlike each other, but some are more unlike than others, and this one is so dramatically unlike that most writers think their own intellectual bafflement is more important than are the facts that have produced it – a professionally self-centred attitude of which our self-educated author is entirely free.

Not that White had, in his turn, neglected Stravinsky's unique uniqueness which, in fact, he was careful to pin-point, either in his own words or those of dependable analysts. Speaking (I hope) as one of them, I felt the guiltier about my past misgivings when I noticed that his two references to my writings about Stravinsky were the two I would have picked if he, or anybody else had asked me which of my diverse essays on Stravinsky's music I considered indispensable. In the first place, that is, he drew attention to my note-for-note analysis of Stravinsky's setting of Dylan Thomas's 'Do not go gentle into that good night',[3] and later he quoted the one sentence from my longest piece on Stravinsky which I should have recommended for continued attention: 'Stravinsky's absorption of Schoenberg's technique was arguably the profoundest surprise in the history of music'.[4]

I do think that the professional quotee's approval is a supreme test: if he agrees that his own contributions have been duly heeded and evaluated, what remains of his professional complaint? The amateur has had it both ways: meeting professional requirements, he has, at the same time, made his own contribution – of which the professional might not altogether have been capable. If anybody could improve on White's monumental study, 'marvellously authoritative' (as *The Times* called it at the time), it was the author himself, the breadth of whose insight was without parallel.

And this is precisely what has now happened: with a new chapter added to Part 1, 'The Man', the second edition, 48 pages longer than the first, not only covers the remaining years of Stravinsky's life in meticulous biographical and musical detail, but contains both countless amendments and indeed additional facts: 'During recent years, fresh information about Stravinsky's early life and adolescent compositions has come to light in the USSR, and this has been incorporated in the new edition'.[5]

Much else has happened, 'during recent years', to the thought and thoughtlessness surrounding Stravinsky's life and work: among the 20th-century

[3] Published in Keller's '*In Memoriam Dylan Thomas*: Strawinsky's Schoenbergian Technique', *loc. cit.* It was this article that was taken up, with a version of 'Towards the Psychology of Stravinsky's Genius' (*cf.* the Editorial Introduction, p. 21, above), in 'Stravinsky Heard' in *Stravinsky Seen and Heard* and can be found again on pp. 133–41, below.

[4] From *Stravinsky at Rehearsal*, *op. cit.*, p. 3; *cf.* p. 21, above, and p. 128, below.

[5] White, *op. cit.*, p. 16. –HK

classics, Stravinsky alone is popular, almost, and the publishing world has continued to make the most of him. Above all, at least in price and size, there was Vera Stravinsky's and Robert Craft's *Stravinsky in Pictures and Documents* (£16, no misprint), which White duly takes into account, though it and his own second edition were published in the same year (1979) – a typical example, this, of his factual alertness, comprehensiveness, and reliability. He simply doesn't miss anything, except what, upon due scholarly and musical consideration, he wants to miss. But if you told me that you had £16 to spare and wanted to enrich your Stravinsky library, I should unhesitatingly advise you to buy the White and save £2.50 for a score: it is one of those rare monographies that will answer – or guide, stimulate, provoke your own answer to – any question about its subject that may have arisen in your mind.

As before, the work falls into three main parts – on the man, his music, and his composing personality – whose virtue is, at the same time, their single drawback: this extensive and intensive amassing of carefully selected facts (including other people's opinions, as distinct from the author's own) does not leave much spatial or psychological room for thought. Insistently, White seems to tell himself: 'Report, don't reflect!' Perhaps it's the ex-amateur's out-dated modesty. Thus, rather tantalizingly, he never tells us in Part III what, after his exhaustive studies, he himself thinks about that profoundest surprise in the history of music, Stravinsky's absorption of serial technique: was it inspired by Webern? By Schoenberg? A bit of both?

> By his own admission, it was the music of Webern (who died in 1945) that triggered off his interest in the 'Method' and provided the 'Open Sesame' to the magic serial cave: but it is significant that this important move occurred only after the death in 1951 of Schoenberg, the pioneer and founder of the 'Method'.[6]

Indeed. But what precisely is the significance? I myself had tried to explain it all psychoanalytically, as an introjection of the dead love-hate object: musically, there was no doubt in my mind at the time of 'In Memoriam Dylan Thomas' that Stravinsky's budding serial technique was Schoenbergian, in that his tone rows *derived* from melodic inventions, rather than Webernian, i.e. based on a priori rows.

I in my turn can now, post mortem, report the composer's own reaction to my identification of his technique. In my analysis of the Dylan Thomas song (which White enthusiastically approves); I had drawn concrete attention to the Schoenbergian nature of Stravinsky's technique. As the piece reached the proof stage, the publisher of the journal in question[7] got a bit nervous: he was

[6] *Ibid.*, p. 480.

[7] The 'journal in question' was *Tempo* (*cf.* note 23 on p. 22, above), which from its foundation in 1939 until 2002 was published by Boosey & Hawkes. The 'publisher' Keller refers to was probably Ernst Roth

Stravinsky's publisher too, and Stravinsky's severely mixed feelings about Schoenberg were common knowledge, whereas the master himself had drawn public attention to his debt to Webern. Would I mind if the galleys were submitted to Stravinsky?

Of course not, I said; the analyst had no right to keep anything from his victim. In the event, however, even I found Stravinsky's response rather surprising. In red pencil, he had written across the last galley: 'Mr Keller is absolutely right'. And thenceforth, he held my writings in great esteem, as I discovered at a subsequent meeting.[8] Not forever, though. Years later, I said somewhere that Benjamin Britten was the greatest composer alive,[9] whereupon I gathered that my name was no longer to be mentioned in the Stravinsky household. In any case, the strength of Schoenberg's influence should not make us underrate Webern's subsequent contribution: it's not a bit of both, but a lot – as one would expect from this widely and deeply absorbent creative character.

Part III only brings us up to p. 569; five documentary and bibliographical appendices (the first comprising 'Various Writings by Stravinsky Reprinted') complete the richest and most riveting accumulation of relevant facts I personally can remember in any field. Even the Index is exceptional: I can't find any mistakes, and therefore suspect that the author himself has checked – or even compiled it? But no: he wouldn't have excluded Appendix E – the bibliography from its coverage. Otherwise, I've only been able to discover a single flaw: 'Few composers (except possibly Webern) have wasted less time than Stravinsky'. You know what he means, of course, because you're only too ready to accept illogicality. Translated into logical language, however, the sentence would read: 'Few composers (Webern possibly among them) have wasted less time than Stravinsky'. It's true, anyway.

(1896–1971), who was Music Publications and Production Director at Boosey & Hawkes from 1945 until his retirement in 1964; *cf.* Helen Wallace, *Boosey & Hawkes: The Publishing Story*, Boosey & Hawkes, London, 2007, and George Newman, 'Ernst Roth: A Personal Recollection' *Tempo*, No. 165, June 1988, pp. 37–40. Presumably the editor of *Tempo*, at that time Anthony Gishford, showed the article to Ernst Roth, who instructed him to let Stravinsky see the text.

[8] Keller's only direct encounter with Stravinsky took place 'at a BBC party', as Milein Cosman recalls (conversation with the editor, 8 November 2010). Stravinsky's presence in London for BBC concerts is detailed in note 2 on p. 174, below. *Cf.* also p. 167, below.

[9] In 'How Great is Britten? or Why I am Right', *Music and Musicians*, November 1963, pp. 12–13 (republished in Hans Keller, *Truth and Music*, *op. cit.*)

XXVI
Stravinsky Heard

The four essays which follow formed the first part, 'Stravinsky Heard', of Hans Keller's and Milein Cosman's *Stravinsky Seen and Heard* (1982), which was itself an expansion of the essay that introduced their *Stravinsky at Rehearsal.*[1] The first of them of them incorporates Keller's '*In Memoriam Dylan Thomas*: Strawinsky's Schoenbergian Technique', published in *Tempo* (No. 35, 1955, pp. 13–20).[2]

I. STRAVINSKY'S CHANGE OF MIND

Across the divisions of style, beyond the wars of musical 'schools', the rival symptoms and rival claims of creative inferiority feelings (unconfessed or at least semi-conscious); across all artificial curtains that separate the seeming irreconcilables of our disunited musical world, there cuts one straight division, the most recent and the most real of them all: the iron curtain between physical and phoney creativity. Not that the physical is the 'A' and 0' of music; but it certainly is the 'A'.

The division was unimaginable so long as there were only musical composers. But once the crumbling of tonality had removed that common background, intuitively comprehensible in terms of sound alone, against which everybody composed, once backgrounds began to vary from composer to composer, making comprehension proportionately more difficult, the road was open to a confusion between the as yet uncomprehended and the necessarily incomprehensible – necessarily, inasmuch as it does not make sense as sound.

Today, we are quite often confronted with unmusical composers producing non-sounding sense; that they cheat their audiences is only incidental to their cheating themselves about their senseless sounds, which they themselves only 'understand' because they know the soundless sense behind, or rather beside the music. It gives birth to a great deal of notation which can't be heard, while sounding sense inevitably contains much that can't be notated. If the composers of downright unmusic are, of course, on the wrong

[1] *Cf.* the Editorial Introduction on p. 21, above.

[2] *Cf.* also 'A Serial Masterpiece' pp. 42–44, above.

side of the iron curtain, there are others whose very heart it tears asunder, with one half on the right side, the other under the dictatorship of soundless intellectualism, musically atrophied. They present the newest and greatest problem of musical culture, for some of our intensest talents are among them. There are only a handful whose heart is altogether pure, unharmed, untouched by the iron curtain which, with inexorable regularity, is drawn up for a fleeting moment and then crashes down again, hitting all but these very few.

Which few? For the duration of our musical crisis, a new, empirical criterion for the existence of genius seems to be emerging. It was only the geniuses amongst the composers writing in a twentieth-century idiom who retained their musicality uncorrupted, making sense of sound and of nothing else. They all belong to the recent past, where they may have made curious bedfellows – Schoenberg, Stravinsky, Britten, Skalkottas,[3] Shostakovich[4] – but even though they may not have known it, their hearts were united in sounding logic, and the sense behind their music (if you can so separate a sense that can only be musically expressed) is spiritual rather than intellectual – a message, revelation, or both, according to the character of the composer.

As time progresses, strange bedfellows get used to each other, not just through habit, but by discovering the affinities which made them bedfellows in the first place – or, if they do not live to see their unity, posterity sees it for them. One of my five geniuses, the father of our musical age, did not live to see the influence he was to exert on what he would have regarded as the most unlikely recipients of his thoughts – Britten and Stravinsky. His influence on Britten is relatively superficial, more psychological than musical, but in Stravinsky, Schoenberg's twelve-tone method eventually produced one of those profound changes of creative mind of which no other great creator, with the possible exception of Picasso, has ever been capable.

[3] As a broadcaster Keller worked for many years to increase awareness of this Greek-born Schoenberg pupil (1904–49); *cf.*, for example, 'Nikos Skalkottas: an Original Genius', *The Listener*, Vol. 52, No. 1345, 9 December 1954, p. 1041, and 'Skalkottas' Violin Concerto', *Radio Times*, Vol. 161, No. 2088, 14 November 1963, p. 6.

Keller's understanding of Skalkottas' music was perhaps as deep as that of anyone else alive at the time. George Hadjinikos, the soloist in the first performance of Skalkottas' Second Piano Concerto, conducted by Hermann Scherchen in Hamburg in October 1953, told Mark Doran that Keller, although he had never seen a score of the work, realised that Scherchen had made a cut in the first movement (Mark Doran, *The Theory and Practice of 'Functional Analysis': A Presentation and Discussion of Hans Keller's 'Theory of Music'*, M.Mus. thesis, University of Liverpool, 1993, p. 7). When Toccata Press was founded in 1981, one of the books Keller said he wanted to write for it was a study of Skalkottas.

[4] Keller briefly discussed Shostakovich's 'creative psychology' in *1975 (1984 minus 9)*, *op. cit.*, pp. 177–82; the indebtedness of the Twelfth String Quartet to Schoenberg's music, in terms both of the form and of twelve-tone technique, is explored in 'Shostakovich Discovers Schoenberg' (*The Listener*, Vol. 84, No. 2168, 8 October 1970, p. 494), and 'Shostakovich's Twelfth Quartet' (*Tempo*, No. 94, Autumn 1970, pp. 6–15).

When Theodor Adorno,[5] our age's musical philosopher-in-chief, wrote his *Philosophy of New Music* in 1949, he was still able to play off Schoenberg against Stravinsky, whose music he regarded as a death-mask of the past (my metaphor); in fact, the whole book develops in the field of tension created by the polarity Adorno postulated between Schoenberg and Stravinsky. Admittedly, at that stage, as indeed for decades before, the two composers represented the fundamental stylistic division of our age, and when I said at the time[6] that they had something more basic in common than many Stravinskyians on the one hand and Schoenbergians on the other (to wit, music), my argument seemed tenuous: there were not many who shared my admiration for either composer. But then, in the twenties, more than two decades before I came in, a seemingly elemental historical clash had occurred: while Stravinsky, via neo-classicism, was diving into the past, Schoenberg, via the tone-row, was jumping into the future. So violent a contrast was too much for the composers themselves to bear: they theorized against each other, and though in later years they calmed down and re-realized that music was music, their ambivalent attitudes towards each other never quite left them.

How then, in the circumstances, was it possible for Stravinsky to turn serial in the fifties and sixties, at first cautiously and indeed tonally, later downright twelve-tonally and even atonally, making nonsense of Adorno's nowise senseless basic thesis? Even for an admirer of both composers, Stravinsky's absorption of Schoenberg's technique was arguably the profoundest surprise in the history of music.

With the help of psychological insight on the one hand and musical insight on the other, it should be possible to explain the late development of this most puzzling of all great composers – most puzzling because truly unprecedented.

All good composers start out from the past; they normally come to create against its background. Most bad composers remain stuck in it and are therefore compelled to use it as a foreground: to copy it. Stravinsky was the first great composer who had it both ways: he kept his past, or rather his pasts, in the glaring foreground, yet composed against them, or, if you like, through them. Anybody can twist a diatonic harmony, but only Stravinsky can re-characterize it by the addition of a wrong note or two.

Apropos of his treatment of Pergolesi's melodies[7] in the ballet *Pulcinella* (1919–20), at that cataclysmic moment when he confronted Schoenberg

[5] *Cf.* note 3 on p. 35, above.

[6] In his review of *Philosophie der neuen Musik*, *Tempo*, No. 16, Summer 1950; *cf.* note 3 on p. 36, above.

[7] Keller's persistence in referring to this music simply as 'Pergolesi's' (as Stravinsky, of course, had believed it to be) had earned him the censure of Jack A. Westrup (1904–75) in one of his two hostile reviews of the essay printed in *Stravinsky at Rehearsal* (1962); *cf. Music & Letters*, Vol. 43, No. 3, July 1962, p. 280. To find Keller still ignoring the various re-attributions in 1982 may seem surprising, but as late as 1979 Eric Walter White had left unrevised his tentative footnote that 'It is possible that not all the music used is by Pergolesi' (*Stravinsky: The Composer and His Works, op. cit.*, p. 284).

across a wider and steeper precipice than any faced by any two artists at any time, Stravinsky asked: 'Should my line of action be dominated by my love or by my respect for Pergolesi's music? Is it love or respect that urges us to possess a woman? Is it not by love alone that we succeed in penetrating to the very essence of a being? But then, does love diminish respect? Respect alone remains barren and can never serve as a productive or creative factor. In order to create, there must be a creative force, and what force is more potent than love?' He felt his 'conscience to be innocent of sacrilege'; indeed, he considered that his attitude towards Pergolesi was 'the only possible one towards the music of earlier ages'. For 'love' read 'hate' without excluding love: we shall see at once precisely why.

We recall Stravinsky's suggestion that 'rape may be justified by the creation of a child'. Paul Valéry changed the metaphor: 'A lion consists of digested lambs'.[8] Now, psychoanalysis recognizes two basic types of love, self-love apart. Genetically the more primitive is identification, which stems from the earliest, sucking stage of infancy and whose prototype is oral incorporation – hence the technical term 'introjection' for the 'absorption of the environment into the personality' (Ernest Jones[9]); hence, too, Valéry's metaphor. The other type, 'object-love', is what we commonly understand by love. In monosyllables, identification is based on the need to *be* someone, object-love on the need to *have* someone. Identification, more primitive, is the more ambivalent of the two, the more aggressive: for one thing you destroy what you eat, for another you want to replace the person you want to be.

Ordinary artistic development always starts with identification: while the composer's own creative ego is still weak, he identifies himself with his teachers and with older masters, and proceeds to imitate them. This is the stage where the past, his future background, is still in the foreground of his creative thought. As his originality grows with the maturation of his creative personality, those father figures are absorbed by his artistic conscience and recede into the background. Once maturity is reached, and if no creative trauma lies in wait for him (such as the encounter with Bach which Mozart had to face as a mature genius), his creative 'love relations' with other composers amount to no more than sporadic flirtations resulting in, say, variations on another composer's theme: these are the children of 'object-love' rather than of identification.

Alone amongst geniuses, again with the possible exception of Picasso, Stravinsky actually developed his capacity for identification together with the unfolding of his intense originality. At the same time, as his commentary on *Pulcinella* indicates, his creative mind also employed a good deal of highly

[8] *Cf.* notes 4 and 5 on p. 46, above.

[9] *Cf.* note 6 on p. 46, above.

aggressive 'object-love' ('rape may be justified by the creation of a child'): he made the aggressive best of both love worlds, though identification remained the basic 'creative force'. No previous composer has shown any desire to compose his way 'into the very essence of a being'.

> And all men kill the thing they love,
> By all let this be heard,
> Some do it with a bitter look,
> Some with a flattering word,
> The coward does it with a kiss,
> The brave man with a sword![10]

There is some special pleading here, but there is a truth too. Stravinsky did in fact himself employ the bitter look, the flattering word, and the sword, but he never killed the past by kissing it, as so many of his followers and all pure neo-classicists did.

Consider such a spotless and gigantic masterpiece as the *Symphony of Psalms* (1930), where identifications with the past span a wide field, stretching back into the archaic: when the opening four-part fugue of the second movement (with the answer in the dominant) raises its voice through what we might call the life-mask of Bach, we realize that the term 'neo-classicism' is no longer good enough – and in Chapter II we shall, at the bottom of it all, unearth the fugue subject's surprising, profound modernism.[11]

Psychologically, the chief fascination of the *Symphony of Psalms* is the nature of its incisive expressiveness. That is to say, the work is expressive through the very suppression of expressionism, through that in-turned, self-castigating aggression which prompted Adorno and myself, independently, to describe it as sado-masochistic. I have been heavily criticized for this characterization; my simple reply is that it is not a devaluation. What it does signify is the complexity of Stravinsky's creative aggression, which manifests itself in his aggressive love and aggressive self-love. Stravinsky's genius utilized its sadomasochism, i.e. both its aggression turned inwards and its enjoyment of such self-attack, towards his unique, tense, meaning-laden suppressionism. His anti-expressionism did not, however, as Adomo thought, result in emptiness, but in fullness fully opposed, in a state of statically intense tension, of dynamic staticism.

The outstanding common trait of Stravinsky's successive styles is indeed their self-restrictive tendency. In point of fact, his urge towards formal stringency and simplicity might well be considered to go beyond the requirements of unity and clarity: he did not discipline his inspiration; rather, he was

[10] *Cf.* note 7 on p. 47, above.

[11] *Cf.* pp. 149–51, below.

more lavishly inspired by self-discipline than any other composer before or even after him, when creators, robbed of universally valid disciplines and afraid of their undesired freedom, have tended to be obsessed with self-disciplinary measures as a matter of pathological course. The source of Stravinsky's self-restrictiveness was not only his in-turned aggression, but also his need for creative identification: identifications with other styles automatically impose severe limitations upon the imagination.

It is in the light of this psychological background, then, that Stravinsky's amazing change of mind towards serialism has to be examined. Now, the simplest, and perhaps the most important fact about his gradual conversion is its chronology: it all happened after Schoenberg's death – we might almost say, by way of creative mourning. Ever since 1916, when Freud published his *Mourning and Melancholia,* we have come to understand that what he called the 'identification of the ego with the lost object'[12] is at the root of all mourning: in concentrated fashion, that very process of 'introjection' takes place which, as we have seen, forms part and parcel of Stravinsky's creative character anyhow.

Grief-inspired incorporations, once our attention is drawn to them, are readily observable by the naked eye. They are especially impressive where the mourned person was a creative or public figure with well-defined, widely familiar character traits: we can all think of more than one widow who was inwardly compelled to burden her psyche with her great or famous husband's peculiarities, however eccentric, and to act out what she understood to be his role; right at the centre of the present essay's world, Mrs Schoenberg was a textbook example. Even on a social scale, the phenomenon makes itself easily felt when a personality dies whose work is hotly contested: public reactions veer in his favour, he is accepted as 'one of us', and unfavourable critics 'introject' him to the extent of turning into advocates. In fact, in the case of Schoenberg himself, while we who had always pleaded for his music prided ourselves on the eventual success of our endeavours, there is little doubt that when it came to it, psychology achieved what we hadn't. A comparison between some of our leading critics' writings before and after his death makes downright grotesque reading: an imaginary public was chided for the critic's own past attitudes.

Stravinsky's character having been predestined to identifications with, incorporations of the past, it is not, perhaps, quite so mysterious any longer that he naturally availed himself of the mourning mechanisms as soon as Schoenberg had become a thing of the past. At the same time, we must, I think, beware of facile explanations: the psychological situation is not as simple as all that. For one thing, why should Stravinsky mourn Schoenberg

[12] *Cf.* note 8 on p. 48, above.

anyway? A condition of mourning is a fairly high minimum of love, the aggressive side of the picture being usually hidden from superficial inspection. With Stravinsky, on the other hand, we need not seek for the aggression; it is the love aspect of which we cannot find much trace. There is no positive evidence that deep love was lost between the two composers; when they landed in Hollywood, they did not venture near each other. In a sense, they must have disliked each other more generously than some music critics disliked both of them, for they were, after all, composers of diametrically opposite orientation, with a corresponding creative intensity behind their mutual dislike. Assuming, however, that there was more mutual love or respect than met the eye (and there is some evidence of suppressed admiration), the proportionate guilt reaction on Schoenberg's death would help Stravinsky towards that state of creative mourning. But it wouldn't be enough. Our psychological budget is still unbalanced; our explanation remains artificial so long as we do not find further items on the credit side of Stravinsky's most revolutionary identification, be they purely psychological, musical, or both.

Facts are better than theories, and nothing is more foolish than not to be wise after the event. Let us look at the precise nature and circumstances of Stravinsky's introjection of Schoenberg's method, as well as at his own attitude towards his change of direction, in order to discover more concretely how it came about. The first thing that strikes us, however, is a further element of confusion, a further inconsistency. Whereas, especially in their early stages, Stravinsky's serial ventures were stressedly Schoenbergian in technical approach, his public utterances almost throughout exalted Webern at the expense of Schoenberg, the implication being that he actually 'had it' from Webern, the real father of the future – a status still accorded to this great minor master by a substantial section of *avant-gardist* opinion which, in reality, is so rigidly old-fashioned that it hasn't changed at all in the course of more than a quarter-century. To my mind, this contradiction reached its manifest climax on a private occasion. In the early stages of Stravinsky's serial technique, when the news had reached the musical world that he admired Webern enormously, I wrote an article for *Tempo* (No. 35, 1955), entitled '*In Memoriam Dylan Thomas:* Stravinsky's Schoenbergian Technique', and containing a complete analysis of his Dylan Thomas dirge. Explicitly and implicitly, I showed that the strictly serial piece, though based on a five-note row, applied Schoenberg's own serial concept very conscientiously.

Now, the reader whose analytic interest in music is limited and who is not specifically preoccupied with the workings of serial technique need not really be bothered with the concrete details of that article, whereas the musicianly reader would not easily forgive me if I kept them from him – especially in view of Stravinsky's subsequent reaction to them. We can easily have it both ways: the next 10 paragraphs, together with the ensuing 5 pages of music type, need not be read; they reproduce my article and analysis in full.[13]

* * * * *

Music examples usually illustrate verbal texts, but the present article is no more than an illustration appended to my analytic music example of the complete central song from Stravinsky's *In Memoriam Dylan Thomas* (Spring, 1954). I think that writers on music should be encouraged to keep to the music, and seriously contend that all the adverse critics of Schoenberg's serial technique, and most of the writers who pass for serial experts, are incapable of a serial analysis and have only the very vaguest notion of what makes a serial piece tick. They quote a bar or two – usually from the opening of Schoenberg's Fourth Quartet — where the note-row is fairly obvious or, anyway, has previously been uncovered by someone else, and then proceed to let obscure theory take the place of clear if complex practice. The reason is simple: they don't hear the row, and if you are unable to imagine a row aurally, it is very difficult, usually indeed impossible, to trace it throughout a piece.[14] Let me hasten to add that I should not dream of reproaching any critic with his tone-row-deafness if he left it at that: for all we know, he may otherwise be a musical genius. If, however, he professes to talk serial 'shop' at the same time, I raise the strongest moral objections.

The result of all this pseudo-articulate obscurantism has been catastrophic, in that the legend has developed that serial technique is something visual, something which could but need not be worked out on paper. Performers do not dream of acquainting themselves with a note-row of a serial piece, and even if they dreamt of it they would rarely be able to do something about it, because there is nobody to tell them that the music is written in serial technique, as for instance in the work under review. A state of performing affairs ensues which is as satisfactory as diatonic conditions would be if executants were unable to imagine the tonic of a piece they were performing.

In these circumstances, only the most supreme artists instinctively surmount their innocent ignorance. At Donaueschingen in 1954, for example, Peter Pears gave a masterly and indeed overwhelming performance of the Dylan Thomas song. When, after the concert, I remarked that the work was written in the strictest serial technique, he seemed amazed; in fact, in his mind serial methods seemed to be bound up with absolute atonality. Why did I enlighten him? Even Peter Pears could profit. He had sung the first note a semitone flat. He could not have done so if he had known the row.

[13] Minor changes (for example, 'in 1954' for 'last autumn') are not indicated here.

[14] Time has proved Keller wrong here: the 'row table', a 12x12 matrix, now allows every music-student to produce 'serial analyses' with relative ease.

Apart from such important practical and specific purposes, the present analysis is intended to give a concrete idea of the nature of serial technique itself. Stravinsky's canonic masterpiece is more suitable for this purpose than any work of Schoenberg's, because it applies the method far more strictly and, at the same time, more simply, primitively (no evaluation, this!) than Schoenberg's music ever did; besides, the application is only melodic, not harmonic, which makes things simpler for a start, since the harmonic aspect of serial technique is its most problematic. In most other respects, Stravinsky out-Schoenbergs Schoenberg, even though his is a five-note row which functions in a vaguely tonal fashion. The tonality of the piece would not, however, be enough to hold it together; in fact, some of Schoenberg's twelve-note music is more tonal than this piece. Nevertheless, since he does not, in principle, care about atonality, Stravinsky disregards one single serial directive, namely what Schoenberg calls 'avoidance of doubling in octaves'. I have marked octave doublings (a) in the refrain 'Rage, rage against the dying of the light', as well as at *Fig. 1*, in order to account serially for certain notes which do not, in one and the same part, form a complete row; and (b) in the last appearance of the opening ritornello (round *Fig. 10*) which, joined by the voice for the first time, shows dodecaphony's typical octave transpositions in the cello part.[15] Throughout the song, Stravinsky freely avails himself of this variational device of Schoenberg's technique.

'BS' means Basic Set, 'R' Retrograde Version, 'I' Inversion, and 'RI' Retrograde Inversion. As with Schoenberg, different characters are derived from the basic set: its initial rhythm remains functional, but is not the lasting property of the series itself, which therefore is a real, subthematic, pre-rhythmic *row,* not a *theme:* a glance at *Fig. 3*, for instance, shows how rhythmic and motivic entities cut across the set and its mirror forms. Significantly enough, Stravinsky adopts Schoenberg's atonical practice of not repeating any notes of the row until all the notes are 'over', unless they are immediately or ornamentally repeated.[16] Other more individual traits of Stravinsky's serial technique, such as varying overlappings and intervals between successive series produced by various transpositions of the row, will be evident from a study of my analysis. Maximal overlapping can be observed in the tenor part in the first, third (*Fig.* 7) and last 'Do not go gentle into that good night': transposedly speaking, the last three notes of the inversion are identical with the first three of the retrograde version, and the last three of the basic set with the first three of the retrograde inversion.

[15] Keller had discussed 'Serial Octave Transpositions' in the *Monthly Musical Record* in July-August and September-October 1956, on pp. 139–43 and pp. 172–77 respectively.

[16] As indeed he had done in the *Symphony of Psalms:* the purpose, then, is not exclusively atonical, but includes a sharper definition of the row *qua* row. –HK

The second 'Do not go gentle ...' (before *Fig.* 4), on the other hand, shows the opposite of overlapping — stretching, if you like. The tenor's C flat on '-ning' is sustained across the parts (C flat in the 'cello followed by B in the viola) while the words 'they Do' double two notes from the 'cello's series (retrograde inversion and retrograde version), one of them in anticipation; after this parenthesis the tenor resumes the C flat that has been kept alive for him by the lower instruments. In other words, the 'cello's C flat quotes from the tenor, whereupon the tenor's A and A flat quote from the 'cello. At the same time, the tenor's 'they Do not' is the middle part of a retrograde row whose first and last notes are the 'cello's B flat on '-ning' (preceding bar) and the viola's C on 'not' respectively. Serially, this is the most complicated passage. The only other irregularity, after *Fig.* 6, is much simpler: taking up the tenor's C, the 'cello's supernumerary C and the ensuing serial oscillation are made possible and, in fact, partially motivated by the canon between the tenor and the first violin, wherein two successive transpositions of the inversion yield three descending semitones followed by an ascending semitone, with the third semitone belonging to a new rhythmic articulation: the 'cello's oscillating motifs are likewise based on three descending semitones, two of them forming a rhythmic unit and sequential model. In the further course of this retrograde version, Stravinsky once more employs the one dodecaphonic device from which he refrains elsewhere in the work – the distribution of the row's notes between the parts: see the D flat in the first violin two bars before *Fig.* 7. The note is obviously over-determined,[17] for at the same time it is part of a linear inversion. There is nothing exceptional in this: all the notes in the horizontal overlappings between the four variants of the row, are, of course, over-determined.

A day or two before writing this note, I talked to one of our leading composers who had examined the present work. He proved utterly unaware of its technique. I thereupon decided to keep my observations as elementary as possible, at the risk of disappointing serial experts. My analysis, however, should make it easy for them to study the many finer points of Stravinsky's application of the serial method.

As for my analytic brackets themselves, where two series overlap by way of repeated closing and opening notes respectively, I have, on the whole, indi-

[17] *Cf.* also note 1 on p. 49. In applying the term to notes that are attributable to more than one row-form, Keller imports a psychoanalytic coinage into serial analysis. In Freudian theory, dreams and symptoms 'regularly have more than one meaning'; thus it may be that 'two interpretations are not mutually contradictory, but both cover the same ground' (*cf.* Freud, 'The Interpretation of Dreams', *The Standard Edition of the Complete Psychological Works of Sigmund Freud*, Vols. IV and V (trans. James Strachey), Hogarth Press and the Institute of Psycho-Analysis, London; corrected reprint, 1958, p. 149). Keller had logical objections to the term in its psychoanalytic usage, explaining his reservations in *1975 (1984 minus 9)* (*op. cit.*, p. 226):

> It is a highly descriptive term, but cannot be accepted as reasonable, in any way tenable: things are either determined or they aren't; they can't be over-determined. If you remove a cause and the event still happens the same way, it isn't a cause – though, in other circumstances, it could be.

cated the widest extent of overlapping. In one or two instances, however, I have departed from this practice for extraneous reasons, e.g., spatial convenience. These divergencies are quite unimportant and of no musical significance.

The song here analysed is a setting of the poem which Dylan Thomas wrote in memory of his father,[18] and forms the middle section of a ternary build whose outer sections consist of purely instrumental 'dirge-canons' that alternate between four trombones and string quartet. In Schoenbergian fashion, the entire work is based on a single row. In the outer sections, however, the row is rhythmically committed, overtly thematic. In consequence, the Pre- and Postlude analyse themselves as it were, yet Stravinsky marks the 'Theme', 'Inversion' and so on throughout the Prelude. In the song itself, on the other hand, i.e., at the very moment when the old contrapuntal technique crystallizes into the new serial method, where the theme becomes a row and will not therefore be heard or seen as a matter of course, Stravinsky's brackets cease. Why, in that case, he has bothered to analyse the first section is incomprehensible.[19] At the same time, it is somewhat depressing to find that the five successive notes of the opening theme seem to remain unrecognized as soon as they go underground. There is a limit to unconscious understanding.

After so much objective criticism, I may be allowed to add that I consider this new work Stravinsky's greatest and most perfect since the *Mass:* it is more coherent than the Septet and establishes stronger contrasts than the preceding Cantata.

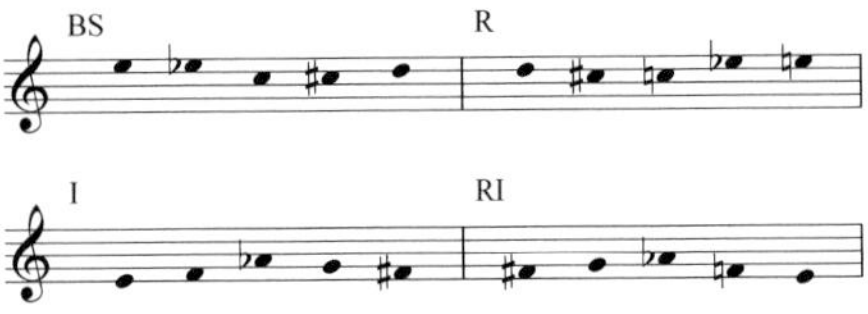

[18] *Cf.* note 2 on p. 42, above.

[19] Stravinsky subsequently explained: 'In correcting the proofs I forgot to erase in the prelude these brackets left over from my final sketches, where they were put *throughout* the work, this complicating the reading of the instrumental and vocal score'. –HK

SONG
Do not go gentle*

*The text is taken from *The Collected Poems of Dylan Thomas*, Dent, London, 1952.

2
Ten.
Vln. I
Vln. II
Vla.
Vc.
- ing of the light…
Though wise men
at their end know dark is right,
Be - cause their words had forked no light - ning
they Do not go gen - tle in - to that good night.
Good men,
dolce
R
RI
BS
I
R: 1

Ten.
Vln. I
Vln. II
Vla.
Vc.
the last wave by, cry - ing how bright Their frail deeds might have
danced in a green bay, Rage, rage a - gainst the dy - - ing of the light
Wild men who caught and sang the sun in flight, And
pizz.
arco
meno f
dolce
sempre poco marc.
RI
R
BS
I

4
Ten.
Vln. I
Vln. II
Vla.
Vc.
learn, too late, they grieved it on its way,
Do not go gen - tle in - to
that good night.
Grave men, near death, who see with blind-ing sight Blind
eyes could blaze like me - te - ors and be gay,
Rage, rage a - gainst the dy -
BS
I
R
RI
7
8
9
arco
pizz.
dolce
meno f

Ten.
Vln. I
Vln. II
Vla.
Vc.
ing of the light
And you, my fa - ther, there on the sad height,
Curse, bless, me now with
your fierce tears, I pray.
Do not go gen - tle in - to that good night.
Rage,
rage a - gainst the dy - ing of the night...
un po
dolce
marc.
pizz.
arco
meno f
p cant.
attacca subito
10
11
R
I
RI
BS

Now, for reasons which need not concern us here but of which I approved, the then editor of *Tempo*[20] sent a proof of the article to the composer before it was published. It came back with stressedly appreciative, wholly confirmatory marginal comments, and without a word of criticism. At the same time, on more public occasions, Stravinsky made his indebtedness to Webern ever clearer – and his ambivalence towards Schoenberg too. There are passages in Robert Craft's *Conversations with Igor Stravinsky*[21] which make one seriously wonder whether the composer really had a proper look at all the Schoenberg works he criticizes (he certainly cannot have heard them all), though in order to keep his ambivalence as tidy as possible in his difficult psychological circumstances, he reserves his most whole-hearted and general condemnation for Schoenberg's literary output: 'Schoenberg's work has too many inequalities for us to embrace it as a whole. For example, nearly all of his texts are appallingly bad, some of them so bad as to discourage performance of the music'.[22] As a matter of fact, German-speaking countries acknowledged Schoenberg's great literary gifts decades before they recognized his musical genius; while nowadays, his texts are even appreciated by foreigners, by critics within Stravinsky's own cultural orbit:

> What is so striking [about *Moses and Aron*] is the enormous significance of the libretto and its unusual form. This text is concentrated to an extreme degree. Psychologically as well as dramatically and ethically, it is of a compactness which we never encounter in the realm of opera. There is no padding here, there are none of the *clichés* with which operatic texts commonly abound … It is a fact that Schoenberg has found a remarkable balance between the literary and the musical elements of his work.

Thus Claude Rostand.[23]

But while Stravinsky's opinions of Schoenberg oscillated between extremes, Webern couldn't put a foot wrong – be it Webern the composer or Webern the man. In fact, Stravinsky's eulogy on Webern in the second batch of conversations between him and Robert Craft (*Memories and Commentaries*[24]) prompted Peter J. Pirie to the somewhat despairing observation that he could not make up his mind 'about the exact intellectual stature of a man

[20] *Cf.* note 6 on p. 125, above.

[21] *Op. cit.* Keller's review of the book can be found on pp. 75–81, above.

[22] *Ibid.*, p 78.

[23] Claude Rostand (1912–71) was a French musicologist and critic. Studying law, literature and music in parallel, he was a student at the Conservatoire de Paris of Jacques Février and Norbert Dufourcq. He was a critic for *Le Monde* and *Le Figaro littéraire* and the French correspondent for *Melos* and *Musical America*, his work also extending to radio and television. He wrote on a wide range of nineteenth- and twentieth-century composers but was especially well known as a defender of the *avant garde*, not least for his *Dictionnaire de la musique contemporaine* (Larousse, Paris, 1970). I have been unable to locate the source of this quotation.

[24] *Cf.* p. 114, above.

who ... sentimentalizes like a teenager over Webern ....'[25] I dislike this kind of description of a genius's reaction to a master, however minor, but the very fact that a by no means insensitive critic was driven to it is an indication of the intensity and purity of Stravinsky's admiration for Webern. There is only one parallel, an acutely striking one, to this kind of public propaganda, on the part of a genius, for a dead master: Schoenberg's own memorial lecture on Gustav Mahler (1912), translated and reprinted in *Style and Idea.* The history of Schoenberg's relation to Mahler is itself one of passionate ambivalence, and the lecture is a guilt reaction if ever there was one, 'mourning and melancholia' *par exellence.*

What I had to introduce as an element of confusion, the seemingly impenetrable cloud hanging over Stravinsky's 'true' feelings about Schoenberg and Webern, seems to turn into the first step towards the solution of our problem. My metaphor is carefully mixed: the cloud is substantial, solid; we may step on it and look beyond. The fact is that all feelings are 'true', and if they contradict each other they are all the truer, stronger: if either side isn't strong, it gives in and is liquidated. Stravinsky's unconscious was prepared to incorporate and mourn Schoenberg on condition that Webern could be absorbed at the same time, and that the manifestly aggressive side of the psychological deal could be confined to Schoenberg, so that Webern could bathe in Schoenberg's glory as well as his own.

Our next and final two steps seem now clearly marked. We have to find out what made it possible for Stravinsky to be attracted by Webern to such an extent, and what made it necessary to retain Schoenberg.

Now it so happens that apart from Stravinsky himself, Webern is the only great sado-masochistic figure in the history of music. In his case, masochism and in-turned sadism are markedly stronger than in Stravinsky's; self-restrictiveness turns into self-destruction. What I mean is that Webern had been misunderstood by his followers with such absolute consistency that we must make him at least partly responsible for this historical, and by now historic misapprehension: it is as if he had worked towards being killed after his death. Much of the prestige of his work amongst composers depends in fact on the suppression of that which it expresses or purports to express, namely, emotion. Urged on by his masochism, Webern drove his heart-felt *espressivo* style beyond the extremes of compression towards partial or sometimes wholesale suppression. With Stravinsky, such suppression is

[25] Peter J. Pirie (1916–97) studied piano, composition and conducting at the Guildhall School of Music, working after the Second World War (during which he was imprisoned as a conscientious objector) as a critic and reviewer, writing especially about twentieth-century British music, not least in *Frank Bridge* (Triad Press, London, 1971) and *The English Musical Renaissance: Twentieth Century British Composers and Their Works* (Gollancz, London/St Martin's Press, New York, 1979). He also wrote *Furtwangler and the Art of Conducting* (Duckworth, London, 1981). Pirie's review of *Memories and Commentaries* appeared in *The Music Review*, Vol. 22, 1961, p. 239.

suppressionism: it is artistically intended and hence functional, i.e., itself expressive. With Webern it is unintentional, accidental from the artistic point of view, though essential psychologically. In that sense, Webern's art is pathological, neurotic, whereas Stravinsky's isn't. Neurosis is unrealism; in art, it is a failure of adjustment to psychic reality. Inasmuch as Webern did not say what he had to say and what he thought he was saying, and inasmuch as this was not due to technical deficiencies (which, in my view, it virtually never was), he was a neurotic master (the only one in our history apart from Brahms, who tended to deny his feelings when he became afraid of them, fearing them to be 'sentimental').

It can easily be seen how Stravinsky was gladly prepared to swallow (incorporate) this sado-masochistic character – so long as he did not have to swallow it whole. Let us be a little more concrete and turn to the musical effects of Webern's sado-masochism – his sparse, ultra-transparent textures, cleaner, it must be said, than anything our entire musical history had had to offer until then. Once Stravinsky was incorporating the twelve-tone method, which itself offers many self-restrictive possibilities to those (and only to those) who want them, once his hostility towards atonality was on the wane, Webern's textures must have exercised a particular fascination on the suppressionist: it is one of the supreme paradoxes of musical history, as indeed of history in general, that pathology can produce health. (The opposite, alas, is also true, as can be observed in the Nazi interpretations of Wagner, Nietzsche, and even Bruckner.) If Webern was ever capable of musical development – in healthy circumstances one of the inevitable consequences of an *espressivo* style – his sado-masochism soon drove the capacity out of his system; and Stravinsky, the anti-expressionist and professed anti-developer *par excellence,* must have been happy to hear the unfinished result – unfinished because the twelve-tone method, a developmental procedure if ever there was one, suppresses itself in Webern's work. How Stravinsky managed to use the method undamaged, yet undeveloping, remains one of the miracles of genius; but one thing is certain – that he could not have done so without, on the one hand, his absolute loyalty to physical musical reality, to sounding sense, and on the other (or not so other) hand, Schoenberg's help.

We thus come to the last step in our investigation. When everything psychological is said and done, what was it in Schoenberg's own twelve-tone method that attracted Stravinsky so intensely and lastingly that it made all the psychological complications we have described worthwhile? And even on the assumption of a topically favourable psychological climate such as I have outlined, of potent stimuli towards identification exciting this perpetually identifying creative character, what was it, musically, that overcame a lifetime of musical resistance, an era of official musical polarity? Had Stravinsky 'killed the thing he loved', had he treated Schoenberg's twelve-tone method as savagely as Webern treated his own, our explanation would not be far to seek; it could, in fact, remain on the psychological level. But he didn't. On the contrary, with the exception of Nikos Skalkottas and the partial exception of Roberto Gerhard, Schoenberg's method has not, to date, found as realistic a follower as Stravinsky.

So far, when speaking about twelve-tone technique, I have kept my remarks general, hoping that they would so make essential sense to the uninitiated, while the versed would pin them down to the relevant concrete details. But when explaining Schoenberg's specific attraction for Stravinsky, I shall have to be mildly technical, without, however, saying anything that presupposes a great deal of technical knowledge.

While for Webern the tone-row is usually abstract, which is to say that it does not readily crystallize into something of melodic significance and therefore remains largely inaudible, the Schoenbergian tone-row is *abstracted from a melodic idea,* an initial inspiration: by and large, it *is* this idea without its rhythm – a succession of notes derived from a tune, and uncommitted to the rhythm of the tune: my term for it is 'sub-thematic'. It may be a little longer than the tune, in which case the rest of the row may be used towards the continuation; or it may be a bit shorter than the tune, in which case the tune will comprise more than one rotation of the row. In any case, however, the characteristic trait of the Schoenbergian row is its original concreteness – its function as a melodic motif, retaining its melodic aspect even when it is divested of its rhythm, or rather, when endowed with a new rhythm. It is due to the melodic idea from which it springs, and the melodic quality which it therefore retains, that the Schoenbergian row is ultimately and spontaneously audible. As Chapters II and III will hope to show, the musical importance of such concreteness and audibility cannot be overrated, nor has it yet been fully appreciated.

The vast majority of serial composers evince exactly the opposite approach, to which Webern inclined, which he was even the first to practise – without, however, fully subscribing to it. With them, the serial idea, the idea of a particular series or a special kind of series, comes first, and the music afterwards. The more pronouncedly phoney ones among them have even gone so far as to write of Schoenberg's rows contemptuously as 'music-making rows' (*Musizierreihen*[26]), comparing them unfavourably with their own 'structural' rows. I cannot explain to the reader what exactly a 'structural' row is, or why it is more structural than a 'music-making' row, because I have never understood the term myself; suffice it to say that you don't know a structural row when you hear it.

[26] In 'Schoenberg's *Moses and Aron*' (*The Score and I.M.A. Magazine* 21, October 1957, pp. 30–45), Keller reveals that he 'picked up' this new technical term 'in a German periodical'.

However, what drew Stravinsky to Schoenberg's method, despite the vast difference in compositional outlook between the two, was, I suggest, its 'music-making' significance. Again and again, I used to point to this, as it seemed to me, obvious trait of Stravinsky's serial technique, long before he did so himself. When he finally did (in *Memories and Commentaries*), he made no mention, of course, of Schoenberg, but the way in which he described his technique left no more doubt about the correctness of my diagnosis. The crucial passage runs as follows:

> Robert Craft: Would you analyse your own composing process in any part of one of your more recent pieces — in, for example, the little *Epitaphium*?[27]
>
> Stravinsky: I began the *Epitaphium* with the flute-clarinet duet ... In the manner I have described in our previous conversations I heard and composed a melodic-harmonic phrase. I certainly did not (and never do) begin with a purely serial idea and, in fact, when I began I did not know, or care, whether all twelve notes would be used. After I had written about half the first phrase I saw its serial pattern, however, and then perhaps I began to work towards that pattern. The constructive problem that first attracted me in the two-part counterpoint of the first phrase was the harmonic one of minor seconds.[28]

Compare this with Schoenberg's categorical statement in a letter to Josef Rufer (quoted in the latter's *Composition with Twelve Notes;* the translation is mine): 'The original idea of a row always occurs to me in the form of a thematic character'.[29]

The road to our understanding is clear. Across the divisions of style, beyond the wars of their schools, Stravinsky and Schoenberg eventually met on the basis of concrete, audible, sounding sense. By way of creative mourning, Stravinsky, who had always tended towards ambivalent identification, became aware of the concrete possibilities in Schoenberg's method and proceeded to incorporate it, insisting on getting Webern into the bargain.

[27] For flute, clarinet and harp (1959). Keller wrote an approving paragraph on the work in 'The New in Review: Donaueschingen, 1959', *The Music Review*, Vol. 21, No. 1, February 1960, pp. 79–80:

> By far the most important first performance was by far the shortest – that of Stravinsky's recent *Epitaphium* 'for the tombstone of Prince Max Egon zu Fürstenberg', given by members of the Südwestfunk Orchestra at the beginning of a Webern chamber concert. An impressive and masterly piece (which, meanwhile, has been heard in the Third Programme too). Flute and clarinet alternate with a harp in a seven bars' texture containing eight rotations of its tone-row. The originality of the form is characteristic: according to the new, 'advanced' conservatism, an aphoristic structure without pointillism is an impossibility. Not for Stravinsky. The duration of the piece is eighteen seconds.

[28] *Memories and Commentaries*, *op. cit.*, p. 105

[29] *Cf.* note 3 on p. 50, above. The quotation here comes from p. 86 of the German original (corresponding to p. 92 of the Searle translation).

With the unerring certainty of genius, he split his mourning attitude between the two composers (some of his remarks about Webern sound as if the Schoenberg pupil had died yesterday) and took from either what he needed, leaving the unrealistic aspects of Webern as well as the developmental and expressionist aspects of Schoenberg on one side. Fascinated, yet uncorrupted, by some of the most recent, partly un-sounding developments of musical composition, he continued to make sense of sound and of nothing else, an advanced aim to those whom even he regarded as more advanced than himself. Look after the physical reality of your music, he told them and still tells them, and the spirit will look after itself. Unlike them, he is not an arm-chair composer; he remains what this book shows him to be – a music-maker.

II. STRAVINSKY'S UNCHANGED MIND

Two questions remain or arise, according to whether or not you share what you may regard as my prejudices – which I, however, consider severely tested working hypotheses: if you share them, these questions have been with you all along, at least on a pre-conscious level. In any case, each deserves a chapter on its own.

The first is burning – ablaze, in fact: convincing as our interpretation of Stravinsky's change of creative mind may be, how was it possible for a great creator to be capable of it all? Must we not agree with my hypothesis that whatever happens in the creative life of a genius, however surprising his metamorphoses, his diametrically opposed, successive creative attitudes may be to the outside observer, they will invariably be found to have profound determinants in his own psyche, palpable causes, tangible endo-psychic precedents which, though they must have remained latent until external stimuli produced the manifest change of mind, are an essential part of his creative character? A genius' revolution, in a word, must have an evolutionary aspect.

Come to think of it, is it not stunning that the critical fraternity, though preoccupied in conscientious detail with Stravinsky's sensational absorption of serial technique, has never yet as much as asked itself what, in the music preceding it, can be said to have led up to it? Twelve-tonery is, after all, a far- and deep-reaching way of musical thinking – which a mere talent may adopt, play with, 'use' without the underlying musical substance requiring this particular procedure, but which a genius would never as much as consider if his creative substance did not urge him towards it, if it did not, in fact, contain the seeds of serial technique itself. I thus accuse, above all, the Stravinskyians amongst critics, musicologists and analysts, of not taking their idol seriously enough: how can they not wonder how it all happened, external stimulation apart, how Stravinsky's own mind had prepared for the event, without his being aware of the fact? When, in Chapter I, we examined Stravinsky's psychological budget and calculated 'the credit side of his revolutionary identifications', we naturally ignored this factor of an independent, internal incentive – not because we doubted its existence, but, on the contrary, because without it, any budgeting would have been senseless: it is not an item on the credit side, but the very condition for the opening of a credit account.

Those internal causes must, surely, always have formed an element in his composing methods, must have established themselves as a characteristic, concrete expressive means which, however unconscious to begin with, made the overt, conscious change of mind possible. Let's face it, either we can unambiguously show even the most anti-serial Stravinsky to have harboured, nevertheless, unconscious serial tendencies, or else we are confronted with the disconcerting alternative of having to deny him genius or ourselves insight – an inconceivable dilemma. Remembering, however, that Schoenberg himself composed with unconscious tone-rows long before he consciously discovered his twelve-tone technique, and that even the classical composers (yes, Beethoven, even Mozart) can be shown – as I demonstrated decades ago in great detail in a paper on 'Strict Serial Technique in Classical Music'[30] – to have practised Schoenberg's own technique without the remotest awareness of what they were doing, we need not feel grotesquely unrealistic, artificial rather than artistic, if we decide to examine or re-examine the passionately anti-Schoenbergian, neo-classical Stravinsky's methods of unification in an attempt to uncover downright serial thought processes – at the very stage in his development when his conscious mind ridiculed serial technique, and decades before he made dodecaphony his conscious own or, we may come to conclude, before Schoenberg's death allowed him to let his own serial inclinations emerge into consciousness.

The one neo-classical theme we have so far alluded to is the subject of the opening four-part fugue of the *Symphony of Psalms*' second movement, which we heard through the life-mask of Bach; had we listened a little more closely, or rather, a little more widely, thus perceiving the theme's integration with the entire work in general and the first movement in particular, we could have heard the life-mask of Schoenberg, too.

Or could we? Serial integration we can certainly diagnose very concretely, and with wellnigh traumatic surprise too, but there is no need, no reason to claim that at that early stage, Stravinsky 'had it' unconsciously from Schoenberg, who did not, after all, invent the method; he merely intellectually discovered and isolated and systematized a natural mode of musical thought that had been operative in many a masterpiece long before he was born.

[30] *Tempo*, No. 37, 1955 [pp. 12–16 and 21–24]. –HK

In any event, so simple and straightforward is Stravinsky's unconscious application of the row technique in the present instance (or his conscious application of a technique of whose strictly serial nature he must, in that case, have been unaware) that despite the fact that the history of composition can hardly offer a greater technical sensation than a piece of essential, indispensable serialism in Stravinsky's greatest neo-classical masterpiece, the uninitiated reader is not, this time, invited to turn his back on our technical demonstration; on the contrary, Stravinsky will enlighten him, as he seemed to enlighten himself, about the very nature and purpose of serial thinking. The concluding thought of Schoenberg's only essay on twelve-tone technique ('Composition with Twelve Tones', in *Style and Idea*[31]) seems highly relevant at this point:

> In music there is no form without logic, there is no logic without unity.
>
> I believe that when Richard Wagner introduced his *Leitmotiv* – for the same purpose as that for which I introduced my Basic Set[32] – he may have said: 'Let there be unity'.

If the reader remembers the *Symphony of Psalms* at all (a greater, deeper work than which Stravinsky never created), he will readily recall what I have isolated on the left-hand side of my music example, i.e., the first movement's nowise concealed accompaniment which, I can now inform him, gives us a simultaneous double exposition of the four-tone row – a basic set together with its transposition – that serves to establish unity not only within the movement, but actually between movements: the fugue subject on the right-hand side is based on another transposition of it, and on the transposition's rotations which, significantly enough, behave exactly according to the twelve-tone rules formulated by Schoenberg a few years earlier, and laughed at by Stravinsky's conscious mind – by what he and we then thought was Stravinsky.

Thus, the row is and remains totally independent of any of its rhythmic articulations; it does not, in a word, remain a rhythmic entity. Again, as in the case of the Dylan Thomas dirge, octave transpositions do not adversely affect its identity, though the melodic innovations they introduce are sufficiently drastic to hide this very identity which, sub-thematically, produces the intensest unity between what thus become dissimilar shapes. Lastly, though the context is, of course, tonal, the row's configuration is defined, re-defined and thus maintained in vastly different harmonic circumstances: there is no harmonic identity between whichever of the two left-hand rows we choose to call the basic set and its two transpositions.

[31] *Op. cit.*, p. 244.

[32] Note to the virginal reader: the 'basic set' is the original (initial) form of the tone-row, as distinct from its 'mirror forms' – the inversion, the retrograde version, and the retrograde inversion. –HK

I have extricated these particular occurrences and rotations of the row in order to provide a quick and clear, yet comprehensive example of Stravinsky's serial technique in the Symphony; a complete analysis of its role in the unification of the work would, of course, reach far further. But my example is, structurally, of central significance, and for my part, I have no doubt that Stravinsky deliberately employed these successions of intervals and their inversions; what he did not realize, and indeed, psychoanalytically speaking, repressed, was the circumstance that through so acting, and especially because of his extra-rhythmic, extra-diatonic approach to his successions of intervals, he landed himself straight in the strictest possible serial technique, albeit of as primitive a type as Schoenberg himself had employed early on, in one of his first consistently twelve-tonal structures (the fourth movement of his Serenade, Op. 24, composed seven years before the *Symphony of Psalms*). By 'primitive type' I simply mean the absence of any mirror forms, such as inversion, retrograde, and retrograde inversion, all of which the more specifically interested reader will have found, or might now wish to revert to, in the Dylan Thomas dirge.

We remember that much later, when Stravinsky had consciously serial ideas, he 'did not know, or care, whether all twelve notes would be used'. No wonder that when he began unconsciously, he didn't care either: Schoenberg himself hadn't cared before his own serial technique reached his consciousness.[33] The twelve notes are, in fact, the only theoretical aspect of twelve-tone technique the result, that is of the decision to unify without the help of

[33] An interview with Stravinsky by Jay S. Harrison in *The New York Herald Tribune* (21 December 1952, section 4, p. 5) reinforces his un-doctrinaire attitude to dodecaphony:

THE R: Do you know, Mr. Stravinsky that there has been much talk recently about the possibility of your embracing twelve-tone, atonal principles?
MR. S: Talk is talk, and cheap. Certain twelve-tone things I like, certain I don't. For instance, I have tremendous respect for the discipline imposed upon the twelve-tone man. It is a discipline that you find nowhere else. But on the other hand, there are too many twelve-tone swindlers working today.
THE R: Swindlers?
MR. S: Swindlers. Not, of course, Schoenberg, Berg, or Webern. These are masters, wonderful musicians, luxury composers. But some others do not hear what they are writing. That, however, is another matter.
THE R: You, too, naturally have a discipline. What is yours?
MR. S. Mine is tonality. After all, it is not easy to write tonal music. Most atonal composers are against tonality because if they weren't they would have to be tonal. And that would make them *triste*.

tonality. They are, therefore, Schoenberg's only personal contribution to the method he discovered, its consistent application apart. At the same time, the *Symphony of Psalms*' four-note row is not the shortest possible: in the aforementioned essay on the classical twelve-toners, I showed that at the beginning of the development section of the finale from his famous G minor Symphony, Mozart uses a three-note row – and, ironically enough, lets it behave more anti-tonally than the maturest Schoenberg allows more than one of his twelve-tone rows to behave; that of the *Ode to Napoleon,* for instance, while starting anti-tonally, eventually contributes to a triumphant E flat conclusion.

It is abundantly obvious, then, that the serial mode of thought came quite naturally to Stravinsky – that he was able to practise it instinctively, with unconscious certainty about *what* had to be done, *how* things had to be done and how they could *not* be done if the row was to serve unification and, hence, comprehension; even Schoenberg's constructive negative rule is heeded as a matter of natural, instinctive course: none of the row's notes recurs after another one has been sounded, and before the row as a whole has unfolded.

I have suggested that Picasso was perhaps the only other great creator capable of comparably profound changes of mind – and I would now go further and submit that in his case, likewise, an 'unchanged mind' must eventually be demonstrable across even the most violent changes, each of which must needs have tapped latent, yet well developed and well-defined sources; it is, I humbly propose, up to my brothers-in-analytic-arms in the present book's other artistic world to find them – unless they have done so behind my back. The underlying assumption is, admittedly, that Picasso was a great creator, a genius, but while I am not entitled to pronounce upon visual art, it is my very ignorance through which the power of Picasso's genius cuts the way the downright elemental force of serial logic cut through Stravinsky's pseudo-elemental prejudices against it; mourning without melancholia killed them and freed it.

I was almost going to conclude this chapter by saying that any musician would be aghast if nobody had yet explored the endo-psychic determinants

---

THE R. Then you think twelve-tone music is limited.

MR. S: Of course it is. It is like prison. Twelve-tone composers have to use the twelve tones. I can use five, eleven, six—anything I like. I am not obliged to use more. I do as I wish in the scale or mode I prefer. I am also able to work in series, like the atonalists, if I want to. But what is important is that I do not have to.

of Picasso's changes of mind – but then, which musician before the present one cared about Stravinsky's? I am indeed aghast that nobody did – unless the same resistances have been at work which kept Stravinsky's spontaneous serial thought firmly locked in the safe of his unconsciousness. After all, he himself couldn't find the key until after Schoenberg's death.

III. THE MUSIC-MAKER'S FUTURE

The other question which remains or arises in view of Stravinsky's change of mind flows from my working hypothesis that however conservative a genius may be or seem, his very genius will, inevitably, be of profound relevance to the future of his art – potentially and/or actually so: Bach and Mozart, for instance, were almost notoriously conservative geniuses, at least in the ears of many observers, contemporary observers (even composers) in the case of Bach, posthumous observers in the case of Mozart. Yet Schoenberg, for instance, regarded himself as a pupil of both Bach and Mozart, nor would it be difficult to show what he learnt from them. What, however, the historical investigator never considers is that part of a conservative genius' influence on the future which is or was destined to remain potential – the influence that never happened. We are, nevertheless, justified in calling it an influence if we can demonstrate that in certain circumstances beyond the genius' control, it could, should have happened.

Take Mozart, the greatest amongst his string quintets, at least four of them, on the one hand, his two piano quartets, his string trio (the so-miscalled 'Divertimento') and the two violin-viola duos on the other. Out of nothing, without any truly helpful precedent, he created supreme masterpieces in each of these media, some of which evince an originality of both structure and texture which can only be compared to the originality of the greatest string quartets of Haydn and Beethoven. Yet, while Haydn duly became the founder of the Austro-German string quartet and Beethoven its almost unreachable prophet, Mozart did not succeed in proving himself the founder or prophet of a comparable tradition in any of these areas of instrumental combinations. Why not? The traditions never really happened. Strictly speaking, his G minor Piano Quartet was to remain the only supreme masterpiece of its textural kind;[34] the two-viola quintet, likewise, never found its way back to Mozart's elevated level; the string trio, after Beethoven, had to wait until Schoenberg to throw up another great masterpiece; and the violin-viola duo never returned to Mozart's level of weighty mastery at all.

The point is that it can easily be shown why it wasn't Mozart's fault that things didn't happen; it was the fault of his successors, however great their

[34] Though equally flawless, his other piano quartet, in E flat, makes life easier for itself as a texture, which is that of a mini piano concerto. –HK

genius. For as soon as we examine the different textures of these instrumental combinations, we find that unlike the string quartet, each of them harbours profound problems so far as their sheer sound is concerned, problems which needed a Mozartian ear in order to be either overcome or simply ignored. However, the historical fact is that after Mozart, there was no Mozartian ear – which, it will be admitted, wasn't his fault. Yet it is because there was no Mozartian ear after Mozart that we call him a conservative.

Or, very conscientiously and equally concretely speaking, there was one, almost – Mendelssohn's. After Mozart, that is to say, Mendelssohn's was the only ear capable of overcoming, or ignoring, most textural problems – situations, that is to say, which presented problems to all other composers – without even needing practical experience, practice: one would have thought that the texture of the *Midsummer Night's Dream* Overture, for instance, needed a lifetime's aural experience. Mendelssohn's inner ear, in a word, seemed indistinguishable from his physiological ear, in that his aural imagination differentiated as subtly as did his perception. But his genius, though towering, was not, of course, of Mozart's order. Nevertheless, he was not only the one composer after Schubert and before our own age whose quartet textures reached classical perfection, but also the only composer altogether who did actually continue what was the richest, most radical and, potentially, the most fruitful of Mozart's textural innovations – the two-viola string quintet: his two works in that medium are the only ones that bear comparison with Mozart's quintet textures, the only ones which show no sign of any problem existing. Without the Mozartian model, they would probably never have been created; and their musical substance, too, proves them his worthy successors — so that in this single respect, at least, it is difficult to consider him an uninitiating conservative. There are two other respects – the string trio (Beethoven, Schoenberg) and, overridingly, the piano concerto: what would have happened to, and about the piano concerto without Mozart? We tend to forget both what had happened, or rather hadn't, before he came in with his unprecedented masterpieces, and what did happen to Beethoven as a result of them. No matter, what is of crucial importance in our present context is a concrete understanding of Mozart as a *potential* innovator, for actual *or* potential innovation is, according to a working hypothesis which the majority of readers will share, inseparable from the phenomenon of genius, one of its *conditiones sine qua non.*

Stravinsky is, of course, our age's conservative genius *par excellence.* Britten would indeed be another, but does not occupy a polar position *via-à-vis* our age's revolutionary *par excellence* – and the fact that Stravinsky came to adopt the latter's revolutionary methods does not detract from his conservatism: he came to conserve them, too. His actual influence on that part of the future which has, meanwhile, become present is nothing or little to write home about: there is Britten as a recipient, of course, but that's about it, for all the many remaining results of Stravinsky's influence are nothing short of deplorable, and easily descend to the film-musical plane of kitschy anti-kitsch – suppressionism without anything to suppress. Nor indeed is it easy to imagine that Stravinsky's various, contrasting conservatisms will be capable of exerting a fruitful influence on any future creativity – with the sole exception of his last and most surprising act of conservatism, that revolutionary, yet evolutionary change of mind which produced the conservation of Schoenberg's, yet also Stravinsky's characteristic method.

'Characteristic' is the doubly operative word: the 'music-making row' is characteristically Schoenberg's, and as both Stravinsky said and we showed in Chapter II,[35] it was the only way in which he himself could think serially, as opposed, very much opposed, to the serial *and* extra-serial thinking of the vast majority of anti-conservative contemporary composers, all of them well on the other side of Chapter I's iron curtain. As an observer whose professional activities have involved him in familiarizing himself with the widest conceivable variety of contemporary scores,[36] I give it as my empirical opinion that at the present, critical juncture in the development of composition, even considerable talents find themselves, under the pressure of influential, 'advanced' forces, on the other side of the iron curtain; and that nowadays, it needs not only deep musicality, but also sheer moral strength to remain on, or defect to, this side, Stravinsky's.

The question of his influence on the future is amongst the most difficult with which genuinely musical criticism can concern itself at the end of the twentieth century – because we now have to face two phenomena for which there is no precedent, phenomena which lie outside musical history, if history is the story of the same causes producing the same effects. The phenomenon of Stravinsky's own creative personality is without the remotest parallel: Picasso may be a comparable mind-changer, but he is not a suppressionist, nor is there any sign of Stravinsky's suppressionism as such being capable of exerting a favourable influence. So far, in fact, this influence has proved a mere, powerful excuse for saying nothing – a pseudo-creative activity which is more popular nowadays than it ever was. Quite often a contemporary composer will have met the demands of his conscience if, instead of saying something, he makes absolutely clear what he is not going to

[35] P. 146, above.

[36] Keller's acquaintance with the newest music was indeed considerable:

> I happen to be in charge of new music at the BBC [as 'Chief Assistant, New Music'], and I have revised our score-reading system and our rules of acceptance and rejection in a way which makes it incumbent upon me to read any new score submitted myself – native or foreign. In addition, I read for the Society for the Promotion of New Music, as well as for competitions.

Cf. 1975 (1984 minus 9), *op. cit.*, p. 176.

say, what he feels aggressive about – what, in his view, is improper artistic behaviour. Not seldom with Stravinsky's help, he will have accumulated a bunch of anti-sentimental gestures, of ruthless ostinatos, of spiced-up, unfunctional demi-semi-diatonic harmonies which will inform the listener to which camp the composer does not belong; such an introductory exposition of the composer's premises will easily prove so enjoyable to the composer that it will soon lose its introductoriness and replace the creative act altogether: again for the first time in the history of music, it has become possible, permissible, even reputable, to say what one is against and leave it at that. In both composition and performance, avoidance poses as art. Stravinsky's unique personality as such, then, cannot foreseeably exert an auspicious influence on his successors – or if it can, it is too unique for us to be able to divine the unforeseeable. Schoenberg's uniqueness is a very different story: its traceable relations to Beethoven's uniqueness have made it possible for us to foresee his influence in terms of Beethoven's, even though the historical situations surrounding the two could hardly be more dissimilar.

Which brings us to the other phenomenon without precedent – our present historical situation, or rather, often conflicting situations, whose complexity and complications seem to be reaching their extended climax at the end of the century: in comparison, what surrounded and immediately succeeded Schoenberg was historical simplicity itself. Mind you, he had indeed started it all, in that the total abandonment of tonality paved the way not only for unmusicality in the guise of atonal incomprehensibility, but also for the replacement of creation with game-playing: where there are no rules, the mere definition of, and subsequent adherence to new rules feels like a creative achievement, to both the composer and his ever more un-aural audience; those new rules, as opposed to the *a posteriori* rules of diatonic harmony, need the eye rather than the ear in order to be understood and followed, and in order for such following to be understood.

Am I talking, amongst many others, about twelve-tone rules? That depends on the individual twelve-tone row you have in mind. One and the same rule, that is to say, will be easily audible when applied to a row of Schoenberg's, or Skalkottas', or Stravinsky's, but exclusively visible when applied to most other people's. In Chapter I, we have drawn attention to the legend of serial technique being visual.[37] Unfortunately, the legend becomes reality where the music is a mere phantom, albeit a highly successful one. It is in view of Schoenberg's or Stravinsky's serial technique that one can safely speak of a legend; but then, most of our current historical situations have become unsafe, sundry visual games lending them the illusion of safety.

[37] P. 133, above.

In principle, it is perfectly easy to determine when and how it all started. It was when instead of thinking music, the composer started to think *about* music. There is no harm in that, so long as there is something to think about – so long as the composer has thought, invented music in the first place, and proceeds to think about it. And by 'music' I don't mean anything elaborate or complex: a tune, a little motif may have occurred to a composer, and he may proceed to think about it, about its character, its harmonic implications, its thematic possibilities and, yes, its constituent intervals, which might indeed prompt him to interpret the motif serially.

If, on the other hand, he thinks about it before it exists, and if, therefore, he reflects upon its constitution, its elements, before they have given rise to an audible entity, he runs the risk of thinking extra-musically, of thinking about things whose existence is visible, but not audible – and let us not forget that in our present state of uncertainty, many a mind which, constitutionally, belongs on this side of the iron curtain may well feel tempted to defect to the other side in order to partake of the safety of thought about music, in the illusory hope that such thought might, eventually, produce music. But that is he and now; we have not yet completed our answer to the question when and how it all started. If, at this point, I enlist the help of philosophy, it is not in order to obscure what, essentially, must remain a simple question, but, on the contrary, in order to simplify a state of creative affairs which, until now, has been obscured even by the most conscientious and the most musical thinkers.

A great deal has happened to philosophy since Kant's *Critique of Pure Reason,* but the beautiful truth of its gigantic cornerstones remains, I submit, unharmed. Let us translate his 'categories of thought' into simple language: it is as true today as it was when he first thought of the fact that it is impossible for us to imagine anything outside the dimensions of time and/or space. Just think of something, anything: it cannot be spaceless and timeless. Now, so far as music is concerned, the indispensable dimension is time and, hence, rhythm: it is impossible to think of any music, any snatch of a tune, any harmony even, outside time. So far as harmony is concerned, you may object: thinking of a dominant seventh's resolution to the tonic, you might say, you aren't concerned with its rhythm, but exclusively with this logical succession of chords, the establishment of harmonic tension and its expected resolution. True enough, but it is a *succession* of chords that defines, therefore, its harmonic rhythm, outside which you can't auralize the event; for it is an event and hence needs time in order to materialize, however mentally. And even if you invent a single chord, it will not only sound a beginning and an end but, if it *is* an invention, imply something preceding and/or succeeding it which, again, will imply a process, harmonic rhythm.

Nor, sticking to our subject, need we worry about harmony at the moment, for what I am concerned with when completing my reply to the question when and how it first happened is, simply, melody. Melodic, or rather rhythmic invention is indeed the elemental creative act; strictly speaking, it is always rhythmic, for there is music without harmony and music without melody and music without both, but no music, no melody and no harmony without rhythm – which is just another way of saying that there is no music without time. I don't want to repeat myself, but I certainly want to repeat Stravinsky:

> I heard and composed a melodic-harmonic phrase. I certainly did not (and never do) begin with a purely serial idea and, in fact, when I began I did not know, or care, whether all twelve notes would be used. After I had written about half the first phrase I saw its serial pattern, however, and then perhaps I began to work towards that pattern.[38]

Having thought music, he began to think about it, which was not what his alleged idol did – Webern. It was the method of the unconscious or pre-conscious idol, Schoenberg – technically speaking, not all that unconscious either, as witness his enthusiastic approval of my emphatically Schoenbergian analysis of his Dylan Thomas dirge. But Webern inverted Schoenberg's procedure: no doubt Schoenberg explained to him that the row was the basis of the piece and, theoretically preoccupied, did not add the all-important circumstance that this basis naturally derived from an invention, that a row as such did not, musically, exist. The row as such is, as it were, the Kantian thing in itself,[39] which we can't hear; as soon as we auralize it, we rhythmicize it. We can, of course, see it – translate it into space, whereupon it ceases to be the thing in itself and doesn't begin to be anything else, for you can't hear it. It is as simple as that: it all started with Webern, the first composer to think about music before thinking music – despite his profound musicianship which, amongst his heirs and successors, affected only profound musicians. Or the one profound musician amongst them?

It would, perhaps, be unfair on Marx to regard him as the father of the iron curtain and all that goes with it – of all the immoralities and inhumanities the development of communism has yielded. In fact, so far as Marx's own personality is concerned, and while one can detect much misjudgement, it would be difficult to trace any immoral or uncultural motivation. Likewise, we mustn't blame Webern for what has happened not only in his name, but as a result of his replacing composition with pre-composition – a practice

[38] *Memories and Commentaries*, *op. cit.*, p. 105.

[39] In my submission, a mistranslation (of *das Ding an sich*) down the ages: it ought to be 'the thing as such'. –HK

which, by now, is almost universal. His musical personality, his creativity and, last but first, his sheer musicality were strong enough to overcome – in the majority of creative instances if not always – the handicap which his unprecedented approach to composition had produced for himself – an approach which, however, seemed motivated in much the same way as it is nowadays, inspired, that is to say, by the fear of insecurity and the proportionate temptation the rules of the game offered. And so he applied the rules before there was anything to apply them to, thereby lending an inaudible aspect to the very audible substance of his work, an aspect of which the work of the inventor, or rather, the discoverer of the rules is altogether free. But then, the very fact that he discovered them, however unconsciously, the very fact that he first encountered them in their application to musical thought (including, of course, his own), made it all the easier for him to adhere to the absolute primacy of musical invention, of specific, characteristic musical thought, which was a clearly demonstrable function of his creative character, anyhow.

At the same time, Webern's introduction of precomposition, of thought about music before any music had been born, foreheard and, alas, fore*saw* a typically modern attitude to musical creation, an at least partial loss of spontaneity, of old-fashioned inspiration, which came to pervade even the safest regions on this side of the iron curtain. We must not forget that even a Benjamin Britten, surely one of the concretest and most spontaneous inventors of our time, experienced yet enough 'thought about' before those concrete ideas occurred to him to be able to say that in his head, he had more or less finished something, and 'only had to fill in the notes' – a statement which a Mozart or Beethoven would have met with total incomprehension, even though Beethoven himself seems to have introduced thought about music into the world of the creator. But invariably, it was thought about something that had happened, on however primitive a level: there were decades of thought about the initial, incredibly simple-minded version of the 'Joy' tune, for instance, thought about how to turn simple-mindedness into extreme simplicity.

The disconcerting question of Stravinsky's influence, at least his potential influence, on future generations of intense talent is becoming a little easier, for he was amongst the very few composers of his time who were utterly unaffected by soundless music, by thought about what had not yet been thought. It is precisely in the area of serial technique that the potential force of such a composing attitude cannot be overestimated — and, paradoxically, Stravinsky's Schoenbergian influence could, in this respect, produce more actuality, more real results amongst future composers than Schoenberg's own. For Schoenberg himself, through his discovery of the dodecaphonic rules and their logical definition, came to play, quite guiltlessly, a far more ambiguous role: the way he silently composed was soon forgotten (at least so far as the order of creative events was concerned), his application of the rules so well remembered that many a dutiful twelve-tone composer composed stricter twelve-tone music than Schoenberg ever did in his life; it was, after all, Webern himself who was the first, ominous victim of this misunderstanding of Schoenberg's approach to composition, which flowed from his unconditional loyalty to the primacy of concrete, rhythmic invention. The rhythmless, temporarily musicless row was invented with and by Webern: his first creative steps are a retrograde version of Schoenberg's – but unlike the tone-row's mirror forms, this one does untold harm to the basic idea!

Stravinsky, quite unbothered by the rules, in whose verbal articulation he didn't show the slightest interest, cannot possibly be misunderstood the way Schoenberg has been and still is; his serial technique, his music-making rows – or rather, his row-making music – will either be understood or met with utter, harmless incomprehension.

Such incomprehension would be harmless inasmuch as it could not result in a misrepresentation, misuse and, truly musically speaking, an abuse of Stravinsky's technique comparable to the abuse Schoenberg's own technique continues to suffer (especially when it is improved upon); but if composers' deafness to Stravinsky's own serial invention should become at all widespread, it would be symptomatic of the greatest harm musical history can do to itself – the admission of extra-musicality, and hence unmusicality, into the ranks of its creators who, after all, are the only possible guardians of musicality. If they fail, musical history as we know it must either come to an end, or at least go into hibernation, with the prospect of an arctic winter.

It is not my intention to paint a gruesome picture of the future of music, but since its gruesome present is scarcely appreciated, the proportionate dangers which the future harbours have to be outlined for the purpose of both therapy and prophylaxis – or, in plain language, of confining music to the musical, however illiterate musically, and keeping it from the unmusical, however literate musically.

For the difference between the reason why quite a few of Mozart's innovations were condemned to remaining a potential influence and the cause of the threatening mere potentiality of Stravinsky's influence is extreme, and explicable with brutal simplicity: in order to materialize, Mozart's influence needed a Mozartian ear – whereas Stravinsky's needs an ear. As a musical culture, we have indeed sunk so low that the act of spontaneous improvisation, previously a first-hand experience for the most insignificant composer as well as the most substantial, has grown into so secret a science that there is many a musical composer who has hardly ever been in touch with it and, worse, does not miss its absence.

'In the manner I have described in our previous conversation I heard and composed a melodic-harmonic phrase.' That is all I am talking about – the ability to hear something without prior intellectual machinations which are designed to justify whatever the composer will eventually allow himself to hear. In this respect, Stravinsky's habitual professions that he 'had it' all from Webern could not have been wider of the mark, for it was Webern's abstractly constructed tone-row which introduced the element of a *priori* justification into serial technique, whereas Schoenberg, however complex his theoretical reflections after the creative event, confined himself to hearing and composing a melodic-harmonic phrase when it came to that moment of self-convincing and hence persuasive invention which the typical contemporary composer, musical or not, does without. Justification, a pseudo-creative concept which would have been incomprehensible to Mozart, has taken the place of conviction and persuasion. What convinces and persuades, however, is the idea itself – whereas what justifies is something else. The unconvincing, indeed meaningless ideas are legion which derive their justification from a complexly constructed tone-row whose very complexity is a delusion, for the simple reason that you can't hear it.

Concretely speaking, then, it isn't so much the notated stages of Stravinsky's serial technique which, one hopes against hope, will find a creative ear or two that will continue his music-making, as that which precedes his application of the technique, that to which the technique is applied, that which, in the case of each individual work, gives birth to its technique – the 'melodic-harmonic phrase' whose 'serial pattern' is discovered *a posteriori.* One has to be in close and constant contact with contemporary composing minds in order to appreciate that as pseudo-creative things stand at the moment, a shatteringly extended moment, the aforementioned typical composer of our undeveloping age needs almost super-human courage for the mere, sheer purpose of having an idea. It was this purpose which Hans Pfitzner threw into relief in his famous controversy with Alban Berg: he suggested that the new, atonal school had replaced the (untranslatable) *Einfall*[40] with constructivism.[41] How unfair he was to Schoenberg! And how

[40] 'A sudden idea', 'a spontaneous notion' would be the closest translation. –HK

[41] Pfitzner (1869–1949) was an arch-conservative who in 1917 attacked Busoni's *Sketch for a New Aesthetic of Music* (Schmidl, Trieste, 1907; rev. edn. Insel Verlag, Berlin, 1910) with an essay entitled 'Futuristengefahr' ('Futurist Danger'): 'All Busoni's hopes for western music are for the future, seizing up the past and the present as a stuttering beginning, a preparation' (*Gesammelte Schriften*, Vol. I, Filser, Augsburg, 1926, p. 221). He then attacked the musicologist Paul Bekker whose book *Beethoven* (Schuster und Loeffler, Berlin and Leipzig, 1911) he accused of elevating intellect and analysis above *Einfall*, which was 'an organic musical whole which cannot be dissected or analysed' (*Gesammelte Schriften*, Vol. II, pp. 139–62), offering Schumann's *Träumerei* in evidence. Alban Berg then joined the debate by analysing it – which Mosco Carner (*cf.* note 3 on p. 102, above) described as being 'like searching for the beauty of a rose by tearing off its petals' ('Pfitzner *vs.* Berg or Inspiration *vs.* Analysis', *The Musical Times*, Vol. cxviii, No. 1661, May 1977, pp. 379–80; reprinted in *Major and Minor*, Duckworth, London, 1980, pp. 253–57). *Cf.* also Owen Toller, *Pfitzner's* Palestrina*: The 'Musical Legend' and its Background*, Toccata Press, London, 1997, pp. 87–88 and 91–94. Pfitzner's opera is in part an allegory of the tension between tradition and innovation, Palestrina and the Camerata in the opera representing Pfitzner and the new music of his own day.

unfair the Schoenbergians were to him! For so far as the Webernite tone-row is concerned, which in due course was to become all too prototypical, a paradigm for every twelve-toner who lacked invention (and, alas, not only for him), Pfitzner's allegedly outmoded, old-fashioned tirade has retained its dynamic topicality down the decades, for almost three quarters of a century. But about Stravinsky's serialism he would have been just as wrong as he was about Schoenberg's. Ironically, therefore, one would have to explain Stravinsky's serialism in terms of Pfitzner's anti-serialism in order to define its potential influence on a future which, without it, will hardly deserve to be differentiated from the present: so long as the way back and forward to music-making is not found, we are not really entitled to talk of a 'future' at all; that shatteringly extended moment is in the process of proving itself a wellnigh infinite present.

About the crucial importance of the music-maker's future there is no doubt: it is a matter of life and death; and future ears, if any, hold his future in their hands. The mixed metaphor is purposive: too many are the hands nowadays which are not ears' hands. It has to be admitted, of course, that handed ears do still exist, but as well as being in a frightening minority, they only include one or two that have remained wholly uncorrupted by what happens on the other side of the iron curtain; in the serial world, perhaps not even one or two. The conclusion at which we arrived at the end of Chapter I[42] now seems substantiated and can be confirmed with factual, indeed empirical assurance: 'Look after the physical reality of your music,' he tells them, 'and the spirit will look after itself'.

IV. THE UNANSWERED QUESTION

In addition to the two questions we have tried to answer, there is one which seems destined to remain unanswered in our time, and compared to which those two are child's play. It is, nevertheless, a question which we cannot allow ourselves to escape – the less so since in the case of the great composers of the past, the answer is, in principle, available, and has, in fact, been given in quite a few instances; Thomas Mann, for example, answered it in respect of Wagner,[43] and Adorno even attempted an answer in the case of Schoenberg. He thought he had answered it in respect of Stravinsky, too, but that alleged death-mask evaded it, denying Stravinsky creative substance. The question, then, is what Stravinsky's music conveys; what those of us who understand it are puzzled by is not only his creative character, which we have tried to shed

[42] *Cf.* p. 147, above.

[43] Mann's writings on Wagner were collected as *Wagner und unsere Zeit*, ed. Erika Mann, Fischer, Frankfurt, 1963, and translated by Allan Blunden as *Pro and Contra Wagner*, Faber and Faber, London, 1985.

light on, but also the character of the creations themselves, that which distinguishes them from any other major creative output.

We are moving dangerously near a fallacious question which, according to Hugo Cole, lies 'beyond the questions "How is music constructed? How is music shaped by context?"' He describes it as 'the ultimate, never-to-be-answered question', but fails to realize that as he and everybody else puts it, it is wrong: '"What is music about?" In Bach's case at least, many would agree that behind the notes there is something exalted, supremely ordered, akin to the universal. The listener who, in answer to a questionnaire of Vernon Lee's, wrote "Bach is Angels and tops of trees and mountains" spoke, naively, for us all'.[44]

Speak for yourselves, thank you very much. Never in what I claim is my understanding experience of Bach's music have angels, tops of trees, or mountains played the remotest role, nor indeed do angels and tops of trees occur in my mental life, while mountains mean skiing to me and, admittedly, pocket-score-reading on the way up in the lift. I am not being flippant: the fallacy lies in the implication of the mere possibility of a simile, or similes. Messrs Lee and Cole are suggesting that what Bach's music expresses also finds its way into our consciousness through our experience of certain symbols and/or divine messengers. And they miss precisely that which the question claims to be about: what tops of trees and mountains (if not angels) tell us comes, exclusively, from within us; what Bach tells us comes from him. The ineluctable implication that we project meaning on to Bach as we project meaning on to tops of trees and mountains is really the supreme act of arrogance, ignoring as it does that which we could never have experienced without Bach, because he introduced us to it, discovered it for us.

'Something exalted, supremely ordered, akin to the universal' behaves a little more respectfully toward the discoveries in which Bach lets us participate, and cannot, in fact, be called fallacious – but merely irrelevant: there are plenty of things, utterly unrelated to, and dissimilar from, music, to which that 'something' is equally relevant, higher mathematics for instance. Stravinsky himself would have answered that ultimate question quite logically: 'Nothing'. He did, after all, tell us that his music didn't express anything – a remark which has been misunderstood from the word 'express'.[45] For what he implied was, quite obviously, that his music did not convey any of those things which we spontaneously regard as expressible; programme music does, and essentially, Stravinsky characterized his own music by way of a

[44] Hugo Cole (1917–95), British critic, cellist and composer, writing in 'Bach's angels' (a review of Wilfrid Mellers, *Bach and the Dance of God*, Faber, London, 1980, published in *The Listener*, 31 December 1981, p. 827). Cole had already discussed Vernon Lee's *Music and its Lovers* (Allen and Unwin, London, 1932) in his *The Changing Face of Music*, Gollancz, London, 1978.

[45] *Cf.* note 4 on p. 83, above.

negative definition: it was not concerned with extra-musical life. Nor, for that matter, is Bach's, even where he uses extra-musical life towards structuring his pure music, however impure such formal assistance.

As soon as we say that *x* is 'about' *y*, we imply that x narrates, or ponders, or expresses, or explains, or elucidates, feelings about – but what in any case makes us more closely aware of – *y*. The further implication is that *y* is namable; we have, in fact, named it. If, on the other hand, the question is 'never to be answered', how can it be posed; or if it is posed, why can't it ever be answered? What, in other words, does it mean, and what is the rejoinder to my claim that in the circumstances as just defined, it is meaningless? 'About' implies conceptual thought, or a musical imitation of conceptual thought, such as the telling of a story through music.

So long as we cling to conceptual thought as the only means of realizing truth, in the sense of both conceiving and presenting it as real, so long as we don't realize that there are truths inaccessible to conceptual thought altogether but accessible to musical thought, as well as truths whose understanding is exclusively musical, although verbal thought can refer, allude to them, establish associations with them, we shall never get anywhere near a conceptual understanding of musical understanding. As children, we had to grow up verbally, which is why we make words the ultimate arbiter. If one allowed a highly musical child's mind to develop, in the first place, musically, this unique member of humanity, once fully developed, could teach us a thing or two about the inadequacy of conceptual as opposed to musical insight. In the history of humanity, Mozart's seems to have been the only mind which, spontaneously and unconditionally, clung to musical thought as the primary source of perception and understanding.

Perception? A theory of cognition which took musical cognition into account would have to accept the fact that without a – primarily emotional – *experience of* any given music, its perception, and hence its understanding, cannot take place. The truth it has to tell has to be experienced in order to be recognized: *it is cognized emotionally and can then be recognized intellectually* – analytically, for instance, though still not through words, but rather through what we did in our complete music example from the Dylan Thomas dirge.

Whether answerable or not, the question of what music is about had better be left alone in the circumstances – which, if their musicality is remembered and fully retained, do not allow us, we have just noted, to think in terms of 'about' anyway. However, the question, not of what Stravinsky's music is about, but of its character, of what distinguishes it from anybody else's music, we can at least investigate along the conceptual lines that have proved helpful in the case of other composers; though we may not be able to answer it, we might at least contribute the first steps towards an answer.

Wagner we accept, instinctively, as Stravinsky's opposite, the expressionist *par excellence* as opposed to the one and only suppressionist. Yet there is one negative trait which the two share – and exclusively, too: they seem to be the only great composers who arouse violent hostility in highly musical musicians. In the case of Wagner's music, I consider such reactions inevitable – and here I am going beyond what other thinkers, such as Thomas Mann and, incidentally, Adorno too, have found out about the nature of his music. For the likely fact is that Wagner's inspirations make us identify with feelings which we experience as bad, evil; and that there are those amongst us who can't forgive him, who blame him for having corrupted them, however temporarily – for the duration of a performance. But without *experiencing* these feelings, we cannot understand their psychological truth: it was Wagner's artistic duty to convey his psychological discoveries through the persuasiveness of his music. The shady side of *any* Wagnerian figure in his mythological world offers us confirmatory verbal thought which refers, alludes to those evil feelings, which establishes convincing conceptual associations with them.

I personally have no doubt that on top of it all, Wagner's music conveys truths altogether inaccessible to conceptual thought, and for which we only have empty words, such as 'metaphysics'. And the very combination, the amalgam of evil and the nameless, the other world, the timeless and spaceless we can't conceptually grasp, is too much for some of us to bear – for the most violent of the Wagner-haters and Wagner-baiters.

No, there is no need to remind me that this is not a book about Wagner – for in an exact negative way it is. Wordlessly speaking, that is to say, I give it as my deeply – unconceptually – considered opinion that the polarity between Stravinsky and Schoenberg (some of which we have seen crumble, anyway) is as nothing compared to the polarity between Stravinsky and Wagner: Stravinsky's music is experienced as the precise negative of Wagner's: it suppresses what Wagner's expresses, without leaving any doubt about the concrete, musically palpable and tangible nature of what it suppresses. Clinically, it is of the greatest significance to observe that the most passionate Stravinsky-lovers one knows are, at the same time, the most conscientious – invariably moralizing – objectors to Wagner's music.

Is the implication, then, that what is felt to be evil is amalgamated with the nameless[46] in Stravinsky's music, too? My answer is not only the *Symphony of Psalms* but also, well above all, his sovereign *Mass* – to which, instructively enough, many a musical believer in the mass as such passionately objects:

[46] For a pious Jew, God is nameless, in that his (Hebrew) name must not be enunciated; a different word is substituted. The present writer, an unpious Jew, approves, so long as it is agreed that musically, this nameless truth is closely definable. –HK

that which he rightly expects from music is being suppressed in the most religious of religious compositions, of all works? Aphoristically, maybe, meaningless words can assume, or at least borrow meaning: Wagner's music offends by turning us evil, whereas Stravinsky's offends by not turning us good.

But that's not the end of the hostile story about Stravinsky's music. Brahms and Webern, when they fail to be as expressive as they want to be, and when their music is therefore open to centrally relevant criticism, are never blamed for their inhibitions: so far as I am aware, I was the first to diagnose them.[47] No, people love these masters' music the more for its neurotic shortcomings, for they are able to identify with the all too human inhibitions which thus manifest themselves. What a relief that the creators of such great music are human after all, what utter relief that the music itself is, sharing as it does the unwillingness to face his own emotions! Stravinsky, on the other hand, faces them all, faces things of which we hadn't even been aware before he told us about – 'about'? no: before he winkingly insinuated – their ill-repressed existence in our own minds. Small wonder that there are those amongst us who won't have it, won't tolerate such superhuman control over clearly acknowledged, elementally powerful feelings, won't accept the mere possibility of such supreme balance between that which is being suppressed and its open-eared suppression! For in order for the suppression to succeed, there must be at least as much natural power behind it as behind the suppressed material itself. Where the music of Brahms and Webern can't get it out (how understandable! how disarming!), Stravinsky's can – but, for the first time in the history of the art, won't. With passionate detachment, it exposes force and counter-force, and counter-forces all those elemental forces to a halt: the apparent staticism thus achieved is the result of opposing, extreme dynamisms.

It is for this reason that Stravinsky's music is not developmental: in it, development is not arrested, but successfully opposed – frontally attacked; its anti-developments are, specifically, traceable. They avail themselves, at their maturest stages, of twelve-tone technique – the developmental technique *par excellence* turned in upon itself. Now, once that inescapable control which is the character of Stravinsky's message, or anti-message, has been traced in concrete, analytic detail, our unanswered question will have been fully

[47] Keller was diagnosing 'inhibition' in Brahms as early as 1946: 'In the music of neither Mozart nor Britten is there a sign of inhibitions (as distinct from restraint). In this respect their exact contrary is Brahms' (*cf.* 'Britten and Mozart: A Challenge in the Form of Variations on an Unfamiliar Theme', *Music & Letters*, Vol. XXIX, No. 1, January 1948, pp. 17–30; republished in 'The Musical Character', in *Benjamin Britten: A Commentary on his Work*, *op. cit.*, 1952, pp. 319–51). The topic was also discussed in the final section ('The Unclimactic Brahms') of 'Music and Psychopathology', *History of Medicine*, Vol. 3, No. 2, Summer 1971, pp. 3–7 (reprinted in *Hans Keller: Essays on Music*, *op. cit.*, pp. 29–36). Keller felt that Webern 'never got as near to spontaneity as Brahms did, say, in the Clarinet Quintet' (*cf.* 'Schoenberg *v.* Webern', *The Listener*, Vol. 82, No. 2117, 23 October 1969, p. 578).

answered. Meanwhile, let us confess that if his kind of inexpressive expression, this overwhelmingly expressive anti-*espressivo* hadn't happened, we would have been able to show, on the basis of our entire history of music, that it couldn't possibly happen: all genius is unique, but this one is the uniquest of the lot.

XXVII
Words about Music

Review of Robert Craft (ed.), *Stravinsky: Selected Correspondence*, Vol. 1 (Knopf, New York/Faber & Faber, London, 1982) and Paul Griffiths (ed.), *Igor Stravinsky: The Rake's Progress* (Cambridge Opera Handbooks, Cambridge University Press, Cambridge, 1982), published in *The London Review of Books*, 30 December 1982–19 January 1983, pp. 15–16

My fairly extensive – and, analytically, intensive – writings about Stravinsky confine themselves to his music and the psychology of his creativity – to the products and the nature of his towering genius. About the human being I have never yet written a word: the greater the genius the less there is of a causal connection or correlation between his life and his art – whence Beethoven came to be *the* communicator of profound, unmixed joy.

On the present occasion, however, it is my duty to tell the potential reader of close on five hundred pages whether Stravinsky the man is worth knowing about. The answer is an unqualified no, unless one is childish enough to enjoy the coincidence, within one and the same mind, of supernormal art and moral sub-normality. I only met Stravinsky once – and had never met such a small-minded great mind before.[1] From the words 'Mr Keller!', exclaimed with hypocritical enthusiasm, I was being flattered out of existence, in that our subject of conversation, my analyses, had to submit, paradoxically, to a sales talk without an ounce of substance, a string of compliments that immediately reminded me of something I'd never heard – a commercial traveller's overtures.

There is nothing in Robert Craft's skilful, conscientious, copiously annotated selection to get me over the shock I then received: on the contrary, there's plenty to revive it. Boring as many of the composer's letters are (which, then, have remained unselected?), about one central fact they seem to leave no doubt – that he treated human beings as mere, sheer material. You may say he had to. Why?

Why, for instance, was it necessary – let's, for once, call a theft a theft – to rob Auden (not a millionaire himself) of his commissioning fee for *The Rake*?

[1] *Cf.* note 8 on p. 125, above.

'I have not sold La Biennale anything but my conducting and musical supervision of the performance,' Stravinsky tells him, 'and most of your problems are off bounds to me.' Despicable, as Craft's commendably honest footnote shows: 'Stravinsky is pretending that the $20,000 for the opera, procured for him from the Italian government by Nicolas Nabokov, was not a commission (which he would have had to share with the librettists) but a fee for conducting the premiere'.

Ineluctably, therefore, one has to wonder what prompted Theodore, Stravinsky's elder son, to refuse to give Craft the composer's letters to his first wife, whose own letters are, therefore, the chapter's sole material. And the second, entitled 'Correspondence with Maurice Delage', is nothing of the sort: its opening Stravinsky letter remains its only one; while conversely, the chapters on Ansermet and Craft himself contain nothing from the addressees. But from Auden, fortunately, there is a lot. I only met Auden once – for many hours, though, discussing music all along.[2] Both as a mind and as a human being, he produced one of my life's weightiest days – whence I am not surprised to find him as the centre of interest of both books. Why indeed should one be? Books are made of words, which many musicians aren't happy with: Auden's conceptual thought is more natural, and hence more interesting than Stravinsky's.

There are choice quotes in Griffiths' second chapter, on 'The Makers and their Work', such as 'No good opera plot can be sensible, for people do not sing when they are feeling sensible'.

Ironically, even Auden's musical observations in Craft's volume can, upon occasion, be more reliable than Stravinsky's. The composer will describe Carl Ebert as 'an experienced musician', just because he wants this current personage to produce *The Rake*, whereas Auden, far more of 'an experienced musician' in the extra-professional sense, is 'a bit worried about the prospect of Ebert directing. We [he and Chester Kallman] saw his *Così fan tutte* and thought it was much too refined and "miniaturised"'. A more musical and alert diagnosis of Ebert's *Così fan tutte*, praised at the time by all the misleading critics, can hardly be imagined.

In a later letter about the star producer of the age, moreover, Auden continues to be absolutely on the musical dot: 'Ebert has asked too much money for the direction etc, etc. As to the latter, it sounds rather conceited to say so, I know, but I believe that I and Kallman could do an adequate job; at least we shouldn't sacrifice the music to the action, as most modern opera directors do, in my opinion'. Thereby, the diagnosis is both widened and deepened: Auden's 'opinion' was sheer musical fact.

[2] A small part of their talk was heard on Radio 3 on 20 November 1971 and, in a shorter version, on 2 April 1972; a copy of the 1971 broadcast exists in the British Library Sound Archive, as P772W.

For the professional musician, Paul Griffiths himself is a problem – which is meant as a relative compliment, since most music critics on the contemporary scene are sub-problematic. The new chief music critic of *The Times*[3] emerges as a conscientious, musical and knowledgeable observer; what does not emerge is musicianship proper. In fact, he doesn't know that difference between description and analysis, and describes where he thinks he analyses, while evincing, at times, highly articulate incomprehension when reacting to other people's analytic thought.

In the circumstances, it saddens one to hear him speak with the authority he doesn't possess: is it too patronising to suggest that in view of his position, Mr Griffiths might consider an unconventional personal course of action – to master one or two disciplines of the art of music itself? Meanwhile, his (or the publisher's?) description of the book's authorship makes a dishonest impression Paul Griffiths does not deserve. 'With Igor Stravinsky'? The composer's contribution is confined to an exceptionally vapid 'programme note' of less than seven hundred words, and a more substantial 'tribute' to Auden of less than four hundred words – whose history and purpose would be utterly obscure without the explanation Robert Craft provides in his own volume:

> On June 28 1965, Christopher Burstall, a BBC Television producer, wrote to Stravinsky asking him to participate in a documentary program about Auden, 'answering an unseen questioner'. Stravinsky wrote back … that he would be 'pleased to contribute to the program' but that the filming would have to be done in his Hollywood home. He asked for a 'question from Mr Auden himself. I would then compose an answer of ca. two minutes duration and read it from … "idiot cards"'.

Robert Craft, in his turn, prints Auden's letter of gratitude, but not the tribute itself, whose proper place would have been in his book, not Paul Griffiths's, which alleges the composer's collaboration. What does Stravinsky's unintentional contribution amount it? Two republications totalling a wordage of just over two-thirds of the present review.

The rest of this 'handbook' for 'the serious opera-goer or record-collector as well as the student or scholar' is, I am happy to report, immeasurably more honest: the other two collaborators have each contributed a chapter. Josipovici's is 'Some thoughts on the libretto', which arrive at the shattering conclusion that *The Rake* 'is the piano tuner's answer to the train driver', whatever that may mean: Stravinsky's brothers 'used to call him "the piano tuner" because of his obsessions with and constant repetition of notes that he liked', and the train driver is Wagner or Berg or Schoenberg or suchlike.

[3] Griffiths (b. 1947) served as chief music critic there from 1982 to 1992, before emigrating to write for *The New Yorker* and, from 1997 to 2005, for *The New York Times*.

Robert Craft's 'note on the sketches and the two versions of the libretto' is what I would describe as the musician's contribution to a book which will undoubtedly serve its purpose, so long as this purpose is not meant to include strictly musical enlightenment. Not that the main author's contribution is musically flawed – but from a genuinely musical point of view, its musical information is, realistically speaking, superfluous, in that it does not go beyond what the musical opera-goer or record-collector can find out for himself, on the basis of his own experience of the work.

My God's-eye view of what, after all, is a well-intentioned, serious effort will seem unfairly niggling unless I throw it into a perspective which, itself, is in urgent need of rational examination. For the fact is that most 'good' books about music, or the few books about music which can be described as 'good', in that they don't misinform and don't mislead, are subject to the same criticism as is Paul Griffiths': they are, strictly musically speaking, superfluous – their factual and historical and biographical information apart. And inasmuch as they are superfluous, they are musically harmful, for they threaten to replace what should happen, or should have happened, in the listener's own mind with a surrogate which he comes to depend on and which, at the same time, remains meaningless so long as it isn't supported by his own musical experience. Once it is thus supported, however, it merely tautologises: all description of music, as distinct from its analysis, is, in this sense, pleonastic.

Yes, I am calling on musicographers of the world: words about music, which centuries of climactic musical development were able to do without, need justification and must not, in any circumstances, run the risk of replacing musical understanding. They have increased in proportion as music has become either a problem or, at the very least, a subject. Natural art and its experience are neither, and words about music are only justifiable if they promote rather than inhibit or indeed replace, the development of natural artistic understanding. For a start, if all descriptions of what the reader has hardly heard yet yielded to analysis of what he has heard, instinctively understood, and so recognises in the analysis as a verbal articulation of his own understanding, a major step would be taken towards once again making musical experience – musical.

Part Two

MILEIN COSMAN
Prints and Drawings

Drawing Stravinsky

Milein Cosman contributed this introduction to her drawings of Stravinsky to the programme of the Camden Arts Festival in 1982, to accompany an exhibition of the drawings in the Camden Arts Centre that ran from 13 to 28 March.

Little did I know when, in 1954, I set out for Venice on the occasion of the premiere of *The Rake's Progress* that I would be seized by a perdurable obsession. I had agreed with the magazine *Opera* to do sketches of the performance, as I had been anxious to see Venice again. Having admired those marvellous Picasso drawings of the young Stravinsky, I had no desire to draw him myself. At the first rehearsal at La Fenice, I ran into a conductor who asked me to come to a reception at the hotel where the Stravinskys stayed, in order to meet the composer. He entreated me to bring my sketch-book, but I greeted his suggestion to draw Stravinsky at such a gathering with horror. I find that kind of social event inimical to my work, although normally I don't feel inhibited about sketching in public places. But as soon as I caught a glimpse of Stravinsky both the formal setting and indeed Picasso were forgotten – replaced by an overwhelming urge to draw him to which I had to yield. He sat, a tiny figure, in a huge armchair, surrounded by a crowd of people; half-kneeling, at quite few yards' distance, I could just catch sight of parts of his face through the gaps in the throng, and as I was about to finish his profile, the tall figure of Carl Ebert[1] wholly obscured what little view I had enjoyed. At this point a man from Rome, looking over my shoulder, became aware of my ordeal. He introduced me to Mme Stravinsky and made me show her what I had done. She was most encouraging and promised to arrange a proper sitting for the next day.

Perhaps it was her warmth and enthusiasm (I had no idea at the time that she was a very fine painter!) which freed me of trepidation when I arrived at the hotel the following noon. Nor, waiting in the lobby, did I worry when, after half an hour, Mme Stravinsky apologised that her husband had not yet appeared: he was still asleep. The ensuing hour was devoted to a crescendo of

[1] *Cf.* note 3 on p. 93, above.

apologies. Another person waited with me, a French-speaking Russian whom Mme Stravinsky had introduced to me; I had heard the name Wakevich and duly proceeded to compliment him on his stage designs. He retorted that he'd never painted in his life, and it gradually dawned upon me that the man was the conductor and composer Igor Markevich, now gravely insulted: the atmosphere grew intolerably sticky, and there was still no sign of Stravinsky.

It was close on 2 p.m. when, at last, he appeared; he now felt like lunch, rather than drinks. A fair-sized party went out to eat on the terrace. Mme Stravinsky bravely tried to keep her word and suggested I should finish the sketch out there. By then I, too, was hungry and the sight of a huge entrecôte nearly made me faint, as did the idea of staring at, and drawing, Stravinsky in the process of eating. To sketch people eating, babies apart, is an indiscretion. I rapidly finished the profile, even though the composer was now facing me; Markevich's hostile glances speeded me along. As I took my leave, I vowed never to approach Stravinsky again.

But when he came to London in 1958, in 1959 – to conduct a concert performance of *Oedipus Rex* – and in 1961,[2] I had to draw him again: the challenge thrown out in Venice proved irrepressible. However, I did not feel up to facing a situation remotely like the earlier trauma; in fact, I never was to meet him again. After a rehearsal (in BBC Studio I, Maida Vale) for *Oedipus Rex* – in which Cocteau took the part of the Speaker; hence, and because of his long association with the composer, his presence – Elizabeth Lutyens tried to take me to the artist's room, and to make me show him my sketch-book; eventually, she went in alone and showed him a few sketches herself, which he signed approvingly. During rehearsal, I tried to keep myself well hidden from his view, and I am grateful to him for seeming unaware of my intrusion, and for being an ever-changing delight to watch (rather like Venice). I loved not only the intensive, athletic way in which he moved as he conducted, but the incessant changes of his face, in turn that of an absorbed musician, a bespectacled horse and a cuddly toy mouse.

In 1965, the last time he came to London, he was very frail and hobbled up to the Festival Hall platform to conduct part of a concert of his music. I was sitting in one of the front stalls. Just before the end I could not resist jotting a few back views of Stravinsky in tails on the white spaces of my programme.

He has haunted me for decades now and continues to pursue my work – one of the strongest visual impressions of my life.

[2] Stravinsky conducted *Agon* on 10 and 12 December 1958 (*cf.* note 3 on p. 71, above) and the performance of *Oedipus Rex* for which these rehearsals took place at a late-night concert on 9 November 1959; his presence in 1961 was for a performance of *Perséphone* on 29 October 1961. In all of these concerts he conducted the BBC Symphony Orchestra in the Royal Festival Hall.

A Note on the Illustrations in this Book

Most of the drawings in this book were done at rehearsals for BBC concerts Stravinsky conducted in 1958, 1959 and 1961. As well as the sketches of the premiere of *The Rake's Progress* (Venice, 1954), this publication has given me the opportunity to include some sketches from *Petrushka*, produced by the Festival Ballet in 1951. The etchings in the book were, of course, made subsequently – in the late 1970s and '80s.

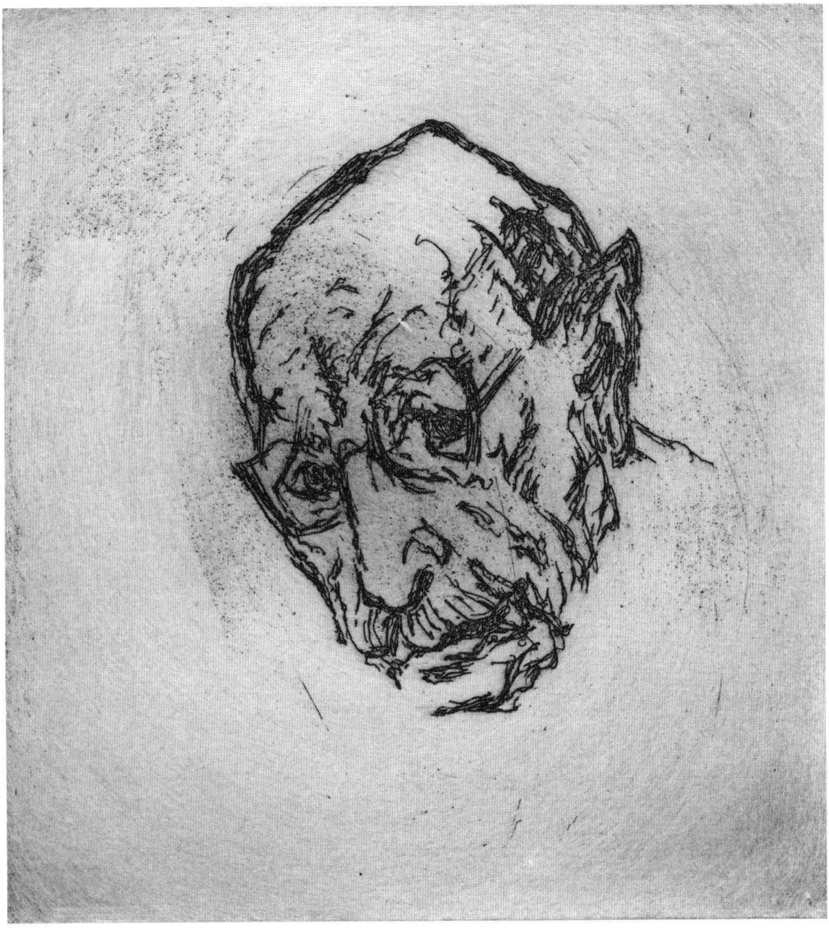

Index